# Education, Aspiration and Upward Social Mobility

Aqsa Saeed

# Education, Aspiration and Upward Social Mobility

## Working Class British Women

palgrave
macmillan

Aqsa Saeed
Oxford, UK

ISBN 978-3-030-82260-6 ISBN 978-3-030-82261-3 (eBook)
https://doi.org/10.1007/978-3-030-82261-3



This Palgrave Macmillan imprint is published by the registered company Springer Nature Switzerland AG.
The registered company address is: Gewerbestrasse 11, 6330 Cham, Switzerland

*'If she does not take the initiative, if she does not evolve the inner richness of her being, if she ceases to feel the inward push of advancing life, then the spirit within her hardens into stone and she is reduced to the level of dead matter. But her life and the onward march of her spirit depend on the establishment of connections with the reality that confronts her'. (Based on Iqbal, 1930, p. 14)*

*'Insiders and outsiders in the domain of knowledge, unite. You have nothing to lose but your claims. You have a world of understanding to win'. (Merton, 1972, p. 44)*

# Acknowledgements

To all my family and friends, and particularly my two younger sisters, who have supported me in myriad ways, I would like to express my heartfelt gratitude.

Thank you to my informants who gave me their time and confidence in sharing their stories with me. The responsibility for any mistakes and omissions of course remains entirely mine.

# Abstract

This research is concerned with the barriers and opportunities experienced by working-class British Pakistani women who aspired to higher education and to obtaining professional jobs. It examines the career trajectories of nine second-generation British Pakistani women who were born in the 1970s and 1980s in a working-class area of a former textile town in the North of England. These women pursued educational qualifications as the means to acquire new knowledge and experiences and in order to secure higher-status jobs. This is in marked contrast to the traditional trajectory which they saw other British Pakistani women following, of marrying and having children soon after leaving school. My informants viewed a career outside the home as affording advantages in terms of personal and social development, family pride and economic rewards. While, at the time of the research, some of them were still caught up in 'making themselves' in terms of their careers, others had already secured professional jobs. The women in this study reflect on changing ideas about British Pakistani womanhood, their educational routes to social mobility and the effects of problematic perceptions of Pakistani Muslims in schools and workplaces. In this book I explore the kinds of cultural capital relevant to their careers, the obstacles they faced and how they negotiated these. I conducted in-depth biographical interviews using a qualitative approach that was designed to be culturally sensitive, revealing how relationships with parents, siblings, peers, neighbours, teachers and colleagues, as well as local contexts and opportunities, feature in informants' lives. The study is a contribution to the small but growing literature that sets out to understand social mobility through qualitative research methods, exploring the processes involved. It also illuminates the life stories of a specific group of British Pakistani women at a particular time in their community's history.

# Contents

# List of Tables

# 1

# Introduction

There has been a great deal of research on the relative failure of working-class ethnic minority students in terms of educational achievement, on the limits operating on their social mobility and on the causes of these limits (Abbas, 2003; Ahmad, 2001; Basit, 1997; Broecke & Nicholls, 2007; Hussain & Bagguley, 2007). My focus in this research is rather different. It is concerned with working-class Pakistani women who have pursued further and higher education, obtained qualifications and in some cases entered professional occupations. My interest is in how these women managed to overcome the barriers they faced, what resources and opportunities they were able to exploit and what strategies they used.

Persisting inequalities have been documented in the relative chances of working-class and middle-class people obtaining higher-level occupational positions (Bukodi & Goldthorpe, 2018; Goldthorpe & Mills, 2008; Heath, 1981; Payne, 2007). While at one time it was claimed that a substantial increase in social mobility had taken place in Western societies during the twentieth century, research has shown that this is only partially true. There was an increase in absolute mobility in the middle of that century with the increase in the number of people from working-class backgrounds obtaining professional and other middle-class occupational positions. However,


A. Saeed, *Education, Aspiration and Upward Social Mobility*,
https://doi.org/10.1007/978-3-030-82261-3_1

*relative* mobility—the relative chances of working-class and middle-class people obtaining such positions—remained more or less the same (Erikson & Goldthorpe, 1993).

The increase in absolute mobility occurred as a result of an expansion in the number of middle-class jobs, and a subsequent contraction in working-class ones, rather than as a result of any equalising effect of the broadening of access to secondary and higher education that took place during the period (Goldthorpe & Mills, 2008). This does not mean that the education system has played no role in the processes by which people are recruited to different positions in the occupational structure (Heath et al., 1992). Indeed, particular levels of qualification have become increasingly necessary for obtaining higher-level posts. However, differential educational achievement on the part of working-class and middle-class students has resulted in little change in relative social mobility. Where previously middle-class young people obtained middle-class positions through family connections and through the background knowledge, skills, attitudes and forms of behaviour they had learned at home, now these have first to be transformed into educational qualifications if they are to achieve such positions. Similarly, *which* working-class young people gain middle-class occupations is now determined, to a large extent, by whether they manage to obtain higher-level educational qualifications.

Much sociological research on the education system has been concerned with this persistence of social class inequalities in educational achievement despite the dramatic increase in access to secondary and higher education that occurred from the middle of the twentieth century onwards. This work has identified a range of factors that depress educational performance on the part of working-class and ethnic minority children, including cultural conditions in the home and community and discrimination on the part of schools and teachers in terms of the kinds of curricular knowledge presented, modes of pedagogy and selection decisions—for example, in allocation to ability groups (Banks, 1971, ch4; Craft, 1970; Keddie, 1971; Troyna, 1991).

There has been a small amount of research on working-class and ethnic minority young people who have succeeded in the education system, concerned with documenting the resources and strategies they use.

Watkins and Noble (2013), for example, explored how the disposition to learn through self-discipline is developed within the homes of Chinese children, which then supports their success at school. Similarly, Vincent, Ball, et al., 2013a, b report on the strategies and expectations adopted by black middle-class families to support their children's educational success. However, none of this has focused on the case of Pakistani students. Moreover, my informants come from an area—to which I shall give the name Milltown—which on most objective indicators is among the most deprived places in England. This class context is important in understanding how they have lived and in particular the resources and opportunities they could access.

Brown et al. (2013) argue that social mobility research has generally overlooked 'the mass of research on student identities, aspirations and experiences of school, college and university'. And they go on to comment that: 'while this points to a weakness in mainstream mobility studies it also points to a failure of the sociology of education to engage in broader debates around intergenerational mobility, notwithstanding its engagement with wider debates on social inequalities and social justice' (p. 638).[1] Equally importantly, many writers have underlined the need to focus on gender and ethnicity, and examine how these are interrelated with social class (Friedman, 2013; Lawler, 1999; Loury et al., 2005; Peach, 2005; Rollock et al., 2011). My research directly addresses these gaps in the literature: I am interested in the experiences that led to the formation of the career identities of upwardly mobile working-class British Pakistani women.

## Historical and Cultural Background

All nine of my informants were educated in Britain, their parents having migrated to the UK from Pakistan. Many single Pakistani men came to the UK in the 1950s as economic migrants from Azad Kashmir and other

[1] For more recent work on social mobility that is concerned with wider debates on social inequalities and social justice mainly beyond schooling/education, see Littler (2018), Exley (2019) and Mohamed (2020).

parts of the Punjab (Anwar, 1979; Kalra et al., 1999; Mohammad, 2005). Relatively cheap housing, sometimes in slum clearance zones, and favourable employment prospects in textile mills attracted early migrants to the old northern mill towns such as Oldham, Rochdale, Burnley, Bolton, Blackburn and to the city of Bradford. Migrants' poor English usually limited them to manual jobs. Whilst the 1962 Immigration Act restricted such migration from Pakistan, it allowed the wives and families of men already here to join them to set up permanent home in the UK. Pakistani communities are now spread widely but unevenly across the UK, with the majority of Pakistanis living in the North of England and the Midlands (Anwar, 1979; Kalra, 2000; Mohammad, 2005).

Early migrants clustered around the employment opportunities available in northern industrial towns (Kalra, 2000). Ethnic segregation in the workplace was common. Very often, Pakistani men worked different shifts in the textile factories from White workers, and, where their working hours coincided, Pakistanis often worked on different floors. However, since the 1970s, the textile mills have closed down, and people have experienced high levels of unemployment as a result. Pakistanis living in deindustrialised areas in the north-west have poorer employment prospects than Pakistanis living in London and newer towns in the south-east, such as Milton Keynes (Garner & Bhattacharyya, 2011).

My research took place with women who had been brought up in Milltown, one of the northern industrial communities in which Pakistanis settled. Pakistanis are the main ethnic minority group in the town, making up around 10% of the population. They are largely concentrated in particular neighbourhoods, and the site of this research is one such pocket of Pakistani settlement, where my informants had been brought up.

## Current Material and Social Realities

In the recession of the 1980s Milltown's textile industry was almost completely closed. The lack of other viable industries in the local economy meant that the unskilled and semi-skilled jobs that textiles had provided were not replaced. Milltown is now one of the most economically and socially deprived areas in the country, and the vast majority of Pakistani and Bangladeshi households live in some of the most deprived parts of the town. The 'objective probability' (Bourdieu & Passeron, 1977, pp. 204–205) of upward mobility is low. Moreover, Garner and Bhattacharyya (2011) have argued that it is difficult to achieve social mobility in such locations where social ties within the community are strong but durable employment prospects are weak.

Pakistani communities in different parts of the UK vary in the degree to which they are physically segregated from the White English communities around them and also in their levels of average wealth and income (ODPM, 2006, pp. 147–152). These two features are related. Pakistani communities in Northern England are deprived communities in terms of durable employment prospects not only because of the early and serious deindustrialisation in the local textile industry but also as a consequence of having limited contact in their neighbourhoods with White English populations (Garner & Bhattacharyya, 2011). Whilst there are multiple sources of segregation, including discrimination (e.g., in access to housing), such ethnic clustering can limit employment and social mobility (Garner & Bhattacharyya, 2011, p. 17; Casey, 2016).

Research by Wrigley (2000) in one of the northern textile towns in which Pakistanis settled found that 'Morale is often low ... where no new industries have emerged on any scale to replace the cotton mills which first attracted immigration from Pakistan. One of the consequences of this economic disappointment is the degree of isolation of the Muslim communities from other parts of the population' (p. 99).

The residential segregation of Muslim communities featured in debates about multiculturalism, race and citizenship after rioting broke out in a former textile town, Oldham, in May 2001.[2] In the months that followed, the town and others like it featured prominently in a frequently repeated narrative of segregation, 'parallel lives', troubled multiculturalism, disenchanted youth and White working-class racism (Alexander &

[2] Rioting featured within a context of police clashes, high racial tension between different ethnic groups and feelings of disenchantment by White voters with the post-industrial realities of a multicultural town with high levels of economic deprivation among both the White and South Asian populations (Dunkley Jones, 2007).

Knowles, 2005; Cantle, 2001). These riots demonstrated the exacerbation of tensions within the community resulting from increased economic deprivation.

Subsequently, divisions and antagonism were sharpened further by several factors including reaction to the attacks launched by Al-Qaeda in the United States on September 11 2001, a series of coordinated suicide attacks in London on July 7 2005, the transatlantic aircraft plot in August 2006 to detonate liquid explosives carried on board ten airliners, the controversy in European democracies over the hijab as a marker of cultural segregation and whether it should be banned in public places (Elver, 2012) and the summer of violence in 2017 (Warsi, 2017). These events became early symbols, for some, of a nation under threat from discontented young Muslims, be they radical Islamists, streetwise rioters, hijab-wearing young women or non-English-speaking minorities whose failure to integrate was felt to threaten the national order (see Saeed, 2016). Within these narratives, the particular constellations within which local identities are created, racialised and contested became dramatised. Serious questions relating to social justice as regards social and educational inequalities came to be occluded by the stereotyping of all Muslims.

The majority of girls born in Milltown's Pakistani community left school at around 16, were married, had children and became housewives, often in the same area or elsewhere in Britain. However, this was not true of all of them. Against the odds a few stayed on at school, aspired to professional occupations, went on to university and even achieved their ambitions. My focus here is on how they did this, what resources and opportunities enabled them to develop and pursue these aspirations and what strategies they used in doing so.

## Research Focus

My research addresses how it is that some women from an economically deprived, working-class Pakistani community were able to go on to further education and become upwardly mobile. I investigate the formation of these women's educational and career aspirations and the manner in which these were realised, to one degree or another. Whilst an aspiration can be an individual desire or quest, it must also be understood as emanating from, and being shaped and supported within, collective contexts. In this research I shall consider how informants developed aspirations that were significantly different from those of most of their peers. Secondly, I shall question how my informants found the resources within their homes, community, schools, colleges and workplaces to pursue these aspirations. Aspirations and actual trajectories do not, of course, always coincide, and the reasons for this will be given attention. My informants' particular positions within the family, school and workplace resulted, to a large extent, from intersections of gender, ethnicity and class. Living in a Pakistani community in a northern English town and attending local schools shapes the formation and fate of career aspirations. A career trajectory is the outcome both of one's capability to aspire and of the circumstances in which this aspiration must be realised.

My interest in the question of how people born into such circumstances could aspire to and achieve upward social mobility arises from the fact that I too was born and raised in the same place. This gives the study a degree of reflexivity. It means, for example, that I am familiar with the political, social and moral topography of the area from which my informants come and with some of the barriers and challenges that they faced. However, whilst using this as a resource, I have focused exclusively on trying to understand *their* experiences, rather than filtering these through my own. I have drawn on my own experience primarily to provide a characterisation of what it is like to live in this community, though I have also used the research literature for this purpose.

There are practices and narratives within the community that create feelings of belonging. People are bound to the location by a microculture of values and meanings that is inspired by Islam, as established by the parental generation who migrated from Pakistan. Within the context of a Pakistani community in Milltown, it is important for people to be seen as upholding religiously inspired notions of modesty, proper conduct and duty to minimise social censure. Living together in narrow streets, people are highly visible to each other and mostly known to one another. This creates a close-knit community in which bonds of solidarity and mutual support are formed. However, this gaze can also lead to critical appraisal and censure. Community judgements, based even on mundane everyday activities, can undermine the honour of families. Deviant behaviour, including non-traditional career choices, may be seen as posing a challenge to traditional norms and risks being met with punishing gossip.

The social conservatism that characterises this community can be understood by focusing on the example of purdah. Islam, as understood in the context of Pakistan, places a clear emphasis upon the matter of men and women's mobility; prolonged and intimate contacts between a mature woman and unrelated men reflects badly upon the honour *(izzat)* of the household of which she is a member (Afshar, 1994; Brah & Shaw, 1992; Gilliat-Ray, 2010; Mohammad, 2010). This derives from a cultural perspective which treats the household or extended family as the 'unit' rather than the individual.[3] Saifullah-Khan (1976) argued that it was this that accounted for the pattern of Pakistani women's work in Britain at the time her study was carried out. In the impoverished rural areas of Pakistan from which many migrants came, only the wealthy could afford to observe segregation by gender. However, in the new British Pakistani communities stable male wages from the mills permitted ordinary households to practise this highly valued cultural ideal initially, while the new conditions of life in urban Britain made it increasingly necessary to do so: 'Even if there are many Pakistanis in the area very few are likely to be kin of fellow villagers. The … women … must observe purdah from all these unrelated men' (Saifullah-Khan, 1976, p. 232).

This concept featured in other ethnographies conducted in the 1970s, such as those of Anwar (1979) and Werbner (1988). Their research focused on Pakistani residential clusters in the northern towns of Bradford, Rochdale and a Pakistani neighbourhood in Manchester. These ethnographies collectively show that purdah characterised the lives of first-generation migrant women, who mostly lacked formal education (Ghuman, 2002; Modood, 2005; Modood et al., 1997). It generated norms and expectations of appropriate ways of being a woman, leading most British Pakistani women at the time to assume a homemaking role rather than working outside the home (Anwar, 1985; Saifullah-Khan, 1976; Werbner, 1988; 1990).

[3] Purdah is also seen as a way to protect women from 'unsafe' public spaces, an issue which again came to national attention with the murder of Sarah Everard.

However, although the wages of Pakistani men in northern English towns were stable, they were often insufficient to underpin purdah, as is suggested by Saifullah-Khan's argument. As a result, as Anwar (1985) has observed, many first-generation British Pakistani women were economically active within the home as piece-working machinists:

> [C]ultural factors largely prevent Pakistani women from engaging in economic activity outside their homes although many work at home doing sewing for Pakistani manufacturers. (p. 43)

Thus women earning at home gave the family enough money to live while allowing them to practise purdah.

Other writers have pointed out how these cultural preferences intersected with exploitative relations in the labour market, as women found themselves working for low wages in often unregulated conditions within the home. As Phizacklea (1988) put it, in a review of the development of the West Midlands' 'ethnic textile industry':

> [A]ccess to 'family' or community members as low-wage workers is a key competitive advantage for many ethnic businessmen … what is usually glossed over is the extent to which this 'family' and 'community' labour is female and subordinated to very similar patriarchal control mechanisms in the workplace as in the home. (p. 31)

By contrast, Pnina Werbner (1988, 1990) emphasised the positive rather than restrictive aspects of Pakistani gender relations. Writing of Manchester in the 1980s, she shifts the focus from Pakistani women as exploited workers or passive objects of male control and protection to a view of them as social agents, actively engaged in building and sustaining relations within and between households, their earnings as machinists converted into gifts and used to cement and create friendship ties. If men are the acknowledged breadwinners, then, women, by forging social links across different kinship networks and social strata within the Pakistani population, were the makers of community (Werbner, 1990).

Despite the very different interpretations they offer, for each of these writers the association between Pakistani women and the domain of the household and family is seen as central to the workings of the British Pakistani community: men as fathers, brothers and husbands are the 'providers'; women as the wives, sisters and daughters are the managers and negotiators of the domestic domain and in Werbner's view of the ethnic social field as well.

Some writers argue that the daily reality of purdah has persisted for subsequent generations of working-class British Pakistani women (Mohammad, 2005). The less educated parents of this second generation present great obstacles to daughters negotiating alternative careers outside the home. Some argue that the durability of traditional purdah has resulted from the continuing links with Pakistan, leading the community to uphold socially conservative ideals (Afshar, 1994)

Studying a Mirpuri[4] community in Reading, Mohammad (2010) argues that women face limits to the amount of time they can spend in public spaces and restrictions on the time of day they can be out in the public sphere away from home. For example, attending training courses in other locations would be problematic. There is thus a 'constant tension between permitting young women to take up opportunities and progress in the education system and concern for the family honour and for the daughter's marriage, which remains the main goal for the majority of parents' (Mohammad, 2010, p. 153).

Nevertheless, purdah is a cultural and moral framework subject to negotiation and change. Dale et al. (2002) reported from the Pakistani community in Oldham that although engaging in proper conduct in the public sphere was essential for daughters wanting to continue into further education, there was nevertheless room for them to successfully negotiate attendance at colleges by reassuring parents that they would not engage in behaviour that would damage the family's reputation, despite their being in mixed-sex spaces.

There are signs of increasing variation in the interpretation of purdah and in families' attitudes towards post-compulsory education, in different parts of the UK. Muslim parents in London, especially, often play an

[4] This refers to people who migrated from the Mirpur region of the Punjab in Pakistan.

instrumental role in encouraging their daughters to succeed both academically and professionally.[5] Ahmad (2001) gives reasons why daughters were motivated to take a degree and why parents encouraged them. For women, potential financial independence was an insurance policy against parents dying early or a marriage failing, rather than an alternative to marriage. Despite parents' active encouragement, however, women were not expected to be breadwinners. Men were expected to be the family earners and therefore strongly encouraged to take vocationally orientated degree subjects. Women, on the other hand, were encouraged to study subjects they enjoyed. Ahmad (2001) did not support the findings of research conducted in East London that found high levels of education correlated with renunciation of 'traditional' values and practices, such as arranged marriages (Bhopal, 1997; Bhopal & Myers, 2008). But her work does emphasise the benefits of having an educated daughter in the family: for example, daughters' education could sometimes bring prestige and material wealth.

However, the situation was rather different in the community from which my informants came. The pressure of rather traditional interpretations of purdah remained. Furthermore, by contrast with Hussain and Bagguley's (2007) study of South Asian women in sixth form or university in Leeds and Birmingham, the parents of my informants were not highly educated, if formally educated at all, and did not have much knowledge of the British education system.

## Organisation of the Book

In this work I shall begin by looking, in national terms, at gender and ethnic differences in the obtaining of educational qualifications and changes in these over the past few decades. I will then consider what can be learned from research investigating the sources of educational inequalities. Here I shall focus, in particular, on the theoretical resources provided by the work of Pierre Bourdieu. Following this, I will outline the

[5] For Carey and Shukur (1985), purdah in London is described as relaxed for second-generation Bangladeshis.

methods I used in investigating the lives of Pakistani women who had obtained higher-level educational qualifications and professional occupational positions. The remaining chapters will outline my findings. A more detailed outline of the contents of subsequent chapters is as follows:

Chapter 2 begins by looking at changing gender differences in overall achievement and then examines ethnic and class differences in achievement levels. Schools have been significant in widening the expectations of appropriate careers for women and supporting women to obtain the qualifications necessary for broader occupational access. However, I shall consider why gender inequalities in career development within organisations persist. I shall present the broad trends in educational achievement of British Pakistanis and whether this is translated into professional jobs. The ways that class can affect educational outcomes and employment prospects is also discussed in this chapter. Trends relating to gender, ethnicity and class provide a backdrop to the career aspirations and choices of British Pakistani women such as my informants.

In Chap. 3 I explore the various *explanations* advanced for educational inequalities—particularly those relating to social class, gender and ethnicity. To this end I outline some of the theoretical ideas of Pierre Bourdieu about the reproduction of social inequality which I will use in my analysis. Central to Bourdieu's approach, of course, is the concept of cultural capital. I shall also consider how social expectations of gender roles have influenced educational provision and how the underperformance of some ethnic minority groups has been explained in the literature. My analysis will include consideration of home, school and wider societal factors.

In Chap. 4 I discuss the method that I used to collect data about informants' aspirations and career trajectories. The biographical research interview can produce relevant and nuanced data in the form of stories with which to understand how aspirations are developed and careers constructed. The interview as a special relationship between the interviewer and interviewee is explored with an emphasis on the process of reflexivity. However, I shall also discuss the limitations of this method.

In Chaps. 5, 6, 7 and 8, the interview data is analysed by considering how the experiences within the family, educational institutions, the neighbourhood and workplace shaped the career aspirations and trajectories of my informants. In Chap. 5, I locate them as second-generation Pakistanis, born and brought up in Britain, but note how, at the same time, they had distinctive aspirations by comparison with many of their second-generation British Pakistani peers. I explore the formation and strength of their aspirations and begin to present their experiences in acquiring the cultural capital needed to underpin these aspirations.

In Chap. 6 I explore the roles of parents, siblings and peers in the formation of careers. I investigate parents' influence over daughters' aspirations, how parents' roles and expectations changed in response to successful negotiation with daughters and how parental participation could be both intense and distant in different social spheres, such as the family, community and schools. Lack of mainstream cultural capital and the presence of ethnically distinct forms of cultural capital are considered.

Chapter 7 analyses how educational structures and cultures contributed to nurturing aspirations, raising expectations and facilitating the meeting of goals such as achieving educational qualifications, while at other times they put up barriers. Relationships with teachers and the informants' own responses to opportunities and obstacles within this sphere are also discussed.

Finally Chap. 8 focuses on the navigation strategies employed by my informants within the Pakistani neighbourhood, the school and the workplace. Their strategies reveal the complexity involved in the task of modifying gender, ethnic and class identities to create career trajectories and social mobility.

The conclusion, Chap. 9, summarises the main themes covered in the book and considers the wider implications of my analysis. I shall also assess the extent to which Bourdieu's theoretical ideas have been useful in understanding the aspirations and career trajectories of my informants. This chapter too reflects on the affective aspects of the journey to achieve social mobility, drawing on a growing body of literature that reveals the emotional costs incurred by some groups of working-class people to achieve social mobility, and shows how my informants fared in this process.

## References


Abbas, T. (2003). The Impact of Religio-Cultural Norms and Values on the Education of Young South Asian Women. *British Journal of Sociology of Education, 24*(4), 411–428.

Afshar, H. (1994). Muslim Women in West Yorkshire Growing Up with Real and Imaginary Values Amidst Conflicting Views of Self and Society. In H. Afshar & M. Maynard (Eds.), *The Dynamics of 'Race' and Gender: Some Feminist Interventions* (pp. 127–147). Taylor and Francis.

Ahmad, F. (2001). Modern Traditions? British Muslim Women and Academic Achievement. *Gender and Education, 13*, 137–152.

Alexander, C. E., & Knowles, C. (2005). *Making Race Matter: Bodies, Space and Identity*. Palgrave Macmillan.

Anwar, M. (1979). *Myth of Return: Pakistanis in Britain*. Heinemann Educational Publishers.

Anwar, M. (1985). *Pakistanis in Britain*. New Century.

Banks, O. (1971). *The Sociology of Education* (2nd ed.). Batsford.

Basit, T. (1997). *Eastern Values, Western Milieu*. Ashgate.

Bhopal, K. (1997). *Gender, Race and Patriarchy*. Ashgate.

Bhopal, K., & Myers, M. (2008). *Insiders, Outsiders and Others Gypsies and Identity*. University of Hertfordshire Press.

Bourdieu, P., & Passeron, J. (1977). *Reproduction in Education, Society and Culture* (R. Nice, Trans.). Sage.

Brah, A., & Shaw, S. (1992). *Working Choices: South Asian Women and the Labour Market*. Department of Employment Research Paper, No 91.

Broecke, S., & Nicholls, T. (2007). *Ethnicity and Degree Attainment*. Research Report RW92. Department for Education and Skills.

Brown, P., Reay, D., & Vincent, C. (2013). Education and Social Mobility. *British Journal of Sociology of Education, 34*(5–6), 637–643.

Bukodi, E., & Goldthorpe, J. H. (2018). *Social Mobility and Education in Britain. Research, Politics and Policy*. Cambridge University Press.

Cantle, T. (2001). *Community Cohesion: A Report of the Independent Review Team*. Home Office.

Carey, S., & Shukur, A. (1985). A Profile of the Bangladeshi Community in East London. *Journal of Ethnic and Migration Studies, 12*(3), 405–417.

Casey, L. (2016). *The Casey Review: A Review into Opportunity and Integration*. www.gov.uk/dclg. ISBN: 978-1-4098-4953-7.

Craft, M. (1970). *Family, Class and Education: A Reader*. Longman.

Dale, A., Shaheen, N., Kalra, V., & Fieldhouse, E. (2002). Routes into Education and Employment for Young Pakistani and Bangladeshi Women in the UK. *Ethnic and Racial Studies, 25*(6).

Dunkley Jones, R. (2007). *Understanding Race Relations in Oldham.* Unpublished Paper.

Elver, H. (2012). *The Headscarf Controversy Secularism and Freedom of Religion.* Oxford University Press.

Erikson, R., & Goldthorpe, J. H. (1993). *The Constant Flux: A Study of Class Mobility in Industrial Societies.* Clarendon Press.

Exley, D. (2019). *The End of Aspiration? Social Mobility and Our Children's Fading Prospects.* Policy Press.

Friedman, S. (2013). The Price of the Ticket: Rethinking the Experience of Social Mobility. *Sociology, 48*(2), 352–368.

Garner, S., & Bhattacharyya, G. (2011). *Poverty, Ethnicity and Place.* Joseph Rowntree Foundation.

Ghuman, P. (2002). South Asian Adolescents in British Schools: A Review. *Educational Studies, 28*(1), 47–59.

Gilliat-Ray, S. (2010). *Muslims in Britain: An Introduction.* Cambridge University Press.

Goldthorpe, J. H., & Mills, C. (2008). Trends in Intergenerational Class Mobility in Modern Britain: Evidence from National Surveys 1972–2005. *Journal of the National Institute of Economic and Social Research, 205*(83), 83–100.

Heath, A. (1981). *Social Mobility.* Fontana Paperbacks.

Heath, A., Mills, C., & Roberts, J. (1992). Towards Meritocracy? Recent Evidence of an Old Problem. In A. Heath & C. Crouch (Eds.), *Social Research and Social Reform.* Clarendon Press.

Hussain, Y., & Bagguley, P. (2007). *Moving on Up. South Asian Women and Higher Education.* Trentham Books Limited.

Kalra, V. (2000). *From Textile Mills to Taxi Ranks: Experiences of Migration, Labour and Social Change.* Ashgate.

Kalra, V., Hepburn, P., & Penhale, B. (1999). *Tackling Barriers into Employment for Pakistani and Bangladeshi Young People.* Oldham Metropolitan Borough Council.

Keddie, N. (1971). Classroom Knowledge. In M. Young (Ed.), *Language and Control.* Collier-Macmillan.

Lawler, S. (1999). 'Getting Out and Getting Away': Women's Narratives of Class Mobility. *Feminist Review, 63*(Autumn), 3–24.

Littler, J. (2018). *Against Meritocracy: Culture, Power & Myths of Mobility*. Routledge.

Loury, G., Modood, T., & Teles, S. (2005). *Ethnicity, Social Mobility and Public Policy: Comparing the USA and UK*. Cambridge University Press.

Modood, T. (2005). The Educational Attainments of Ethnic Minorities in Britain. In G. Loury, T. Modood, & S. Teles (Eds.), *Ethnicity, Social Mobility and Public Policy: Comparing the US and the UK*. Cambridge University Press.

Modood, T., Berthoud, R., Lakely, R., Nazroo, J., Smith, J., & Beishon, S. (Eds.). (1997). *Ethnic Minorities in Britain: Diversity and Disadvantage*. Policy Studies Institute.

Mohamed, H. (2020). *People Like Us. What It Takes to Make It I Modern Britain*. Profile Books.

Mohammad, R. (2005). Negotiating Spaces of the Home, the Education System, and the Labour Market: The Case of Young Working-Class, British Pakistani Muslim Women. In G.-W. Falah & C. Nagel (Eds.), *Geographies of Muslim Women: Gender, Religion and Space* (pp. 178–200). Guildford Press.

Mohammad, R. (2010). Gender, Space and Labour Market Participation: The Experiences of British Pakistani Women. In S. Mc-Grath-Champ, A. Herod, & A. Rainnie (Eds.), *Handbook of Employment and Society. Working Space*. Edward Elgar Publishing.

ODPM. (2006). *The State of the English Cities Report*. ODPM Publications.

Payne, G. (2007). Social Divisions, Social Mobilities and Social Research. *Sociology, 41*(901), 901–915.

Peach, C. (2005). Social Integration and Social Mobility: Spatial Segregation and Intermarriage of the Caribbean Population in Britain. In G. Loury, T. Modood, & S. Teles (Eds.), *Ethnicity, Social Mobility and Public Policy: Comparing the USA and UK* (pp. 178–203). Cambridge University Press.

Phizacklea, A. (1988). Entrepreneurship, Ethnicity and Gender. In S. Westwood & P. Bhachu (Eds.), *Enterprising Women: Ethnicity, Economy and Gender Relations*. Routledge.

Rollock, N., Gillborn, D., Vincent, C., & Ball, S. (2011). The Public Identities of the Black Middle Classes: Managing Race in Public Spaces. *Sociology, 45*(6), 1078–1093.

Saeed, T. (2016). *Islamophobia and Securitization. Religion, Ethnicity and the Female Voice*. Palgrave Macmillan.

Saifullah-Khan, V. (1976). Purdah in the British Situation. In A. L. Barker & S. Allen (Eds.), *Dependence and Exploitation in Work and Marriage* (pp. 224–245). Longman.

Troyna, B. (1991). Underachievers or Underrated? The Experience of Pupils of South Asian Origin in a Secondary School. *British Educational Research Journal, 17*(4), 361–376.

Vincent, C., Ball, S., Rollock, N., & Gillborn, D. (2013a). Three Generations of Racism: Black Middle-Class Children and Schooling. *British Journal of Sociology of Education, 34*(5–6), 929–946.

Vincent, C., Rollock, N., Ball, S., & Gillborn, D. (2013b). *The Educational Strategies of the Black Middle-Classes*. Institute of Education University of London.

Warsi, S. (2017). *The Enemy Within: A Tale of Muslim Britain*. Penguin UK.

Watkins, M., & Noble, G. (2013). *Disposed to Learn Schooling, Ethnicity and the Scholarly Habitus*. Bloomsbury Academic.

Werbner, P. (1988). Taking and Giving: Working Women and Female Bonds in a Pakistani Immigrant Neighbourhood. In S. Westwood & P. Bhachu (Eds.), *Enterprising Women: Ethnicity, Economy and Gender Relations* (pp. 177–202). Routledge.

Werbner, P. (1990). *The Migration Process, Capital, Gifts and Offerings Among British Pakistanis*. Berg.

Wrigley, T. (2000). *The Power to Learn. Stories of Success in the Education of Asian and Other Bilingual Pupils*. Trentham.

# 2

# Educational Inequalities in the UK: Gender, Ethnicity and Social Class

As explained in the Introduction, my focus in this research is on the educational and occupational careers of young Pakistani women born in the 1970s and 1980s in a working-class community in a northern English town. In this chapter I outline the broad trends in women's education and careers in the UK for the population as a whole. I provide national and some local statistics relating to gender, ethnic and class differences in educational and occupational achievement relevant to the cohort to which my informants belong. This provides important background for my study.

## Gender and Achievement: Patterns of Change in Britain

In the past, educational provision for girls and women throughout Britain was linked to what was judged to be appropriate to their gender-specific role in society. These expectations related to ideas both about what women are capable of (they were often seen as having different capabilities from men, with these generally being viewed as of lower status) and



A. Saeed, *Education, Aspiration and Upward Social Mobility*,
https://doi.org/10.1007/978-3-030-82261-3_2

about what role they did and should play in society (such as bringing up the next generation and sustaining men so that they could do their work).

In the nineteenth and into the twentieth centuries there were largely separate curricula for the sexes, in line with these assumptions about their different personalities, interests, educational needs and roles in society. Up to the mid-twentieth century, access to academic schooling, higher education and the professions was available only to a small number of women who often had to struggle to achieve it. Women's visibility in the male educational and career spheres was often seen as sexually threatening and widely subject to scorn (Robinson, 2010). The arguments used to block the participation of women reflected masculinist attitudes. It should be noted that these also pointed in the direction of separate schooling rather than the complete denial of an academic education to girls and women.

At this time, most people, including many women, believed that the ideal role for a woman was primarily located in the domestic sphere and any education should be a preparation for this. The exact nature of the role varied according to social class. Purvis (1989), for example, documents how upper and to some extent middle-class girls were prepared for engaging in those activities deemed to be characteristic of a lady such as embroidery, art and music. Other middle-class girls were often educated with a view to becoming governesses. By contrast, working-class girls were educated, if they were educated at all, to do domestic work although of course many of them also did other kinds of work, including factory work.

Over the course of the twentieth century, in the UK and some other Western societies, both sets of ideas changed to a considerable degree, previous views of women's incapacities were abandoned, and assumptions about the roles they can play in society changed. Reasons included domestic technology reducing housework, plus the shift away from heavy manual jobs as a result of technological developments and the expansion of service industries, administration and management. World War II is often seen as a key turning point, when many women took over 'male' jobs from men on the home front, demonstrating that they were capable of doing these (Arnot et al., 1999; Oakley, 1974).

In the first wave of feminism in the west, in the late nineteenth and early twentieth centuries, women campaigned for suffrage. They demanded equality with men and political and social inclusion. They not only wanted the right to vote but also access to previously male-dominated spheres such as education. In the second feminist wave, influenced by the women's liberation movement of the 1970s, some women questioned gender as a social construct. They adopted a political agenda, aimed at the liberation of both genders from the confines of narrow socially constructed roles. Particular themes on this agenda were sexuality, reproduction, the family and work (see Rupp (2001, pp. 5469–5472; Whittier, 2007, pp. 1872–1875).

From that time, feminists have objected to education being organised on gender lines. Subsequent educational changes that were brought about in part by feminist campaigning opened up opportunities for more women to choose lifestyles that did not limit them to the domestic sphere (Arnot, 1993; Arnot et al., 1999; Weiner & Arnot, 1987). After 1970, there was common provision between the sexes and a largely shared curriculum. Much of the debate in the 1980s was about why, having been given the option, girls nevertheless tended to choose subjects seen in patriarchal terms as 'feminine' and to avoid so-called masculine subjects. Today there is less scope for choice of subjects up to GCSE, so that boys and girls experience largely the same curriculum. However, beyond GCSEs, echoes of the earlier gendered patterns of choice still persist.

## Gender Inequalities in Attainment

In England and Wales, educational achievement is measured in terms of different types and levels of qualification, for example, GCSE, A Level and undergraduate degree. Moreover, at each of these levels courses are available in a wide range of subjects, and there is also differentiation between these academic qualifications and vocational ones. Obtaining particular educational qualifications is the key to many careers. Gender-based differences in exam results have therefore been used to understand educational and career inequality.

Until the 1980s girls experienced relative average underachievement in many GCE O Level/GCSE subjects. Arnot et al. (1999) have shown how the situation then changed. The DFES report *Gender and Education: The Evidence on Pupils in England (2007)* shows girls performing better than boys in most subjects at GCSE and A Level. The gender gap was almost 10% overall: 63.4% of girls achieved 5+ GCSEs or equivalent in 2006 but only 53.8% of boys. This trend has continued and girls continue to outperform boys at GCSE.[1]

Post-16 participation rates in education have also changed: by 2006 girls were more likely to stay on in full-time education after 16 (82% of girls versus 72% of boys). Girls were also more likely to be entered for A Levels than boys with 54% of entries being female, in contrast to the 1950s and 1960s when only one-third of A Level entrants were girls.

Gender differences in pass rates are much narrower at A Level than at GCSE but they are still evident. On average, girls achieve at a 4% higher rate across all subjects at A Level. This is in the context of a very high pass rate. Girls outperform boys in attaining an A grade for the majority of subjects, which is a significant change over the last ten years. Evidence from international research shows similar patterns in some other countries. Of course, in some ways it is unhelpful to view girls' and boys' achievement in binary terms of winners and losers. To understand what is happening in schools requires a broader and more nuanced analysis (DFES, 2007).

## Gender-Related Employment Patterns

While younger women now outperform their male peers in terms of educational qualifications, this does not translate into occupational positions. Platt (2011) explains that despite 'increases in women's labour market participation, the rise in the number of women who delay starting their family or do not have children, and some equalization in

---

[1] Data shows that in 2017/18, 46.7% of girls and 40% of boys got a strong pass (Grade 5 or above) in GCSE English and Maths. Source Data: GOV.UK Ethnicity facts and figures statistics (education-skills-and training/11-to-16-year-old/a-to-c-in-english-and-maths-gcse-attainment-for-children-aged-14-to-16-key-stage-4).

the sharing of household labour (Fisher et al., 2007; Gershuny, 2000), it is still true that women remain overwhelmingly responsible for dependent children and for providing and organising their care, with the consequences for other aspects of their life that such responsibilities bring' (pp. 52–53). Those responsibilities are important in understanding the variation in employment conditions between men and women in terms of occupations, pay, hours, shift work and unemployment rates.

Platt (2011) discusses various trends relating to gender and employment. Women are less likely to be in paid work than men, and women's work is more likely to be part-time to supplement the family income rather than to pursue a career. Men are more likely to work non-standard hours, as a result of shifts or overtime than women. Occupations also still tend to be gendered. Women are more likely to be in caring and clerical professions and men in managerial or skilled manual occupations. Women's average full-time earnings still fall short of men's. Societal structural constraints and discrimination as well as different choice patterns narrow the opportunities for most women. However, there are now more women (and probably a higher proportion of women) in managerial positions and other professional occupations than there were in the past.

In summary, over the past 70 years there have been major changes in the level and nature of women's educational opportunities and achievement, employment, marriage and living arrangements. These have led to a significant transformation in the gender order. We see that girls' educational attainment is now, on average, higher than that of boys'. However, where there is freedom to choose school subjects, gender differences emerge: boys tend to favour mathematics, physical sciences and IT, whereas girls tend to choose the humanities and biological sciences. These choices lead to fewer girls entering careers in engineering, technology, mathematics and computing. As these are better paid jobs, this is one of the factors that leads to girls continuing to earn less than men overall in professional careers. Finally, Platt's (2011) work shows that women's qualifications at school and university do not lead to higher-level occupational positions to the same extent as those of men. She argues that women are held back by domestic responsibilities which oblige them to take part-time or lesser paid work or prevent them from finding paid work at all. Women are more likely to be constrained in their paid labour market participation by their being responsible for childcare and their part-time status.

Of course, gender differences are not the only 'inequalities' relevant to my study. In the next section, I shall consider the effect of differences in the educational performance of boys and girls from different ethnic and class backgrounds.

## Ethnic Inequalities in Education

There has long been concern about ethnic differences in educational achievement in the UK, in the wake of substantial immigration from the Caribbean and South Asia in the 1950s, 1960s, and 1970s. Thus, Gillborn and Gipps (1996) demonstrated that the average achievement at GCSE level of African Caribbean pupils in many LEAs was significantly lower than that of other groups, representing a continuing cause for concern. However, not all ethnic minority groups achieved at a lower average level. Indian pupils, for example, consistently appear to achieve at higher levels than pupils from other South Asian backgrounds and their White counterparts in most urban areas. Chinese children have long had higher than average levels of achievement.

Pakistanis are the most numerous ethnic minority group in the UK after Indians, with the major period of immigration of Pakistanis taking place in the late 1950s and early 1960s prior to the restrictions of the 1962 Immigration Act (Brown, 2006; Kalra, 2000). Within the Pakistani group nationally, both males and females achieved lower than the national average, in terms of the proportion obtaining five A*-C grades at GCSE level. In 2004 the average was 48% for boys and 58% for girls, whereas for Pakistani boys it was 39% and for Pakistani girls 52%.[2] Since the time when most of my informants were at school, the gap between Pakistanis

[2] Source: ONS SFR 37/2004 National Statistics http://www.education.gov.uk/rsgateway/DB/SFR/s000528/sfr37-2004.pdf). I am using older data because it is closer to the cohort that my informants belong to.

and pupils from other ethnic backgrounds has narrowed. However, in 2011–12, Pakistani girls and boys in Milltown still achieved almost 10% below the national average of 59% gaining 5 A*-C GCSEs (including mathematics and English) and also below the achievement of White pupils in the town.

A contributing factor to this low performance is the lack of educational attainment by the migrant generation. Seminal research by Anwar (1979) in Rochdale reported that many Pakistani migrant men had limited skills in the English language and few qualifications relevant to a working-class northern Milltown. Twenty-two per cent were illiterate. Whilst 46% had matriculation-level qualifications from Pakistan, these had no value in the UK labour market and were anyway irrelevant to the manual jobs the migrants took. In Milltown, the Pakistani population had the lowest average skill levels in the borough, with more than half having no qualifications. Most women of the first generation were housewives with no qualifications, although some did earn money working as home-based machinists for the textile factories, as did the women in the study by Anwar (1979).

In contrast to Milltown, Ghuman (2002) found among South Asians nationally that because education was seen as a means of social mobility young people frequently stayed at school after 16, developing higher vocational aspirations and a strong positive attitude to work, in contrast to their White peers. Abbas (2002) also reported that South Asians in Britain are more likely than White people to remain in further education. The former improve their GCSE results by re-sitting and then are more likely to embark on A Levels. In addition Basit (1997, p. 130) argued that some students show remarkable assiduity in pursuing their objectives by completing A Levels with re-sits.

## Attainment at Degree Level by Ethnicity

Whilst there were very few first-generation Pakistani migrants with degree-level qualifications, a trend is apparent amongst the second generation towards acquiring such qualifications. Hussain and Bagguley

**Table 2.1** Percentage with degree-level qualifications (level 4/5) by age, sex and selected ethnic groups, England and Wales, 2001 (adapted form)

| Age groups | 25–29 | 30–44 | 45–59 | 60–64 | 65 and over |
|---|---|---|---|---|---|
| White males | 29.8 | 22.4 | 19.1 | 14.1 | 12.6 |
| White females | 29.7 | 21.5 | 17.8 | 12.7 | 11.3 |
| Pakistani males | 33.2 | 27.2 | 22.8 | 19.4 | 12.5 |
| Pakistani females | 25.6 | 17.4 | 13.1 | 9.6 | 6.7 |

Source: SARS, Census of Population, 2001. Taken from Hussain and Bagguley (2007, p. 13). (The labels used in the original table in Hussain and Bagguley (2007) were problematic. They referred to respectively British, Indian, Pakistani and Bangladeshi males and females. I have changed the first label to White so that all the labels refer to descent, not place of birth.)

(2007) show that in 2001 British Pakistani women, aged 25–29 years old, were 3.8 times more likely to have a degree than those 65 and over (see Table 2.1).

The comparable ratio for White women is 2.6. Although the 25- to 29-year-old Pakistani women are still less likely to have a degree than their White counterparts (25.6% vs 29.7%), these percentages are remarkably similar given the differences in their parents' education and occupations. If 25- to 29-year-old Pakistani women are matched with White women with similar parental backgrounds, a much higher proportion of Pakistani women would be found to have degrees.

Findings such as those in Table 2.2 below have led Kay (2007, p. 128) to argue that there has been a significant change in the educational position of younger British Pakistani women:

> [A]lthough a clear majority of Pakistani and Bangladeshi women looked after their home and family full-time, this was becoming less common among the growing number of women who are obtaining good educational qualifications.

**Table 2.2** Change in numbers of first-year UK-domiciled full-time first-degree female students by ethnicity from 1994–95 to 2004–05

| | White | Indian | Pakistani | Bangladeshi |
|---|---|---|---|---|
| Percentage increase | | | | |
| 1994–5/2004–05 | 43.3% | 84.8% | 158.7% | 273.7% |

Source: Calculated from HESA Table 10b. Taken from Hussain and Bagguley (2007, p. 12 adapted form)

Modood (2005) notes a similar trend that: 'ethnic minorities in general manifest a strong desire for qualifications and once they begin to acquire qualifications, they seek more' (p88).

Although people from ethnic minority backgrounds are more likely to have degrees than their ethnic majority counterparts, they are less likely to obtain first- or upper second-class honours. This situation has not improved in almost a decade. Broecke and Nicholls (2007) report in *Ethnicity and Degree Attainment* that whilst aspirations may be high among ethnic minority students (as shown by the numbers who embark on degree-level qualifications), their achievement in attaining excellence in qualifications is still lagging.

Richardson (2008) speculates on the reasons for the lower attainment at degree level by ethnic minority students. These include lower entry qualifications, inappropriate choice of subject, discriminatory teaching and assessment practices and conceptions of learning and approaches to study that adversely affect the quality of their learning. Lesser degree-level attainment among British Pakistanis can also be explained partly by their higher levels of economic poverty, requiring them to work full-time whilst studying (Broecke & Nicholls, 2007). The role of each of these factors remains to be explored. Leese (2010) suggested that 'new students' expressed a need for more structured activities on campus to help them to fit in to university culture and for more support from academic staff, particularly in the form of clear communication of what is expected of students (p. 239).

In spite of the sharp increase in university attendance by the second generation of British Pakistani women, some writers argue that there should now be a focus on factors that affect the translation of qualifications into higher levels of jobs (Modood & Shiner, 1994). One reason for this is that while people from ethnic minority backgrounds are over-represented in higher education in relation to their proportion in the population, they are less likely to apply to and attend higher status universities (Modood & Shiner, 1994). Consequently they are less likely to be able to enter some professions.

## Ethnicity and Labour Market Disadvantage

People with qualifications generally have lower levels of unemployment than those without (Hussain & Bagguley, 2007). As we have seen above, British Pakistani young women have acquired qualifications in disproportionately high numbers (Lindley et al., 2006). However, these women with qualifications nevertheless have lower than average participation rates in the labour market. This is an example of Platt's finding that qualifications do not automatically secure social mobility or favourable employment returns for all ethnic groups equally (Platt, 2011, p. 46 and Shain, 2020)

Data show that Bangladeshi and Pakistani women graduates with level 4+ qualifications (a degree or equivalent) are five times more likely to be unemployed[3] than White British women peers and more likely to be unemployed than male graduates from the same ethnic group (EOC, 2006).

Although the chances of British Pakistani women entering a profession are higher than for their parents' generation, this progress has not been evenly experienced across the country. The professional success of Pakistani women in some areas of the country, particularly London, has led The Change Institute (2009) to report that:

[3] The data do not show whether they are unemployed and 'seeking employment' or just 'not employed'.

> increasing numbers of young bilingual Pakistanis are successfully entering Higher Education and moving into the professional sphere. (p. 35)

and that

> Pakistani women are becoming more visible in all walks of life, corporate, media, political and community-based, and that leadership is being demonstrated through a growing number of women who are taking a leading role in politics and other arenas as councillors, mayors, journalists, and by women in high profile jobs in the public sector. (p. 45)

However, levels of success, in terms of education and occupation, are significantly affected by social class differences in this community, as in others.

## Social Class

Class is a very significant factor in educational attainment and career opportunities and progression. Nationally, across all ethnic groups, pupils eligible for free school meals have lower average Attainment 8 scores than those not eligible. The proportion of pupils achieving 5 A*-C GCSEs (including English and Mathematics) in Milltown's more deprived communities is substantially lower than attainment levels in the borough as a whole. This is true in some wards that are mainly White as well as those with high percentages of Pakistanis.

Of course, each ethnic group has its own class profile. Child poverty is highest among British Pakistanis and Bangladeshi households (Khan & Shaheen, 2017, p. 14). In the case of Northern England, British Pakistanis in working-class families are over-represented by comparison with the mainstream class profile. Indeed, in Milltown itself, the Pakistani community is skewed even further towards the working class than that of the town as a whole. The class composition of British Pakistanis as a group, and of Pakistanis in Milltown in particular, may explain a significant part of their educational underachievement and employment disadvantage.

Some writers have developed this theme and focused on how ethnic and employment penalties affect Pakistanis differently in different areas, based on class differences. Heath and McMahon (1997) define 'ethnic penalty' in terms of discrimination and other factors relevant to employment:

> We use the expression 'ethnic penalty' to refer to all the sources of disadvantage that might lead an ethnic group to fare less well in the labour market than do similarly qualified Whites. In other words, it is a broader concept than that of discrimination, although discrimination is likely to be a major component of the ethnic penalty. (Heath & McMahon, 1997) as cited in Platt (2011, p. 80)

Dale et al. (2002) conducted research in Oldham where they found that South Asians felt they had to obtain superior qualifications to those required from people of a non-Asian background in order to compensate for the ethnic penalty in the labour market. These authors argue that negative and out-dated stereotypes of Muslim women held by employers remain a significant barrier to employment. But Platt (2011) explains that there are additional reasons other than employer discrimination why people from certain, particularly poor, backgrounds do not obtain work. A lack of qualifications is not the only barrier to entering competitive jobs. Lacking information about job opportunities, living in areas where there are few such opportunities, limited public transport to the workplace and lacking specific work experience can all operate as barriers in the lives of working-class Pakistanis as well as working-class people from other ethnicities (Heath & Cheung, 2006, p. 19). Employment penalties are seen to operate regardless of the level of education, and disadvantage is based on comparisons with similarly qualified Whites (Heath & Cheung, 2006).

Of course, an ethnic penalty will not affect all ethnic minority groups, or all members of any particular ethnic group, equally (Heath & Cheung, 2006, p. 24). Such a situation can be exacerbated for women such as my informants because of the degree to which their homes are isolated from the mainstream community. The extent of such segregation of Pakistani communities from the White English populations around them differs across the UK, as do their levels of wealth and income (ODPM, 2006, pp. 147–152). Segregation and poverty are correlated. Segregated Pakistani communities in Milltown are deprived in the absence of new and durable employment following the closure of the local textile industry. Whilst there are multiple reasons for segregation including discrimination, for example, in access to housing, ethnic clustering can limit employment and social mobility as the day-to-day needs of the Pakistani community evolve to be met within a small geographic area (Garner & Bhattacharyya, 2011, p. 17). This can make it easier for those who stay within the supportive networks of the familiar Pakistani community and thus avoid the emotional and monetary costs of venturing beyond the community and forging links within the mainstream. My informants, however, did move into the mainstream, and in the following chapters, I will consider why and how they did so.

## Conclusion

In this chapter I have shown that changes in the expectations of appropriate careers for women have meant that women now have more educational opportunities and alternatives to life as a housewife. At school, women have access to a broader range of subject choices than ever before in Britain. Girls' levels of achievement now equal if not exceed those of boys in many subjects at school. However, girls' subject choices continue to differ from those of boys to some extent. Girls' preferences for the humanities over physical sciences, mathematics and IT mean that careers in these better paid areas are often closed to them.

While educational qualifications play a major role in occupational recruitment, women's qualifications do not on average translate into higher occupational positions to the same extent as do men's. There are also gender inequalities in career development within organisations, resulting to a considerable extent from the predominant role that women still play in bringing up children.

Pakistanis have lower GCSE attainment rates in comparison with most other ethnic minority groups in Milltown. A contributory factor may be the limited number of parents with a Western education who can serve as role models and mentors. Nevertheless, increasing numbers now stay on to pursue further study, often to degree level. However their educational career routes, including the universities they attend, affect their attainment at degree level, which still lags behind that of other ethnic groups. This in turn affects the occupational positions they can obtain.

The next chapter will focus on explanations that have been developed for inequalities in educational and occupational achievement.

## References

Abbas, T. (2002). Teacher Perceptions of South Asians in Birmingham Schools and Colleges. *Oxford Review of Education, 28*(4), 447–471.

Anwar, M. (1979). *Myth of Return: Pakistanis in Britain.* Heinemann Educational Publishers.

Arnot, M. (1993). A Crisis in Patriarchy? British Feminist Educational Politics and State Regulation of Gender. In M. Arnot & K. Weiler (Eds.), *Feminism and Social Justice in Education: International Perspectives.* The Falmer Press.

Arnot, M., David, M., & Weiner, G. (1999). *Closing the Gender Gap Postwar Education and Social Change.* Polity.

Basit, T. (1997). *Eastern Values, Western Milieu.* Ashgate.

Broecke, S., & Nicholls, T. (2007). *Ethnicity and Degree Attainment.* Research Report RW92. Department for Education and Skills.

Brown, J. (2006). *Global South Asians Introducing the Modern Diaspora.* Cambridge University Press.

Dale, A., Shaheen, N., Kalra, V., & Fieldhouse, E. (2002). Routes into Education and Employment for Young Pakistani and Bangladeshi Women in the UK. *Ethnic and Racial Studies, 25*(6).

DFES. (2007). *Gender and Education: The Evidence on Pupils in England.* DfES Publications.

EOC. (2006). *Moving on Up? Bangladeshi, Pakistani and Black Caribbean Women and Work.* Equal Opportunities Commission.

Fisher, K., Egerton, M., Gershuny, J. I., & Robinson, A. (2007). Gender Convergence in the American Heritage Time Use Study (AHTUS). *Social Indicators Research, 82*(1), 1–33.

Garner, S., & Bhattacharyya, G. (2011). *Poverty, Ethnicity and Place.* Joseph Rowntree Foundation.

Gershuny, J. (2000). *Changing Times: Work and Leisure in Post-Industrial Society*. Oxford University Press.

Ghuman, P. (2002). South Asian Adolescents in British Schools: A Review. *Educational Studies, 28*(1), 47–59.

Gillborn, D., & Gipps, C. (1996). *Recent Achievements of Ethnic Minority Pupils* (HMSO, Ed.). London.

Heath, A., & Cheung, S. Y. (2006). *Ethnic Penalties in the Labour Market: Employers and Discrimination*. Department for Work and Pensions.

Heath, A., & McMahon, D. (1997). *Education and Occupational Attainments: The Impact of Ethnic Origins*. The Stationery Office.

Hussain, Y., & Bagguley, P. (2007). *Moving on Up. South Asian Women and Higher Education*. Trentham Books Limited.

Kalra, V. (2000). *From Textile Mills to Taxi Ranks: Experiences of Migration, Labour and Social Change*. Ashgate.

Kay, T. (2007). Daughters of Islam, Sisters in Sport. In C. Aitchison, P. Hopkins, & M. Kwan (Eds.), *Geographies of Muslim Identities*. Ashgate.

Khan, D., & Shaheen, F. (2017). Introduction: Analysing and Responding to Racial and Class Inequalities. In D. Khan & F. Shaheen (Eds.), *Minority Report: Race and Class in Post-Brexit Britain*. Runnymede.

Leese, M. (2010). Bridging the Gap: Supporting Student Transitions into Higher Education. *Journal of Further and Higher Education, 34*(2), 239–251.

Lindley, J. K., Dale, A., & Dex, S. (2006). Ethnic Differences in Women's Employment. *Oxford Economic Papers, 58*(2), 351–378.

Modood, T. (2005). The Educational Attainments of Ethnic Minorities in Britain. In G. Loury, T. Modood, & S. Teles (Eds.), *Ethnicity, Social Mobility and Public Policy: Comparing the US and the UK*. Cambridge University Press.

Modood, T., & Shiner, M. (1994). *Ethnic Minorities and Higher Education – Why Are There Different Rates of Entry?* PSI.

Oakley, A. (1974). *Housewife*. Penguin.

ODPM. (2006). *The State of the English Cities Report*. ODPM Publications.

Platt, L. (2011). *Understanding Inequalities Stratification and Difference*. Polity Press.

Purvis, J. (1989). *Hard Lessons. The Lives and Education of Working-Class Women in Nineteenth-Century England*. Polity Press.

Richardson, J. (2008). The Attainment of Ethnic Minority Students in UK Higher Education. *Studies in Higher Education, 33*(1), 33–48.

Robinson, J. (2010). *Bluestockings the Remarkable Story of the First Women to Fight for an Education*. Penguin.

Rupp, L. (2001). Feminist Movements. In N. Smelser & P. Baltes (Eds.), *International Encyclopedia of the Social and Behavioral Sciences* (Vol. 8). Elsevier Science.

Shain, F. (2020). Navigating the Unequal Education Space in Post-9/11 England: British Muslim Girls Talk About Their Educational Aspirations and Future Expectations. *Educational Philosophy and Theory*. https://doi.org/10.1080/00131857.2020.1769604

The Change Institute. (2009). *The Pakistani Muslim Community in England Understanding Muslim Ethnic Communities*. Queen's Printer and Controller of Her Majesty's Stationery Office.

Weiner, G., & Arnot, M. (1987). *Gender Under Scrutiny: New Inquiries in Education*. Hutchinson in association with The Open University.

Whittier, N. (2007). Social Movements and Gender. In G. Ritzer (Ed.), *The Blackwell Encyclopedia of Sociology Volume IV F-HE*. Blackwell Publishing.

# 3

# Explaining Educational Inequalities

Having outlined patterns of educational and social inequality that are relevant to the lives of my informants, I now want to look at the various explanations that have been put forward for these inequalities. I shall first look at those developed in relation to social class. As part of this I will introduce the work of Pierre Bourdieu, on which I shall rely as an important resource in the later analysis. After that, I will consider explanations for gender and ethnic differences in educational achievement.

## Explaining Working-Class Underachievement

A range of explanations has been put forward to account for lower levels of working-class educational achievement. In the first half of the twentieth century, these focused on genetic differences in intelligence, material poverty (resulting in an inability to afford the cost of secondary education and to keep children in secondary school) and discrimination on the part of schools and colleges. When access to free secondary education became available in the UK in the middle of the twentieth century, there was a shift in the explanations put forward. While some continued to appeal to



A. Saeed, *Education, Aspiration and Upward Social Mobility*,
https://doi.org/10.1007/978-3-030-82261-3_3

differences in inherited intelligence, the emphasis was placed, to a large extent, on differences in cultural background between the social classes. Initially, these were conceptualised in terms of the 'cultural deprivation' said to be characteristic of working-class homes. This consisted of linguistic and cognitive deficits; low educational and occupational aspirations; the prevalence of a short-term perspective emphasising immediate gratification, this inhibiting the ability to plan ahead, to persevere and show initiative; and a lack of appropriate reading material in the home.

In other words, it was argued that many working-class homes were culturally impoverished and that this deficit impacted on the educational performance of their children at school (Craft, 1970). While Craft recognised that there were significant variations among working-class families in the degree to which they supported their children's education, he argued that these families were generally less able to provide support than middle-class families and that this explained their lower average level of educational success.

However, this form of explanation came under increasing attack, on the grounds that it simply took for granted the superiority of middle-class culture. Instead, it came to be argued that rather than being culturally deprived in any absolute sense, working-class children are disadvantaged in school because they do not possess middle-class culture. The problem is not that they lack culture but that, from the point of view of the education system, they have the wrong sort of culture—in other words, one that the system does not recognise as of value. Thus, for working-class children to be successful within the education system and obtain the qualifications necessary to enter higher-level occupational positions would require them to abandon their own culture and set about the laborious task of learning an alien one.

Along these lines, Keddie (1971) emphasised cultural differences between social classes and how the dominant class sought to impose its culture through schooling. She argued that there is a mismatch between working-class culture and the arbitrarily dominant culture imposed in schools, which amounts to cultural imperialism.[1] For Keddie the term

---

[1] See Ingram (2011) for recent research on how tensions between school and home cultures can give rise to identity conflicts for working-class boys.

cultural 'deprivation' is nonsensical because no one can be deprived of the culture to which they belong. On this basis she argued that schools should 'become more flexible in their willingness to recognise and value the life experience that every child brings to school, and at the same time become more willing to examine and to justify what schooling could be about and what kind of life experiences children are being offered' (Keddie, 1973, p. 19).

The most developed and sophisticated version of this kind of cultural difference theory is that put forward by Bourdieu. Although Bourdieu's theory was developed in the context of France and addresses some of the distinctive features of that country, his central concepts do have wider application and have been very influential in recent years in analysing educational and social inequalities in the UK (Robbins, 2004).

Bourdieu views modern capitalist society as made up of two main classes, the dominant class and the working class. Members of the dominant class or 'bourgeoisie' would include private sector company executives, people in high-status professions such as doctors and lawyers and college professors. At the other end of the spectrum, of course, would be factory workers and farm labourers as well as those in routine non-manual occupations. In between these two groupings there are overlapping occupational categories such as small business owners, technicians, secretaries and primary school teachers, which are collectively termed the 'new petite bourgeoisie' (Bourdieu, 1984, pp. 128–129).

Bourdieu views this class structure as having been maintained since the nineteenth century, but argues that the manner in which it has been reproduced has changed over the course of the twentieth century. Where previously this occurred in a direct manner, through the inheritance of wealth and/or of occupational positions, now occupational recruitment increasingly depends upon obtaining educational credentials. So, in the nineteenth century processes of occupational recruitment were, to a large extent, a matter of 'social connections': the direct inheritance of occupations (passed on from father to son, and occasionally to daughter) or the obtaining of positions through relatives or patronage of one sort or another. Wealth could also be used, effectively, to buy positions. Having attended particular schools or universities could also play a role, not least in putting one in contact with potential sponsors or patrons, (an aspect of what Bourdieu calls 'social capital'). However, the manner of occupational recruitment has changed in England, and western societies generally, over the past 150 years (Dore, 1976). An educational credential system emerged, in the form of nationally recognised qualifications, with these playing an increasingly important role, even though not eradicating the role of social connections or the influence of attendance at particular schools and universities. Possession of knowledge and skills was important even under the older system, but the level of knowledge and skill (in particular, literacy and numeracy) seen as necessary for many types of work increased over time, and it came to be required that these abilities be validated through obtaining qualifications. In short, the inheritance of social position now had to operate through the acquisition of knowledge, skills and credentials. Bourdieu argues that this change has the effect of serving an ideological function, giving the impression that this type of society is meritocratic (Bourdieu & Passeron, 1990).

While the rise of credentialism *does* mean that the children of higher-class families must demonstrate their intellectual and motivational superiority through educational achievement, a central theme in Bourdieu's work is that children from the dominant class enjoy a considerable advantage within the education system, because it is their home culture that is privileged there. A substantial segment of parents in that class has direct involvement in the educational process, as teachers in schools and universities, or in other intellectual positions, for example, in the mass media. Furthermore, by virtue of their home backgrounds and their own success in the education system, most adult members of the dominant class share in this culture. Bourdieu argues that this dominant class culture is arbitrarily imposed through the education system, not just in terms of the particular forms of knowledge and skill deemed to be an appropriate part of the formal curriculum, but also through the hidden curriculum, in other words through the manners and style that must be displayed if educational success is to be achieved (Bourdieu & Passeron, 1990).

Bourdieu does not argue that differences in economic power between the social classes entirely determine what happens in the educational field. People compete in particular fields for resources and dominance, and what happens there has some autonomy from other fields, including the economic (Bourdieu & Wacquant, 1992).[2] So, he sees the education system operating as a relatively autonomous field, in which distinctive resources have to be displayed and deployed in the struggle for success. At the same time, this autonomy *is* only relative: there is a significant homology between the economic and educational fields in terms of what resources different agents can mobilise and what opportunities they enjoy. In other words, to a large extent, differences in economic power come to be displayed through differences in lifestyle, mode of dress, aesthetic preferences and in cultural attributes that are directly relevant to educational success. Thus for Bourdieu class analysis must address both economic and symbolic dimensions.[3]

One of the central concepts in Bourdieu's theoretical framework is 'cultural capital'. It is of particular importance for this study because it seems likely that both the successes achieved by my informants, and the barriers they have faced, can be understood in terms of their possessing, or lacking, particular kinds of cultural capital.

## The Concept of Cultural Capital

Bourdieu identifies a range of different types of 'capital'. The primordial form is, of course, economic capital, but he also refers to social capital and cultural capital.[4] Although these are presented as theoretically distinct, empirical research can illuminate the ways in which they are intertwined in social life. In order to understand what is meant by 'cultural

---

[2] The term 'field' in Bourdieu's work refers to a specific context of life. It can refer broadly to economics, politics or education, or specifically to a location such as the workplace or home. People occupy positions within particular 'fields' relative to one another, in terms of power, and cultural and economic resources (Thomson, 2010).

[3] Smyth and Wrigley (2013, pp. 24–27) argue that Bourdieu sometimes seems to understate the importance of economic capital. He begins by showing how cultural capital enhances the effects of economic capital (Bourdieu, 1973), but then later, and especially in *Distinction* (1984, p. 128), he appears to place the two on an equal footing. He then recovers an economic focus through a polemic against neoliberalism, and in *The Weight of the World* (1999).

[4] Bourdieu uses the term 'social capital' to indicate how connections and networks can magnify economic advantages. In places he often refers to further sorts of social capital, such as symbolic, educational, political, and linguistic. I am going to set these aside here because they are simply particular forms of cultural capital. The concepts of gender capital and ethnic capital have been developed by other theorists, and I shall deal with the latter later in this chapter.

capital' we need to begin with the word 'capital' itself, and its meaning in the context of economics.

In the history of that discipline, 'capital' seems to have two related but distinct meanings. First, it is used to refer to money that is lent to others on the understanding that it will be repaid in the future with interest. Secondly, it refers to one of the three main factors of production, the others being land and labour. Here 'capital' means equipment that is used to boost output by making production processes more effective or efficient. The concept that ties these two meanings of 'capital' together is 'investment'. In both cases money is not being used for present consumption but is being 'put to work' in order to accumulate more money or to yield a return in future production.

In the mid-twentieth century, some economists developed the concept of human capital, recognising that people may invest in developing their own skills and knowledge so as to increase their productivity, and therefore their income in the future, and, in many respects, this provides the model for Bourdieu's notion of cultural capital (Bourdieu, 1986; Bourdieu & Passeron, 1977; Moore, 2004). Bourdieu (1977) identifies an analogous process of investment and return as regards knowledge, skills and educational credentials. However, where the economists took for granted that the skills and knowledge concerned were simply those that were technically required for increasing productivity, as we have seen, Bourdieu locates his discussion of cultural capital relationally, in the context of the reproduction of capitalist society and the social divisions involved in this. He argues that the knowledge, skills and attitudes, which represent the culture imposed by the education system, are simply that of the dominant class: it has no inherent superiority to the culture of the working class but rather enjoys a particular privilege of *recognition* (Bourdieu & Passeron, 1977). In the terms introduced earlier, his explanation for the relative lack of success of working-class children and adults in the system appeals to cultural difference, not to cultural deprivation. The reason why working-class culture does not count as cultural capital is simply because dominant class culture has been institutionalised within the education system, immediately putting working-class children at a disadvantage.

The higher chances of educational, and occupational, success that dominant class children enjoy stems both from the fact that they acquire knowledge, skills and other cultural attributes in their homes that will subsequently serve them well within the education system and from the fact that dominant class families specifically work on their children to inculcate such attributes, in a way that working-class families generally do not or cannot do (Lareau, 2003). Yet the failure of the majority of the population to acquire or even appreciate the dominant minority culture is portrayed as resulting from their intellectual inadequacy. In this manner the hierarchical structure of society is legitimised, not least through the use of terms such as 'intelligence' or 'IQ' (Bourdieu, 1973, pp. 80–81).

According to Bourdieu, cultural capital is transmitted in three forms: (i) embodied (through habitus), (ii) objectified and (iii) institutionalised. These refer respectively to corporeal capacities, cultural objects and artefacts, and credentials (Bourdieu, 1990). Habitus refers to the behaviours, habits and attitudes that are learnt throughout childhood, and beyond, and that makes us who we are. Ways of sitting, standing, speaking and thinking, and the rules to do with good manners, become second nature. The body is moulded by this training (Bourdieu, 1990, p. 70). The resulting dispositions are structured because they reflect the social class conditions within which they are acquired (Maton, 2010). Thus, habitus locates us as social persons and gives rise to dispositions that can be predicted to a large degree. As a result, people from different social classes experience school and its culture through the body differently. When people feel at ease in school, they are less likely to experience alienation from its environment. There is a class correlation in positive or negative experiences of school. This is because the logic of the educational field situates working-class children's habitus unfavourably, yet they have to endure this positioning. Language is also caught up in this power-based struggle, in school and beyond. For example, accents are often attributed differential value in power-laden contexts, and may be regarded inappropriately as a sign of intellectual and cultural inferiority.

Habitus is not simply passive, it can be agentic as well, because habitus represents what people do when they confront a situation. The cumulative or immediate effect can be to reproduce the social relations in the field or to change them. Bourdieu's point here is that the agency exercised by middle-class children through their conduct has the effect of normalising or reproducing the social order. Working-class children, in comparison, are less likely to socially engage with the situations in the educational field in terms that are deemed appropriate and that bring them educational success. The transformation needed to improve their condition is not available to them. The effect is to reproduce their inequality through their own alienation. In these terms, agency is an historically embedded process of social engagement, based on a 'capacity to contextualise past habits and future projects within the contingencies of the moment' (Emirbayer & Mische, 1998, p. 963).

Objectified capital takes the form of cultural goods (such as books, artefacts, dictionaries and paintings) that circulate in the culture of the dominant class. Such cultural artefacts serve as cultural capital because they somehow carry the assumption that their owners are superior in intellect and culture. Possession of this type of cultural capital, along with having the appropriate habitus, leads to favourable outcomes for children of that class (Bourdieu, 1984). The third kind of cultural capital that Bourdieu identifies, 'institutionalised' capital, takes the form of qualifications. Whilst appearing neutral and objective, and although some members of lower classes emerge with higher grades, examinations have the effect of eliminating those who are not from the 'legitimate' class.[5] They are the 'clearest expression of academic values and the educational system's implicit choices'. They are tools that inculcate the values of the dominant culture:

> Nothing is better designed than the examination to inspire universal recognition of the legitimacy of academic verdicts and of the social hierarchies they legitimate, since it leads the self-eliminated to count themselves among those who fail, while enabling those elected from among a small number of eligible candidates to see in their election the proof of a merit or 'gift' which would have caused them to be preferred to all comers in any circumstances. (Bourdieu & Passeron, 1990, p. 162)

Qualifications are institutional capital because they represent resources in the labour market that provide access to occupational positions. Modern societies demand social and technical selection. For Bourdieu, a school

[5] It is worth remembering that the system of recruitment by nomination and patronage that exams replaced was even more class-biased.

conceals its social function of legitimating class differences behind its technical function of producing qualifications. Even in the case of a qualification which is technical, the school has also performed a social function, which will be significant in bringing future power and privileges (Sullivan, 2001).

Up to now, I have focused on explanations for social class inequalities in educational outcomes. However, considerable attention has also been given to the role of gender and ethnicity.

## Explanations for the Educational Underachievement of Girls

In the nineteenth century, and well into the twentieth, there were significant differences in the average educational achievement levels of males and females in the UK. Up to the 1960s this largely reflected differences in educational provision for the two sexes, these being rooted in beliefs about biological differences and distinct social roles (Arnot et al., 1999; Silva, 2005). Early explanations, then, pointed to inherent differences between the sexes in capability and orientation. It was common to regard women as intellectually inferior. They were seen as weak-minded and overly dependent on their emotions, and therefore treated, like children, as properly dependent on men. Moreover, they were destined for motherhood and domestic duties, so that it was generally believed that, if much of an education was required, it should be directed towards preparing them for these future duties. Women were expected to become full-time mothers and housewives, which meant minimal participation in the public sphere (Arnot et al., 1999, p. 34). As McDermid (2000, p. 107) notes, as an ideal: 'All women were expected to conform to the ideology of domesticity, which disapproved of working women and which located feminine virtue in a domestic and familial setting'. Men's future roles, in contrast, were focused to a much greater extent on the public sphere: they were viewed as the heads of their families and the main breadwinners.

So, prior to the middle of the twentieth century, educational provision reflected these different assumptions about men's and women's capabilities and roles. To a large extent, there was separate secondary educational provision for the sexes and in particular separate curricula. Education was seen as a vehicle for women to develop feminine skills, personalities and interests linked to the domestic sphere. Elementary schooling at most was necessary for working-class girls, focused on 'domestic' subjects. Middle-class girls would attend ladies' academies, where they would learn skills that would prepare them for their future, more genteel but nevertheless domestic, roles. It was regarded as inappropriate for women to choose 'masculine' subjects (McDermid, 2000). Too much formal education for women was thought to risk infertility and amounted to a distortion of their femininity.

One of the earliest challenges to these assumptions was Mary Wollstonecraft's (1792) *Vindication of the Rights of Woman*. She argued that differences in intellectual capability were not natural but socially engendered: women were inhibited from developing critical powers of reasoning, not least because they did not have contact with the public world in the same way that men did. Furthermore, the education that women did receive further limited their minds; their moral education, for example, did not go beyond encouraging a superficial feminine decorum, which developed vanity, immaturity and cunning rather than a deeper understanding of morality. For Wollstonecraft, women should be educated to become independent and useful to society (p. 59). Otherwise they would remain weak and oppressed.

These ideas had little impact on the mainstream development of the education system in Britain in the nineteenth and early twentieth centuries, though they did influence the founding of some private schools and colleges for girls. The female founders and teachers in those institutions held an emancipated view of girls' potential, and instituted a broad and academically challenging curriculum. The new female professionals and educators who came out of these institutions were able to help other women access improved education (Arnot et al., 1999). It was well into the twentieth century, however, before the changes begun by Victorian pioneers brought about significant change in the gender order, even in relation to education.

The educational system was comprehensively restructured after World War II. The Butler Act of 1944 provided free secondary education for all.

There was, however, a continuing ideal of women primarily as family carers and housewives rather than working outside the home. Indeed, restrictions were placed upon the number of girls attending grammar schools and it was later discovered that higher marks were required of girls to pass the 11-plus entrance exam. However, this changed in the 1960s, which also saw the rise of comprehensive schools and a decline in the number of single-sex institutions. Furthermore, the Sex Discrimination Act of 1975 rendered illegal the practice of excluding pupils from particular school subjects on the grounds of gender. By the 1970s there was common educational provision and a curriculum largely shared between boys and girls.

With increasing provision of secondary schooling for girls, and the introduction of a more or less common curriculum, the achievement gap between girls and boys started to close. Furthermore, explanations for underachievement shifted from appeals to biology towards increasing emphasis on socio-cultural factors. In the forefront here were second-wave feminists who developed Wollstonecraft's arguments about the effects of gender socialisation in the home. It was pointed out that from birth male and female babies are treated differently: there are different expectations of, and different responses to, them, which it was claimed bring about significant differences in self-perception, attitude and capability. This explanation parallels that relating to class outlined in the previous section: in effect the argument was that girls had been deprived of cultural capital through a gender-differentiated socialisation process.

However, an equally important explanation put forward in the 1980s to explain girls' underachievement was that there was discrimination against girls within schools. This discrimination took a variety of forms: differential treatment in the classroom (e.g., teachers interacting more with boys than with girls); forms of pedagogy and assessment that favoured boys over girls; and gender-biased curriculum content, from the predominance of pictures of boys and use of illustrations more likely to interest them than girls, through to the actual topics covered. There was also criticism of modes of pedagogy: Arnot et al. (1999, p. 28) claim that girls generally do better than boys on 'sustained tasks that are open-ended, process-based, related to realistic situations and that require pupils to think for themselves' (Arnot et al., 1998, p. 28). It was argued that boys prefer traditional approaches to learning—such as the memorisation of abstract, unambiguous facts and rules. Such differences, and the modes of pedagogy prevalent in schools, were also held to explain differential achievement levels of girls and boys across different subjects.

Using Bourdieu, Arnot (1993) argued that male power in society, and specifically in education, operated in the same way as class power: male privilege in education was legitimated in a concealed way. For Clarricoates (1987) this hidden curriculum perpetuated gendered expectations. For Spender (1980) patriarchy persisted and was expressed in schools through the *malestream curriculum* and male-orientated teaching and assessment. Through studies such as these, new levels of awareness of gender differences in learning styles, responses to different forms of teaching and assessment, content and feedback, gender bias in teaching and examining materials and marking were produced. For example, how different subjects placed different learning demands on boys and girls became apparent.

Towards the end of the century, average levels of educational achievement for girls in 16+ examinations had equalled or surpassed those of boys in most subjects. Indeed, at this point there came to be mounting concern in some quarters about boys' underachievement, with the three sorts of explanation outlined above—appealing to biological differences, differential socialisation, and bias in the education system—being deployed, but now in the opposite direction. The other side of such arguments was, of course, the implication that, comparatively speaking, girls were more likely to possess important forms of cultural capital than boys.

Nevertheless, girls and boys still tended to choose different subjects at A Level, with boys predominating in mathematics, physics and chemistry, for example. Norms that link women with domesticity persisted; women continued to be the main carers of children, which penalised their careers outside the home (Platt, 2011). These societal patterns were seen as playing an important role in shaping the subject-choice process.

## Explanations for the Underachievement of Some Ethnic Minority Groups

In the 1960s and 1970s, explanations for the poor average performance of some ethnic minority children focused on factors external to the school, such as migration processes, family background and cultural differences (Tomlinson, 1987, p. 1). The root of educational inequality was seen to rest explicitly within pupils and their communities (Glennerster, 1972; Reeves & Chevannes, 1988). In particular, home culture was seen to be deficient in not being English-speaking (Hawkes, 1966). Languages and dialects other than Standard English were regarded as intrinsically inferior and a barrier to learning (see Labov, 1969; Rosen, 1972, for a critique of these views). It was generally believed by schools that the way to address the lower achievement of ethnic minority pupils, and to prevent them from depressing the achievement of 'British' pupils, was for them to abandon their distinctive social and cultural beliefs and behaviours and to assimilate into the school and mainstream cultures (Hawkes, 1966, p. 11). Some ethnic minority pupils were targeted with remedial help for their linguistic and cultural 'deficiencies' (Swann, 1985, p. 576). Such assimilationist objectives existed within a broader context of unequal power relations and colour discrimination which treated ethnic minority home cultures as alien and inferior (Tomlinson, 2008, p. 6). This led to the generation of unhelpful stereotypes by teachers, such as South Asians being 'passive' and African-Caribbeans as 'aggressive' (Tomlinson, 1984). Such attitudes perpetuated racial and cultural disadvantage. However, since the family was regarded as the root cause of underachievement, the educational system and teacher expectations were not given attention (Troyna, 1984).

In the 1970s, the explanation for ethnic minority underachievement shifted to processes within schools. In this approach structural issues were not ignored: educational underachievement was not felt to emanate from individuals but rather from the workings of institutions and structures in society. Multiculturalist policies introduced within schools were a response to the evolving view that Britain had become a plural, multi-ethnic society and that minorities should share equal rights with the majority, retaining a degree of cultural diversity but capitalising on agreed common values and aims. It was believed that this would create a more conducive learning environment for all pupils and thereby reduce ethnic inequalities in educational achievement. To overcome ethnocentrism, it was argued, teachers should learn to appreciate and respect other faiths and cultures, provide pupils with positive histories and images of minority cultures, support positive self-identities among minority children and broaden the cultural horizons of every child. It was believed that this could be achieved by changing the curriculum (Tomlinson, 1987). The Swann Report (1985) supported this kind of multiculturalism as an attempt to create social cohesion and consensus, and to raise the achievement levels of those ethnic minority groups that were below average. It identified the following barriers to their higher achievement: intentional and unintentional teacher racism, a curriculum that did not draw upon the experiences of every child, books and teaching materials that presented inaccurate and negative images of ethnic minority groups, examination syllabi and papers that were not relevant to the actual experiences of ethnic minority pupils in schools, lack of active engagement between the school and home, and career teachers not being sensitive to the needs of pupils from ethnic minority backgrounds. In a similar multicultural vein the *Linguistic Minorities in England: A Report by the Linguistic Minorities Project for the Department of Education and Science* (LMP, 1983) treated bilingualism in England as an asset for bilinguals and a potential resource for society as a whole, including monolinguals (p. 12). Respect was to be accorded to the dietary preferences, dress, customs, religions and cultural heritage of each ethnic group.

Whilst multiculturalism countered racism, it did not eliminate it (Parekh, 1989). Indeed, it came to be argued that the most important factor generating ethnic inequalities in education was discrimination by teachers including unconscious bias. For example, Troyna (1991) argued that ethnic minority students tended disproportionately to be placed in lower sets than White students, with the consequence that they were not prepared for examinations at a level which would do justice to their natural abilities. Teachers could also influence the subject choices that pupils made. Ethnic minority parents tended to agree with the choices endorsed by teachers (Tomlinson, 1987). 'Schools can therefore adopt their own system of channeling individuals based on perceived ability' (Abbas, 2004, p. 36). Ethnic minority pupils tended to be under-represented in higher sets and were more likely to be over-represented in those containing children with 'learning difficulties' (Troyna, 1991).[6]

Haw's (1998) research in Bradford discussed at length this theme of problematic relations between teachers and parents, and the teacher's low expectations of Muslim girls in comprehensive schools, even as late as the time of her writing in 1998. She claimed that teachers viewed parents as limiting their children, school being just a 'dumping ground' for girls until they reached marriageable age (p. 125). Ghuman (2002) reported too that teachers felt that Muslim parents did not give girls the same opportunities as boys. This prophecy of lower career expectations could lead to behaviour on the part of teachers that would reduce opportunities for Pakistani Muslim girls, although in my view Ghuman does not provide sufficient evidence to show that teachers might have been wrong about this or that such attitudes were universal among teachers.

Basit's (1997) research was conducted mainly among British Pakistanis from Mirpur living in the east of England. Her research focused on the aspirations of adolescent British Muslim girls from their own perspectives and those of their parents and teachers. Some parents in Basit's research believed that school discouraged their daughters from excelling in education, and daughters thought that schools were motivated only to support those pupils whom they knew for certain were going to continue into further and higher education. Teachers felt that most of the girls they taught would not continue into post-compulsory education because their parents did not regard education as necessary for their futures. According to Basit, this led teachers to regard most of the Pakistani girls as apathetic. Basit (1997) questioned teachers' assumptions that British Muslim girls were restricted within the home and that they experienced 'culture clash' between parental and school values. She argued that family relations were more consensual than these views suggested. The girls largely accepted their parents' religious and cultural demands relating to purdah. They

[6] Gomm (1993) draws attention to both the inappropriateness of the model of ethnic equity which grounds Troyna's (1991) claim that South Asian pupils are being treated inequitably, and to shortcomings in the way in which Troyna handles numerical data to present them as evidence of this claim. For a broader critique of this literature, see Foster et al. (1996).

would dress modestly, limit their visibility in some areas of the public sphere and adhere to the rules governing relations between the sexes. However, this did not mean that parents did not want their daughters to succeed in education.

For Smith and Tomlinson (1989) it was the school a child attends that makes a greater difference to examination attainment than any factor associated with ethnicity. Whilst there are methodological difficulties involved in comparing one school to another, it is nevertheless useful to reflect on how individual schools can make a difference to the achievement of pupils, including those from ethnic minority backgrounds (see the ten case study schools in Wrigley, 2000). Qualitative work by McIntyre et al. (1993) at a school with a significant number of ethnic minority pupils revealed how school factors such as facilities and resources, the need for teachers' help, extra classes and individual attention influenced these pupils' academic success. Interestingly, integral to the success of the school's multicultural policy was the regard the school showed for pupils' perspectives on how their school could adopt a curriculum for a multicultural society (McIntyre et al., 1993, pp. 19–21).

In recent years some have applied the concept of cultural capital to the case of ethnic inequalities. It has been noted, for example, that South Asian Muslim parents tend to be less educated than other groups (Abbas, 2004, p. 30). This suggests that their children often lack cultural capital within the home that could contribute to success at school. However, Modood (2004) has identified features of ethnic minority communities and families that provide distinctive forms of cultural capital, which he refers to as ethnic capital. He compares working-class ethnic minority groups with their working-class White counterparts and argues that young people from ethnic minority backgrounds are encouraged and expected to choose to go into higher education. They possess *ethnic* capital in the form of parental norms and expectations about educational success and professional careers. What he is pointing to here is variation in the frequency of such attitudes in the two communities (see also Strand, 2007). Basit (2012) too argues that aspirational capital is an important element to be found to greater degrees in some ethnic minority cultures. Thapar-Bjorkert's and Sanghera's (2010) research in Bradford emphasised the social capital available within the Pakistani community from parents, siblings and other members, to support young men and women to enter higher education. Modood's (2004), Basit's (2012) and Thapar-Bjorkert and Sanghera's (2010) work can be used to explain why people from ethnic minority backgrounds obtain a slightly higher proportion of places in higher education than their proportion within the population suggests. Transmitting this expectation is key to students' success.

Writers have identified other types of ethnic capital available within ethnic minority homes. Wrigley's (2000, p. 14) work in the North of England emphasises a disposition towards moral seriousness as regards education shown by British Pakistani families and illustrates ways in which more successful schools have worked to support this. In a similar way, Watkins and Noble (2013) argued that ethnic capital amongst Chinese families manifested itself in terms of the disposition to learn through self-discipline, which then supported their children's success at school.

Modood's work with Bindi Shah and Claire Dwyer (Shah et al., 2010) provides a detailed presentation of how ethnic capital operates amongst Pakistanis in Slough (see also Dwyer et al., 2011). Relations between parents, older and younger siblings, extended kin and family friends can come to generate capital through the cultural endowments, obligations and expectations, information channels and enforcement of social norms relating to success in education that characterise and circulate within these relations. These expectations and norms serve as a distinct form of both social and cultural capital. However, in contrast to Modood's (2004) optimism, others have emphasised that many ethnic minority families face an overall deficit in cultural capital. Furthermore, some commentators, such as Ahmad (2001), have pointed out that cultural resources within the home, such as high expectations to succeed, can amount to excessive pressure on young people. In such cases what seems to be ethnic capital in fact yields negative returns. This suggests that we should be wary of overconfident generalisations about the possession of ethnic capital (Watkins & Noble, 2013). It is important to recognise the variation between ethnic groups, and indeed within the same group in different parts of England (e.g., Pakistani communities in London compared with the former industrial towns of Lancashire and West Yorkshire), which in turn reflects differences in patterns of parental education, occupations and career opportunities.

## Conclusion

In this chapter I have reviewed the various explanations that have been put forward for educational and social inequalities, as regards social class, gender and ethnicity. Early investigations in relation to social class pointed to the effects of alleged differences in intelligence between members of different social classes, as well as the effects of poverty and discrimination. Later, the focus shifted to culture. Some argued that working-class families were culturally deprived, but this explanation came to be criticised, and the notion of cultural difference was developed. One of the most influential versions of this approach is to be found in the work of Bourdieu, and I looked at this in some detail—focusing particularly on the concept of cultural capital.

In the final two sections of the chapter I looked at explanations for gender and ethnic inequalities. In the past there was differential educational provision for girls and boys, reflecting biologically based arguments relating to deficiencies in women, as well as the belief that women were, and should be, destined for quite different roles in society from men. These ideas came to be challenged leading to efforts to equalise educational provision between boys and girls. By the second half of the twentieth century girls were achieving at the same average level as boys and often well above this at 16+, 18+ and in obtaining degrees. However, there remained differences in choice of A-Level and degree-level subject between males and females. Furthermore, women continue to be responsible for caring for children, which limits their participation in the labour market and thus their career outcomes.

Over the past four decades, various explanations were presented for ethnic inequalities in education. Cultural deficiencies were used to justify the need for ethnic minority pupils to assimilate into the school environment in order to raise their attainment. Multicultural policies in education and beyond were a response to the racial hostility experienced by ethnic minority groups implicit in those earlier assimilationist policies. This led to an emphasis on cultural difference explanations. Subsequently, though, researchers insisted on the continuing role of racism on the part of teachers and schools as institutions in undermining the educational progress of children from some ethnic minority groups, while others pointed to the effects of the differing qualities and practices of individual schools. Finally, I noted how some writers have developed the notion of ethnic capital, this sometimes being used to explain the disproportionately high representation of ethnic minority students among entrants to further and higher education. At the same time I noted some problems with this concept.

While I have examined explanations for educational inequalities separately in relation to social class, gender and ethnicity, of course their effects are interrelated, and in recent years a number of writers have examined such intersectionality, that is, how these factors combine to shape people's lives (Vincent et al., 2013a, b; Goode, 2019). For example, those living in more affluent and ethnically diverse environments may experience purdah differently from those living in close-knit Pakistani communities in the North of England (Abbas, 2003, p. 422). It is clearly necessary to be sensitive to the complex ways that class, gender and ethnic cultures feature and interact to produce unique habitus and social mobility outcomes for different groups.

## References

Abbas, T. (2003). The Impact of Religio-Cultural Norms and Values on the Education of Young South Asian Women. *British Journal of Sociology of Education, 24*(4), 411–428.

Abbas, T. (2004). *The Education of British South Asians Ethnicity, Capital and Class Structure*. Palgrave Macmillan.

Ahmad, F. (2001). Modern Traditions? British Muslim Women and Academic Achievement. *Gender and Education, 13*, 137–152.

Arnot, M. (1993). A Crisis in Patriarchy? British Feminist Educational Politics and State Regulation of Gender. In M. Arnot & K. Weiler (Eds.), *Feminism and Social Justice in Education: International Perspectives*. The Falmer Press.
Arnot, M., Gray, J., James, M., & Rudduck, J. (1998). *A Review of Recent Research on Gender and Educational Performance*. OFSTED Research Series.
Arnot, M., David, M., & Weiner, G. (1999). *Closing the Gender Gap Postwar Education and Social Change*. Polity.
Basit, T. (1997). *Eastern Values, Western Milieu*. Ashgate.
Basit, T. (2012). 'I've Never Known Someone Like Me Go To University': Class, Ethnicity and Access to Higher Education. In T. Basit & S. Tomlinson (Eds.), *Social Inclusion and Higher Education*. The Policy Press.
Bourdieu, P. (1973). Cultural Reproduction and Social Reproduction. In R. Brown (Ed.), *Knowledge, Education and Social Change*. Tavistock.
Bourdieu, P. (1977). *Outline of a Theory of Practice* (R. Nice, Trans.). Cambridge University Press.
Bourdieu, P. (1984). *Distinction*. Routledge and Kegan Paul.
Bourdieu, P. (1986). The Forms of Capital. In J. G. Richardson (Ed.), *Handbook of Theory and Research for the Sociology of Education*. Greenwood Press.
Bourdieu, P. (1990). *The Logic of Practice* (R. Nice, Trans.). Polity.
Bourdieu, P., & Passeron, J. (1977). *Reproduction in Education, Society and Culture* (R. Nice, Trans.). Sage.
Bourdieu, P., & Passeron, J. C. (1990). *Reproduction in Education, Society and Culture*. Sage.
Bourdieu, P., & Wacquant, L. (1992). *An Invitation to Reflexive Sociology*. University of Chicago Press.
Clarricoates, K. (1987). Dinosaurs in the Classroom – The 'Hidden' Curriculum in Primary Schools. In M. Arnot & G. Weiner (Eds.), *Gender and the Politics of Schooling*. Unwin Hyman.
Craft, M. (1970). *Family, Class and Education: A Reader*. Longman.
Dore, R. (1976). *The Diploma Disease Education, Qualification and Development*. University of California Press.
Dwyer, C., Modood, T., Sanghera, G., Shah, B., & Thapar-Bjorkert, S. (2011). Educational Achievement and Career Aspirations for Young British Pakistanis. In T. Modood & J. Salt (Eds.), *Global Migration, Ethnicity and Britishness*. Palgrave Macmillan.
Emirbayer, M., & Mische, A. (1998). What Is Agency? *American Journal of Sociology, 103*(4), 962–1023.

Foster, P., Gomm, R., & Hammersley, M. (1996). *Constructing Educational Inequality*. Falmer Press.
Ghuman, P. (2002). South Asian Adolescents in British Schools: A Review. *Educational Studies, 28*(1), 47–59.
Glennerster, H. (1972). Education and Inequality. In P. Townsend & N. Bosanquet (Eds.), *Labour and Inequality*. Fabian Society.
Gomm, R. (1993). Figuring Out Ethnic Equity. *British Educational Research Journal, 19*(2), 149–165.
Goode, J. (2019). *Clever Girls. Autoethnographies of Class, Gender and Ethnicity*. Palgrave Macmillan/Springer Nature.
Haw, K. (1998). *Educating Muslim Girls*. The Open University Press.
Hawkes, N. (1966). *Immigrant Children in British Schools*. Pall Mall Press.
Ingram, N. (2011). Within School and Beyond the Gate: The Complexities of Being Educationally Successful and Working-Class. *Sociology, 45*(2), 287–302.
Keddie, N. (1971). Classroom Knowledge. In M. Young (Ed.), *Language and Control*. Collier-Macmillan.
Keddie, N. (1973). Introduction: Tinker, Tailor…The Myth of Cultural Deprivation. In N. Keddie (Ed.), *Tinker, Tailor… The Myth of Cultural Deprivation*. Penguin.
Labov, W. (1969). The Logic of Non-Standard English. In P. Giglioli (Ed.), *Language and Social Context* (pp. 179–215). Penguin.
Lareau, A. (2003). *Unequal Childhoods: Class, Race and Family Life*. University of California Press.
LMP. (1983). *Linguistic Minorities in England: A Report by the Linguistic Minorities Project for the Department of Education and Science*. University of London, Institute of Education.
Maton, K. (2010). Habitus. In M. Grenfell (Ed.), *Pierre Bourdieu Key Concepts*. Acumen Publishing.
McDermid, J. (2000). Women and Education. In J. Purvis (Ed.), *Women's History: Britain, 1850–1945*. Routledge.
McIntyre, D., Bhatti, G., & Fuller, M. (1993). *Educational Experiences of Ethnic Minority Students in the City of Oxford*. Oxford University Department of Educational Studies.
Modood, T. (2004). Capitals, Ethnic Identity and Educational Qualifications. *Cultural Trends, 13*(2), 87–105.
Moore, R. (2004). Cultural Capital: Objective Probability and the Cultural Arbitrary. *British Journal of Sociology of Education, 25*(4), 445–456.

Parekh, B. (1989). The Hermeneutics of the Swann Report. In G. Vera (Ed.), *Education for All: A Landmark in Pluralism*. Falmer Press.

Platt, L. (2011). *Understanding Inequalities Stratification and Difference*. Polity Press.

Reeves, F., & Chevannes, M. (1988). The Ideological Construction of Black Underachievement. In M. Woodhead & A. McGrath (Eds.), *Family, School and Society*. Hodder and Stoughton.

Robbins, D. (2004). The Transcultural Transferability of Bourdieu's Sociology of Education. *British Journal of Sociology of Education, 25*(4), 415–430.

Rosen, H. (1972). Language and Class: A Critical Look at the Theories of Basil Bernstein. Reprinted in J. Richmond (Ed.), *Harold Rosen: Writings on Life, Language and Learning 1958–2008*. UCL IOE Press.

Shah, B., Dwyer, C., & Modood, T. (2010). Explaining Educational Achievement and Career Aspirations Among Young British Pakistanis: Mobilising 'Ethnic Capital'? *Sociology, 44*(6), 1109–1127.

Silva, E. B. (2005). Gender, Home and Family in Cultural Capital Theory. *The British Journal of Sociology, 56*(1), 83–103.

Smith, D. J., & Tomlinson, S. (1989). *The School Effect: A Study of Multi-Racial Comprehensives*. Policy Studies Institute.

Smyth, J., & Wrigley, T. (2013). *Living on the Edge: Rethinking Poverty, Class and Schooling*. Peter Lang.

Spender, D. (1980). *Man Made Language*. Routledge.

Strand, S. (2007). *Minority Ethnic Pupils in the Longitudinal Study of Young People in England (LSYPE)*. University of Warwick.

Sullivan, A. (2001). Cultural Capital and Educational Attainment. *Sociology, 35*(4), 893–912.

Swann, M. (1985). *Education for All the Report of the Committee of Inquiry into the Education of Children from Ethnic Minority Groups*. Her Majesty's Stationery Office.

Thapar-Bjorkert, S., & Sanghera, G. S. (2010). Social Capital, Educational Aspirations and Young Pakistani Muslim Men and Women in Bradford, West Yorkshire. *The Sociological Review, 58*(2), 244–264.

Thomson, P. (2010). Field. In M. Grenfell (Ed.), *Pierre Bourdieu Key Concepts*. Acumen Publishing.

Tomlinson, S. (1984). *Home and School in Multicultural Britain*. Batsford.

Tomlinson, S. (1987). *Ethnic Minorities in British Schools a Review of the Literature, 1960–82*. Gower Publishing Company.

Tomlinson, S. (2008). *Race and Education Policy and Politics in Britain*. The Open University Press.

Troyna, B. (1984). Fact or Artefact: The 'Educational Underachievement' of Black Pupils. *British Journal of Sociology of Education, 5*(2), 153–166.

Troyna, B. (1991). Underachievers or Underrated? The Experience of Pupils of South Asian Origin in a Secondary School. *British Educational Research Journal, 17*(4), 361–376.

Vincent, C., Ball, S., Rollock, N., & Gillborn, D. (2013a). Three Generations of Racism: Black Middle-Class Children and Schooling. *British Journal of Sociology of Education, 34*(5–6), 929–946.

Vincent, C., Rollock, N., Ball, S., & Gillborn, D. (2013b). *The Educational Strategies of the Black Middle-Classes*. Institute of Education University of London.

Watkins, M., & Noble, G. (2013). *Disposed to Learn Schooling, Ethnicity and the Scholarly Habitus*. Bloomsbury Academic.

Wollstonecraft, M. (1792). *Vindication of the Rights of Woman*. Penguin.

Wrigley, T. (2000). *The Power to Learn. Stories of Success in the Education of Asian and Other Bilingual Pupils*. Trentham.

# 4

# Methodology

Most research concerned with social mobility, and quite a lot of work investigating educational inequalities, has employed quantitative data and forms of analysis. While this can be of value, there is much that it cannot capture. In this research, in order to investigate the opportunities for and barriers to higher levels of educational achievement and upward social mobility of working-class Pakistani women, I used a very different approach: the biographical interview method. In this chapter I will outline the reasons for choosing this method and provide some detail about what it involved, what problems arose and how these were dealt with.

## Survey Methods and Understanding Social Mobility

Social mobility is concerned with movement between social classes or socioeconomic strata, its variation over time, across different societies, and its causes. The most commonly adopted method in studying it has been the social survey (Goldthorpe, 2003; Halsey, 1977; Heath et al., 1992). This method generally allows the collection of relatively small



A. Saeed, *Education, Aspiration and Upward Social Mobility*,
https://doi.org/10.1007/978-3-030-82261-3_4

amounts of significant information about a relatively large number of individuals, from which reasonably reliable generalisations can be made about national cohorts. It has been effective in showing patterns of social mobility over time in the UK, and other countries, and in identifying some of the factors affecting these (Erikson & Goldthorpe, 1993; Bukodi & Goldthorpe, 2018). Sociologists have also used such research to show how the variables of class, gender and ethnicity influence social inequality and mobility (Liodakis, 2006; Platt, 2011). Some research relying on survey work has gone beyond this to try to assess the role of attitudes and aspirations, and of cultural capital (Halsey et al., 1980). Here, though, the method is less successful in understanding what is involved, and how these factors vary across different groups.

While there are advantages in collecting quantitative data about large samples of people, there are also disadvantages. Survey research starts with hypotheses, or at least with some set of pre-defined categories, that are necessarily taken for granted in the process of data collection and analysis. There is little scope for re-thinking the assumptions made, or for exploring new aspects of the issue that could be important, during the course of the research. These failings are especially significant when the aim is to investigate the development of aspirations, and the opportunities and barriers to achieving these experienced by particular groups in distinctive contexts.

This is why in the present research I used a qualitative approach to try to capture the social and psychological experiences of my informants in their careers. More specifically I used a life history method, drawing on informants' educational and career biographies. In this chapter I will outline what is involved in the life history method and its advantages in understanding career trajectories within individual lives, as well as some of the problems involved.

## Biographical Interviews

The main method of data collection in my research was in-depth, biographical interviews, a form of case-centred research. This method is key to the burgeoning sub-field of the narrative study of lives in the human sciences, which developed across a range of disciplines especially during the second half of the twentieth century (Cohler, 1988; Riessman, 2008; Roberts, 2002). Varied terminology is used in this field to describe broadly similar methods which nevertheless have specific applications. Indeed, Bertaux (1981, p. 7) claims that there has been some terminological confusion. The different terms used include: 'biographical interviews', 'in-depth interviews', 'narrative research', 'life story' and 'life history method'. Whilst these terms are not synonymous, what they refer to shares many features. Biographical research may aim at complete life histories, focus on one aspect of people's lives, explore events at a specific time in a person's life or deal with particular themes such as social mobility (Bertaux & Thompson, 1997; Erben, 1998). The accounts produced by informants can be referred to as personal narratives, and these have been used as data in many areas of study (Mishler, 1999, p. 17).

There are three broad traditions of biographical research: oral testimony used by historians, the collection of life histories by anthropologists and sociologists (Thompson, 1981) and narrative analysis (Riessman, 2008).

## Oral Testimonies

In studying the recent past, some historians have used oral history interviews together with 'life documents' such as diaries, letters and photographs as well as the more conventional written documents on which historians usually rely. One of the reasons for this is that such data gives them access to the voices and lives of those under-represented in more formal written sources and even in published memoirs and diaries (Denzin, 1989, p. 7; PMG, 1982; Thompson, 2000). Oral history gained ground as a method in the 1970s, at the same time as various 'movements for political and social change, such as feminism, permeated universities and challenged traditional forms of knowledge' (McLeod & Thomson, 2009, p. 36). It was part of a broader approach to social history. It aimed to recover the perspectives of people previously marginalised in the historical record, thus preserving the perspectives of generations that might otherwise be lost (McLeod & Thomson, 2009, p. 35). The growth of recent interest in oral history began in the 1950s and 1960s, initially in the fields of local history and folklore.[1] An important part of oral history interviews is accessing people's subjective perspectives, that is, how they experienced particular events and their views of them, as well as more basic facts about their lives. For example Chamberlain (2006) uses the method to understand the experiences and perspectives of British Caribbean families from the 1920s until more recent times. The histories of this group are largely missing from the written record, so material gathered in biographical research interviews is an essential source of information. There has often been a link between oral history, community histories and political activism (Barnett & Noriega, 2013). Later critiques of the oral history method challenged whether people's accounts represented objective accounts of a past, since the past is always mediated by present circumstances (Thomson, 2007). Such discussions have become part of this field of research, and I shall explore them further later on.

## Life Histories

Life story has been a standard tool of fieldwork in sociology and anthropology since the early twentieth century (Bertaux, 1981, pp. 5–8; Lewis, 1961, 1964). Early uses of 'personal documents' in sociology pre-dated the growth of oral history from the 1950s onwards referred to above. Life history methods and personal documents enabled the researcher to understand the perspectives of particular groups, such as Polish immigrants into the United States, that are not represented in other sources of data (Thomas, 1958). It was also argued that these documents facilitated understanding of processes over time, for example how people's lives were shaped by the process of migration and settlement. Some anthropologists also argued that through the life histories of key individuals, such as native American chiefs, an understanding could be gained of the working of a whole society. Later, this same approach was applied by sociologists to investigating distinctive types of work, usually of a deviant kind—for

[1] See http://www.history.ac.uk/makinghistory/resources/articles/oral_history#early_history.

example, Clifford Shaw's *The Jack Roller* (1930) on robbers and Klockars' *The Professional Fence* (1974) on 'fences' for stolen goods (See Salerno, 2007).

The aim of life history interviewing was to document the course of people's lives and to *discover* what factors had shaped them, rather than basing interview questions on prior assumptions about such influences. *The Jack Roller*, for example, was an intensive study of one boy's life, behaviour and social background. It recorded the delinquent's own account of his experiences and was written as an autobiography. The delinquent mugged people and stole from them, and Shaw was concerned with what could be learned from this about the origins of delinquent behaviour. This process of gathering data capable of generating fresh and unforeseen insights makes biographical research a powerful methodology, since it allows the testing and reformulation of the researcher's assumptions throughout the research process.

Among anthropologists in the 1980s and 1990s there was a move to see the lives of people from different cultures as not completely and 'objectively' different from the researcher's, that is, to see the self in the other. This is illuminated most clearly in the classic text based on research conducted in the Kalahari Desert in Botswana: *Nisa: the life and words of a !Kung woman* (Shostak, 1982, 2000). The American anthropologist Shostak wanted to convey Nisa's life story as having universal relevance. She used an in-depth life story interview with an exceptionally verbally gifted woman to collect her experiences, thoughts and feelings. The story is told by balancing three perspectives: that of Nisa, told in the first person; the second, official voice, that of the anthropologist putting Nisa's story into a cultural context; and the third voice, that of the author as a young woman rather than an anthropologist (Shostak, 1998). The work recognised the mutual sensitivity of Shostak and Nisa. In this work the life story interview is understood as an interaction between the perspectives of two people.

In the 1980s Daniel Bertaux and some co-workers began to use the life history method to study particular occupations. He argues that the method is capable of taking account of the broad purpose of sociology, to focus less on the individual and more on the person as a sociological object, part of a network of social relations (Bertaux, 1981, pp. 6–9). The life history approach can take account of a wider range of factors than is possible in a social survey. Life history material can, like survey research, identify an individual's place in the social order but in addition explain experience through the moral, ethical or social context of a given situation (Bertaux, 1981; Josselson & Lieblich, 1993). In short, studying individuals can thus illuminate the intersection of biography, history and society. One of the advantages of the life history method is that it highlights the role of agency, of the decisions that individuals take in shaping their lives, while at the same time locating these individuals within contexts shaped by macro-structural social forces. Thus, through individual biographies we can understand how social structures shape the barriers to, and opportunities for, social mobility in people's lives. These include traditional forms of stratification such as class, gender and ethnicity.

The main examples of life history research on social mobility are the case studies included in Bertaux and Thompson (1993, 1997, 2007). Bertaux used the life history method to understand the social and psychological aspects of social mobility in the twentieth century. Interview analysis was complemented by information from other sources to advance understanding of people's social mobility experiences. Other case studies explored, amongst other things, the ways in which women's mobility experiences are bound up with their familial roles, the extent to which family ties encourage or inhibit their social mobility, how the family's economic and social resources feature in intergenerational mobility (Bertaux & Bertaux-Wiame, 1997) and how the home and 'cooking cultures' affect mobility.

For example, Bertaux-Wiame (1993) challenges the almost intuitive assumption that upward social mobility is achieved at the expense of one's family ties.[2] This assumption is based on the supposition that those who rise socially have to create a distance from their parents' generation because family ties are inherently conservative, with children expected to follow the life courses of earlier generations. The persistence of family solidarity undercuts the belief that social change is brought about through the struggle of each new generation for its autonomy.

[2] This is contrary to recent work that emphasises the pain of social mobility (Goode, 2019; Hanley, 2016).

More recently, Goode (2019) uses autoethnographic accounts of 'clever girls' from working-class backgrounds to share their individual social mobility experiences. Intersectionality is used as a tool to examine how different forms of structural inequality co-exist and dynamically interact to affect the individual emotionally as well as socially. Their highly personal accounts are presented using various literary and textual forms (poetry, school reports, photographs, diary extracts, 'fragments', time shifts, 'reflexive vignettes', reconstructed conversations, an imagined letter p. 346). The book provides a supportive space for the contributors to reflect on how their various social identities have shaped their social mobility experiences.

There has been surprisingly little other biographical research conducted on social mobility. Yet the biographical method, using the subjective insights of interviewees' experiences from their own point of view, invites career decisions to be located within a wider context, elucidating the varied influences on an individual's career aspirations and decisions. This can include complex and intimate data. People's sense of mobility is affected by social processes on which a survey approach would give little purchase, for example, early family relationships, a migrant or single parent background or parental fear of poverty. In short, some of the factors that are important in understanding social mobility cannot be understood through reliance upon highly structured data collection and measurement procedures, rather they need to be explored in a more sensitive way.

## Narrative Research

Narrative research is a very broad category. Often the term is used in a way that includes life history work and even oral history. However, often there is a concern not just with the content of the stories that people tell but also a focus on how these stories are structured, how they reflect the contexts in which they are told and how they are shaped by the audiences to which they are addressed. In studying this, a range of ideas is drawn from a number of sources: linguistics, ordinary language philosophy and post-structuralist French philosophy (Riessman, 2008). A central theme in much of the work that labels itself as narrative research is the idea that in using language we do not represent a pre-existing world, so that our accounts are not to be judged as more or less accurate; the idea is rather that it is only in and through language use that 'the world' is constituted. So life narratives do not simply report the facts of people's lives; in an important sense they constitute or give meaning to those lives. This line of argument breaks with the predominantly realist approach adopted in most oral history and life history work in the past.

Much biographical research has adopted a realist stance, implicitly if not explicitly, in the sense that interviews were used to collect information about people's past lives, what happened to them, why it happened the way it did and how they felt about it. The assumption here is that people's accounts represent the reality of their lives, more or less accurately. This is true of almost all oral history work and much life history research. Thus, in the research on social mobility by Bertaux and others, the accounts provided from the life stories of the interviewees are treated as descriptions of the reality of their lives (Bertaux & Thompson, 1997). These researchers do not treat what people say as automatically true; its likely validity has to be assessed. Nevertheless, in adopting a realist perspective, they do treat what people say about their lives as potentially representing what actually happened. And the primary concern is to determine in what respects it is, and is not, accurate.

Over time there was, however, growing recognition that the accounts people give about their lives, or about anything else, are formulated using particular linguistic resources, drawing on distinctive cultural genres, and therefore could always have been constructed somewhat differently. Moreover, the decisions speakers and writers make about how to formulate accounts reflect their purposes, the context and the intended audience.

So, for example, the Popular Memory Group at the Birmingham Centre for Contemporary Cultural Studies came to argue that there is a direct relationship between public representations and private memories:

> Private memories cannot … be unscrambled from effects of dominant historical discourses. It is often these that supply the very terms by which a private history is thought through. Memories of the past are, like all common sense forms, strangely composite constructions, resembling a kind of geology, a selective sedimentation of past traces. (PMG, 1982, p. 211)

People's memories can therefore illuminate cultural myths, dominant memories and public histories (McLeod & Thomson, 2009, p. 41). We can understand people's stories by considering how the larger social and historical discourses shape them. In relation to my own research for example, my informants revealed aspects of the Pakistani community's history in Milltown, in making references to the public discussion of halal meat and learning Urdu, as well as in talking about the everyday aspects of their own lives.

However, in many more recent accounts of narrative research this line of argument has been taken further, moving away from realism to a form of constructionism. Constructionists deny, or are not interested in, any purported relationship between what people say and some reality they are describing, for example, what they themselves did in particular situations. Instead the focus comes to be on how accounts are put together and why they take one form rather than another, with the idea that this can tell us a great deal about the different ways in which lives come to be formulated within a society, and perhaps what factors shape this, how particular narrative strategies have particular discursive effects and so on.

For constructionists, it is particularly important to take into account the performative demands of the interview context. It is argued, for example, that what is actually expressed there will be based on whether it fits into a range of versions of the self that are sanctioned in that environment (Dingwall, 1997). The data tells us about the interview itself rather than about some world beyond it (Hammersley, 2008, p. 87; Scheurich, 1995). This perspective abandons any concern with what information the interview account might be held to provide, focusing instead on the processes of social interaction involved and on the cultural resources participants employ (Potter & Hepburn, 2005). A central emphasis is on the ways in which interview data are co-constructed by interviewer and interviewee. From this perspective, nothing exists 'behind' the accounts given in interviews. It is thus meaningless to ask whether what is said in interviews corresponds with reality: it is argued that any reality is itself always a discursive product (Chamberlayne et al., 2000; Crossley, 2000; Riessman, 2008).

So, a constructionist approach to narrative analysis suspends the question of whether or not narratives tell the truth about reality, in order to focus on how they are structured rhetorically to be convincing for some audience and what effects they create 'through the telling'. Generally speaking, the teller of a story must convince the listener, who has not lived it, of its 'authenticity'. This is the 'teller's problem' (Riessman, 2008, p. 87). One of the foci for narrative research, then, is whether and how this problem is solved in particular cases.

## The Approach Taken in This Research

As a sociologist I am particularly interested in my informants' experiences and the opportunities and barriers they encountered. My position is fundamentally realist but I believe that something can be learned from constructionism, and in this respect my position is similar to Mishler's. According to Mishler (1999), narratives are also identity performances. The interview is not just a search for facts and an uncovering of the true and full story. When people are being interviewed, they are performing an identity. This does not mean that what they perform is 'untrue', but rather that it is bound by the context of the interaction which inevitably creates particular expectations. The whole interview can be seen as a narrative with a purpose. A coherence can be found, as we would expect in a plot. This approach can allow more information to be drawn from the data whilst acknowledging that people's memories are mediated by present circumstances. It can be viewed as an eclectic approach shaped by both realist and constructionist traditions.

So my fundamental approach has been to treat the biographical research interviews with my informants as revealing their educational and career decisions and processes more or less accurately. In other words, I will assume, for the most part, that what they told me provides an accurate account, though I am attuned to the possibility of error. But how reliable were these memories? This is a big question. In both the life history and oral history traditions it used to be assumed that informants' testimony was reliable, *on the whole*, so that checking was only required where there was a possible motive for not telling the truth. This seems to me to be a defensible strategy.

The key question here is: how sceptical should we be about people's accounts of the past? It is certainly true that conveying memories is a constructive process rather than simple regurgitation of past experiences and thoughts. People continually reconstitute their memories, influenced by current experiences (McLeod & Thomson, 2009). They seek to make sense of their lives, in particular contexts and for particular purposes, and in so doing reshape their memories retrospectively. The resulting life story they tell will be based on memories that may be real, embellished or imagined—but will be shaped to serve people's current definition of self:

> The process of remembering is a dialectical process, incorporating current questions and preoccupations, as well as the act of remembering, into the memory. It is laced with the hopes, dreams, and regrets from the past that entangle themselves with current recollection, leading sometimes to forgetting, denial and even fabrication. The fact that people do remember, and remember differently at different times in their lives and in different contexts, highlights the complexity of meaning and the transformations that take place in interpretation and reconciliation. Above all, it suggests that memory itself has a history, and that history can provide a clue to how an individual sees him- or her- (or them-) self/selves, and forms an identity. (Chamberlain, 2006, p. 12)

Ken Plummer's two editions of his classic text *Documents of Life* (1983, 2001) reveal that, like Mishler's, his position on how sceptical we should be in relying on people's memories is somewhere in the middle between constructionism and realism. Plummer's second edition shows more awareness of the fact that multiple stories can be told about the same event, that these will reflect people's motives and the audience they are speaking to. However, he retains a concern with the lives behind the stories.

This issue is clearly of considerable importance for a study like mine where biographical interviews are used as a means of understanding past experience and decision-making. Memories do not simply reproduce how past decisions were made because they are constituted and reconstituted over time and will be presented in different ways on different occasions. However, I believe that it is reasonable to assume that they do nevertheless capture much of the original event, particularly when they are recalled and retold at length. In ordinary life we assume that people's memories are reliable to a considerable degree and that they represent what happened in most respects, most of the time. We do not regard them as complete fictions. Indeed, if we were to do this then we would have to conclude that we could have no reliable knowledge of the past, of any kind. Certainly, there could be no stable knowledge acquired from biographical interview data. I do not believe that this is the case. In research, no less than in everyday life, we cannot assume that everything people tell us is simply an imaginative fabrication which bears no relation to reality. Were we to take such an extreme position seriously, it is not only research such as mine that would be impossible; indeed, it is difficult to see how practical everyday life could continue. In my view, then, interviews should be regarded as a fallible source of information about the world that can nevertheless provide reliable data about people's lives and experiences (Hammersley, 2003). It is in the spirit of such methodological caution that I explore in the final section of this chapter my own decision-making in carrying out research and some of the assumptions built into this.

## How the Research Was Carried Out

My approach to interviewing acknowledges that the interview encounter does not merely record the 'facts' of a stable pre-existing narrative but itself produces a particular *telling* and a particular mode of understanding the events and memories being recounted. This is a process in which I am also implicated at many levels. For this reason a degree of reflexivity was built into the research. I wanted to avoid foregrounding the experience of the researcher, giving priority instead to the interviewees' stories, but at the same time I did not want to ignore the ways in which my self became entangled in the research at various stages.

Reflexivity is an important part of the research process because it helps the qualitative researcher to be vigilant in the face of threats to the validity of the research findings. It is a continual process (Hammersley, 2011) and involves a consideration of the ways that the researcher's own gender, class, ethnicity, professional position and biography influence the collection and interpretation of the data. In addition, it requires a continual process of engaging with other credible interpretations when analysing the data. These alternative ideas can be provided by external and wide-ranging sources such as literature, other disciplines and politics.

As explained earlier, narrative research as a methodology promised to provide an understanding of the experiences of my informants that would not have been available using other methods, such as survey research. At the same time I was aware that the stories told would be influenced by my management of the interviews. I wanted to make the circumstances as relaxed as possible so that people would talk at length and on their own terms. The aim was to generate rich data through giving my informants opportunities to explore their stories as far as they wished. Stories we tell are central to who we are (Crossley, 2000).

I interviewed nine women, aged from 19 to 39, separately and in-depth in 2012. All the women were born in Milltown, where they completed their compulsory education mainly from the late 1980s to 2000s. All of their parents had migrated from Pakistan, mainly from the Punjab. This is a very small sample of course, but these interviews generated a large body of unstructured data. Increasing the number of interviews would have made the amount of data unmanageable. Stanley (2008, p. 444) has warned of the danger of being overwhelmed by the data analysis when too large a number of cases is used in life history research. Furthermore, the research was exploratory in nature, given that I was working on a topic about which there has been relatively little previous work: the upward social mobility of British Pakistani women from working-class backgrounds.

In recruiting my informants I took into account several considerations. One was that they must have been educated in Britain. I also wanted to work with women who would be happy to talk at length about their lives. Finding such people could have been more difficult had I been a complete stranger, simply because I might not have been trusted to be the guardian of their stories—here my connection with the area where they grew up paid off. Like my informants I was born in Milltown and attended schools there, though I had subsequently moved away.

I used a snowball sampling method, relying largely on word of mouth. This seemed appropriate in view of my own links with the location of the research, which could be drawn upon to minimise my status as a 'stranger'. My sister had been a key person in my gaining access to some of the informants. She was able to put me in touch with people whom she knew at work, at the mosque or with whom she was friends at the gym. In addition, some of the informants themselves introduced me to other people who would '*enjoy being interviewed*' or '*wouldn't mind being interviewed*'. Two informants were siblings both of whom I already knew slightly. I was vaguely acquainted with four others, but I had not met any of the remaining three previously. As I did not know any of the young women well, their responses at the outset were unpredictable.

This method of recruitment led to participants who were similar in terms of their career aspirations and marital status, but not in terms of what they had been capable of achieving. They all aspired to achieve professional work, and all had avoided an early marriage arranged by parents. Table 4.1 below shows the various career routes taken thus far by my informants. They did not all achieve what they aspired to in terms of having professional careers, and some of them were still in the process of securing professional work, but all had made some progress towards realising their ambitions. Of course, all names have been anonymised.

Most of the interviews were conducted in the front room of my parents' house in Milltown, as this is a quiet and private place in which traditionally visitors are received. As a result of this context, the interviews were influenced by a particular cultural etiquette governing the reception of guests in one's home. This etiquette had a religious basis, informed by the *sunnah*, which understands guests as having 'rights' to be treated exceptionally well, using the best cutlery and crockery and sharing with them the best of what one has. This choice of location also provided interviewees with information about me. However, despite this formality and expectation, there was some improvisation involved. My younger sister complained that I had not tidied the reception room well enough, suggesting that I was being too casual in receiving visitors to whom she had introduced me. I did not share this view, but felt that I had to comply and apologised. For my family, an air of importance hung over the occasions that had become 'Aqsa's interviews'. Family members remained

**Table 4.1** List of informants and their personal characteristics

| Name | Age | Marital status | Attended University/ HE? | Current occupational status and place of work | Highest educational qualification |
|---|---|---|---|---|---|
| Raheela | 39 | Single | Yes | Senior nurse<br>Not in immediate locality | BA |
| Ghazala | 27 | Single | Yes | Social worker<br>Within locality | BA |
| Tahira | 27 | Single | Yes | Dentist, with own practice<br>Just outside locality | BDS+ |
| Shaheena | 27 | Single | Current | Training to become primary school teacher Not in immediate locality | A Levels. Currently studying for a foundation degree |
| Nasreen | 20 | Single | Current | Training in childhood studies—aims to run her own nursery in locality | A Levels. Currently studying for a foundation degree |
| Ayesha | 32 | Single (with one child) | Current | Aims to become a primary school teacher<br>Outside locality | GCSEs, then university access course. Currently studying for a foundation degree |
| Shamila | 27 | Single | No | Local government administrator<br>Within locality | GCSEs |
| Robina | 28 | Single | Yes | Supply teacher within locality and its outskirts | MA |
| Noreen | 37 | Single | No | Retail management and voluntary work<br>Outside locality | GCSEs. Hopes to study for a degree at the age of 40 |

quiet in other parts of the house as they would have done for any visitor. Whilst the interviews took place we were not interrupted. Following the etiquette relating to visitors, all the respondents were offered fruit juice, tea and biscuits, and one was given a meal (albeit from the local take-away) by my older sister.

Does this setting mean that the interview was a social occasion rather than a sound way of collecting data about my informants' experiences and ideas? Did this context determine what was discussed? All qualitative interviews are social occasions and this always shapes the character of the data. It was thus important for me to be aware of how the social context of the interview could influence the data and for me to intervene to generate the appropriate interview conditions.

My own position in relation to my informants was somewhat ambiguous. I had much in common with them, but there were also relevant differences, notably that I had not lived in the town for 15 years. At the same time, my family continued to live there, and I visited quite frequently. In various aspects, then, I was both an insider and outsider.

Strauss and Corbin (1998) point out that having a personal connection with the research can increase one's commitment to it. A number of scholars have written, often in moving terms, about the complexities of identification and positioning in relation to research topics in which they have deep emotional investments (Motzafi-Haller, 1997; Probyn, 1993, 2004) and about the sensitive and sometimes painful interplay of family and personal relationships and academic work (Skeggs, 1997, 2002). The position of academics carrying out work in communities where they had grown up and/or have family connections is sometimes described as 'insider research' (Reed-Danahay, 1997, p. 5). There can be advantages to being an insider because one can understand the 'fine-grained meanings of behaviour, feelings, and values … (and) decipher the unwritten grammar of conduct and the nuances of cultural idiom' (Merton, 1972, p. 15).

To understand their stories required me to participate vicariously in their lives just as my reader would be expected to (Erben, 1998, p. 4). I was in a good position to understand their stories and share them with an academic audience as part of the process of scholarship. I could use intuitive information when analysing their stories to corroborate my interpretations of what they were saying. The fact that I too was an upwardly mobile British Asian woman meant that there were many things my informants said that they did not need to explain and concerns that they would expect me to share. My insider position therefore lent support to what they remembered of their own trajectories. However, having moved away from Milltown 15 years ago, there were points during the interviews where a shared background no longer pertained and at which I therefore required informants to provide greater detail. Similarly, each unique family history needed to be related. Moreover, we did not always share the same knowledge and values, so it was important to listen carefully to the words of the informant and to be aware of how I was using shared knowledge. Even as an insider I had much to learn about my informants' lives.

Tahira, for example, made reference to the cultural assumptions built into one of my questions, referring to this explicitly in the interview to make her point about the differences in cultural capital between working-class and middle-class trainee dentists.

In the context of the wider point that Tahira was making, she regarded the types of question that I asked as reflecting a middle-class discourse that assumed that decisions are made openly, through discussion with parents at least. In this way my questions reflected a voice that was middle-class, although I do not think it created a chasm of cultural asymmetry or social distance in the interview. A sympathetic comprehension and a sense of social ease overcame obstacles that such questions might have raised.

Sometimes it was not a simple case of shuttling between an insider and an outsider position, but rather of working within both simultaneously. For example my presence as a young woman did influence one street interview in unanticipated ways, when an unexpected source helped me to appreciate the community's history more broadly. It was an unscheduled conversation I had with a Pakistani man whilst in Milltown. He stopped me in the street, and when I told him I was doing research in Milltown, he started talking to me about the history of the National Front in the area. He had been a key player in resisting the National Front's attempts to intimidate Pakistanis in the 1980s, and he told me of incidents that led to this resistance. An impromptu interview ensued. The engrossing content of his stories, the passionate flow of his narrative and my own upholding of the rules of research politeness made me persist with talking and listening to him. The data felt raw, and I experienced the respect of being treated on equal terms as a witness to important aspects of men's stories in community history. This contact helped me to appreciate how my role as a researcher could further my access to worlds that I could easily assume wrongly were culturally closed to me. Research can be a risky endeavour, transforming the boundaries of socially acceptable conduct and involving movement between a multiplicity of positions within research relationships (Jewkes & Letherby, 2001; Reed-Danahay, 1997).

I thus learned to use my part-insider, part-outsider status to advantage in the project, allowing me to move through a range of perspectives and preventing too stark a dichotomy between the proximity of empirical engagement and the distance entailed in theoretical analysis. My positioning also forced me to reflect critically on the various discourses of objectivity through which researchers establish their credibility and authority, making me acutely sensitive to how education and power differentials may have shaped my interactions with my interviewees and helped me to meet scholarly standards. I had the power to set the agenda, analyse and interpret the data and present my informants' stories (Erel, 2009). I needed to remain aware that I differed from them and could not assume that they and I always shared the same frame of reference.

I wanted my informants' two overlapping roles, as visitors and interviewees, to complement each other. By receiving guests in the expected manner, I wanted to normalise the setting of the interview rather than it being unfamiliar, so that the interviewees would feel as comfortable as possible. Nevertheless, I followed the conventions of an interview throughout, listening carefully, using body language to show that I was engaged and not interrupting but rather letting people finish making their point. Sometimes I would reiterate what had been said to maintain active listening, to check that I was hearing correctly and to let respondents know that I was listening with interest. This also served to check that my interpretation of their experiences at that point matched theirs.

## Interview Questions

I carried out one interview with each informant, lasting around one and a half to two hours. I began each interview with an open question, asking respondents to talk about key educational decisions that they had made in their lives. I explained that they could interpret the question in any way they chose. I adopted an open disposition throughout. My questions and prompts varied between participants to the extent that different contexts of their stories gave rise to different questions. My aim was to encourage interviewees to tell their stories in their own ways, with a minimum of prompting. I wanted them to control the stories they told and to minimise my own influence on what they chose to tell. Decision-making is a complex process which, to varying degrees, can be explicit and informed as well as intuitive and emotional. I wanted to be able to understand all these aspects of the decisions that my informants had taken.

My experience of using this method revealed that people did indeed talk about themselves at length, with some preferring not to be interrupted by my questions. I think this was facilitated by the non-threatening nature of the questions, which were also wide enough in scope for people to present their biographical narratives as they chose. They could avoid talking about uncomfortable aspects of their lives, without sanction or being 'found out', and there seemed to be plenty of 'safe' areas to talk about, even if that was just rehearsing a choice of GCSE options.

The overall framework of my questioning related to the routes that informants took in their educational decision-making:

Which were the key educational decisions?
Who else was involved in those decisions?
What were the perceived barriers and favourable circumstances leading to the outcomes they wanted to achieve?
How were these barriers overcome, and if they were not, why not?
What have been their post-education experiences?
What opportunities and problems have they encountered in their work?

In the interviews, people described and interpreted the quotidian realities of their lives and in so doing included motives, decisions, feelings, rationalisations, personal details and cultural networks, all of which gave the data considerable richness. The content included factual biographical details and personal thoughts, and reference to conscious and unconscious decision-making.

The life stories elicited in my interviews revealed past and present constructions of identity. For example, Ghazala highlighted her Pakistani identity and how she was encouraged by her sisters and by acting as an 'agony aunt' at school, while Ayesha viewed herself at least initially as unfocused, with parents who were unable to help her. Respondents provided a plethora of examples to support these identity presentations, which acted as loci of educational decisions as well as serving to buttress identity constructions that impacted on those decisions. These examples came to act as facts in people's lives, although I am aware that the power of these identity labels may vary over time, in different contexts, and even between interviews. Some of these early identities impinged upon identity perceptions in the present, or worked as experiences to move away from, and thus were implicated in shaping current identities. Ayesha, for example, understood her current educational decisions as being markedly different from earlier, less-focused decision-making. Sometimes people viewed the history of their 'educational' identities as being marked by disjuncture and uncertainty ('Shall I become a physiotherapist?' 'Shall I continue being a social worker?' 'Shall I continue being a scientist?'). At other times they indicated stable features of identity ('I am an active Muslim', 'I am Asian' or 'I want to be a businesswomen').

Erben (1998) explains that the general purpose of biographical research is:

> to provide a greater insight than hitherto into the nature and meaning of individual lives or groups of lives. Given that individual lives are part of a cultural network, information gained through biographical research will relate to an understanding of the wider society. (p. 4)

Talking about oneself autobiographically always touches on the biography of others; sometimes this is done explicitly. Ghazala compared and contrasted herself with 'other Asian girls'. This can provide useful leads when the researcher is trying to gauge a sense of how individual lives may also say something about the lives of people as representatives of a group or category.

The interviews were not exhaustive since they did not tell me about whole lives and neither did they tell me all the details relating to key educational decisions and their contexts. As a result I did sometimes have to do follow-up work to clarify cultural information. For example I sought clarification from Ghazala following her interview about her job as a social worker through a brief phone call.

## Analysis

I was firmly located in the research as the *manager* of the data collected because it seemed to me that three layers of insight or knowledge emerged and converged in my interviews: the interviewees' understandings of their lives, the interviewer's understanding of their experiences through what they said and academic interpretation of the interview data. Whilst informants were not being asked to theorise their position, they were certainly not being treated as 'cultural dopes' who could not articulate their experiences with fluency and reflect intelligently upon them. Informants' experiences may offer manageable and holistic insights into human complexity. Biographical research retains an emphasis on the linguistic reality of human experience and provides the researcher with rich descriptions. Although I did not question the veracity of informants' stories, I did create as far as possible the necessary conditions for my questions to be taken seriously and answered fully, as a way for full explanations to be given. Atkinson (1998) has argued that the account should seem 'trustworthy' and have 'internal consistency'. These were the broad terms of assessment I used, but when there seemed to be an inconsistency I explored it rather than deeming the data as invalid. Shamila, for example, revealed career-related priorities that seemed to be inconsistent. However, the method allowed shifting perspectives over time to be expressed and the reasons for these to be explored.

There was a standard of systematic thinking that was applied in the analytic process. Exploring the potential of various categories involves continual interplay between the researcher and the raw data, and is a creative, painstaking and laborious process. Our shared way of speaking meant that I found it easy to be able to recall the ways that informants expressed themselves. This helped with immersing myself in the data, thinking laterally about the meaning of particular words and generating initial concepts. These concepts were subsequently identified, developed and related to each other (Strauss & Corbin, 1998). Whilst my insights as a British Pakistani woman facilitated intuitive generation of concepts, I also developed my understanding of concepts by drawing on the literature. Both sources informed my understanding of the properties and dimensions of analytical concepts and of the relationships among them. The analysis involved connecting those sources of knowledge with the interview data. The major themes of social mobility and aspiration developed from the process of theory building and from analysing data. I hope I have written with truth, care, insight and clarity, and in so doing have illuminated important and complex aspects of working-class British Pakistani women's lives for my readers.

## Ethical Considerations

The interviews were audio-recorded and transcribed. Transcripts were anonymised so that participants could not be identified. I offered participants the opportunity to correct or delete material from their interview transcripts and assured them of complete confidentiality. The research questions did not in themselves raise ethical concerns, being sufficiently straightforward for interviewees to be able to give informed consent to participate.

Such informed consent was a key element of meeting ethical standards. I explained at the outset of the interview how long it might take, what the research was about and the nature of an in-depth interview, reassuring the interviewees of my strong commitment to anonymity and confidentiality at every stage of the research. They could turn the audio recorder off at any point. I told them that the recorded data were only for my benefit and would not be shared with anyone else, although the work would become public knowledge in due course. I also made it clear to them that they were free to decline to be interviewed if that was their preference.

A research interview can have positive outcomes for people, although I am aware of the warning given by Goodson and Sikes (2001) that 'participating in life history research can damage the psychological and emotional … health of informants, and of researchers too. It is not to be embarked upon lightly' (p. 99). I think these potentially harmful consequences of the method ought not to be ignored by the researcher for her own sake and for that of her interviewees. I protected myself from the poignancy of the interviews by carrying them out about once a fortnight. However, whilst there are personal risks and consequences that accompany the research process, such as the distress caused by reading literature on racism, these should not come to overshadow the process, to which dwelling on them might well lead.

Most respondents did talk about at least one deeply personal and painful matter that impacted on their key educational decision-making: a painful experience of racism, repercussions of their parents splitting up, being bullied at school or being belittled by a school teacher and feeling socially excluded. I did not want to appear inquisitive and seduce my informants into revealing more about themselves than they would have wished to, because this would have been unethical. For this reason if they digressed too much, for example when Noreen started talking in detail about her friend, I was not dismissive but gently re-stated the purpose of the interview. In this sense there was a topical line that related to key educational decision-making that I kept in mind.

I tried to listen to the sense of what was being said, rather than just the words. In an extreme case I stopped the recording when the respondent talked of the deaths of close family members. I could also see benefits to people of talking about their decision-making. For Ayesha, it gave her a chance to 'realise new things' and remain committed to her decision to complete a degree. It helped people to reiterate their identities and uphold a positive sense of self. Perhaps the extraordinary nature of the interview for them, carrying their experience from the private to the public, and the density and intensity of their thoughts, can explain the relief and sense of accomplishment that some of them felt.

On two occasions I sensed that interviewees wanted to talk for longer than one and a half hours so I let the interview continue. The experiences they were sharing with me were emotionally intimate, such as Ayesha's references to her parents' limitations in being able to help her. Sometimes the talk revealed something that had previously been private, such as a racist insult. It was therefore important that I closed the interviews appropriately so that respondents did not feel the 'chill of exposure' or an immediate need to share more information. In all of the interviews, I spent the last ten minutes of the interview closing it. In that time I talked about practical things such as the confidentiality clause. I asked respondents if they were happy for the interview to come to an end. In this way, I was giving them control over what they wanted to say and ensured that the interview did not end too abruptly. I also let them know that they could contact me to talk further about the interview if they wished and that I would let them have a transcript of the interview which would allow them to change any part of it.

I minimised the amount of information about myself that I shared with the women I interviewed to avoid influencing them by giving them unintended suggestions of the kinds of things I might want to hear. As a rule I therefore decided to keep reciprocity to a minimum throughout the interview, although I did talk more at the beginning of the interview to inform respondents about the project, engaging in non-essential discussion about the interview process, such as how long it would take me to transcribe an interview, to put the respondents at their ease. Oakley (1982) has characterised feminist interviews as being non-hierarchical because they involve the researcher reciprocating with personal information about themselves. While I chose not to do this, I did reflect on the relationship in order to appreciate how power was operating within it. Oakley (1982) assumes that the power in feminist research is more equal than in conventional interviews. However, I think that all research involves the researcher exercising more control. For example, I was able to steer the conversation away from topics and invite expansion of ideas around a particular point. Being aware of how I exercised power was part of my reflexive research responsibility. Also, I was the one who would be telling my story of my informants' career journeys, based on my own understanding and interpretation of the experiences they shared with me. The researcher listens to peoples' narratives, that is, their interpreted stories of their experiences. Her research is then a presentation of a meta-narrative based on an interpreted overview (Stanley, 2008).

I saw my informants' lives as intrinsically interesting but did not strive to make their narratives as exciting and engaging as possible because this would risk 'othering' them and making them stand out as unusual.

I aimed to resolve this dilemma by depicting their lives in a way that showed them respect. The proof of this respect is through my ability to talk about people in a way that makes the reader engage with their humanity (Plummer, 1983; Stanley, 2013).

## Conclusion

In this chapter I began by arguing that the dominant approach to studying social mobility, which relies upon survey data, does not provide much evidence about the sorts of aspirations, barriers, resources, opportunities and experiences that are often very significant for explaining why people are or are not upwardly mobile. Moreover, these are particularly significant in the case of ethnic minority groups. The alternative approach that I have adopted draws upon biographical method, as initially developed in the form of life history studies and oral history work. Recently, this kind of approach has been applied to the study of social mobility by a number of researchers, though not specifically to the case of social mobility within ethnic minority groups (Bertaux & Thompson, 1997, 2007). This work adopted a broadly realist stance, as against the more constructionist approach that has come to dominate much work on narrative. I have done the same, although at the same time trying to learn what I could from constructionism.

I have outlined how I recruited informants for my study and the process of interviewing, noting the flexible and open-ended approach I adopted. Clearly, one of the potential problems with the research method I have used concerns the reliability of the accounts my informants provided of the decisions that they made in the past and the various factors that shaped these. I have argued that any thoroughgoing constructionist approach to interview accounts, treating them as simply inventing the past, is unsustainable and unhelpful. I have outlined a number of strategies I employed within the interviewing in order to try to ensure the fidelity of the information provided. Important here was the exercise of reflexive awareness on my part, as both 'insider' and 'outsider', in relation to my informants and their world, paying particular attention to ways in which I may have influenced the accounts produced.

Finally, I have looked at ethical aspects of the research process, examining some of the issues I needed to take into account and how I dealt with them.

## References

Atkinson, R. (1998). *The Life Story Interview*. Sage.

Barnett, T., & Noriega, C. (2013). *Oral History and Communities of Color*. UCLA Chicano Studies Research Centre Press.

Bertaux, D. (1981). *Biography and Society the Life History Approach in the Social Sciences*. Sage Publications.

Bertaux, D., & Bertaux-Wiame, I. (1997). Heritage and Its Lineage: A Case History of Transmission and Social Mobility Over Five Generations. In D. Bertaux & P. Thompson (Eds.), *Pathways to Social Class*. Oxford University Press.

Bertaux, D., & Thompson, P. (Eds.). (1993). *International Yearbook of Oral History* (Vol. 2). Oxford University Press.

Bertaux, D., & Thompson, P. (1997). *Pathways to Social Class: A Qualitative Approach to Social Mobility*. Clarendon Press.

Bertaux, D., & Thompson, P. (2007). *Pathways to Social Class: A Qualitative Approach to Social Mobility*. Transaction Publishers.

Bertaux-Wiame, I. (1993). The Pull of Family Ties: Intergenerational Relationships and Life Paths. In D. Bertaux & P. Thompson (Eds.), *International Yearbook of Oral History and Life Stories Volume II Between Generations Family Models, Myths, and Memories*. Oxford University Press.

Bukodi, E., & Goldthorpe, J. H. (2018). *Social Mobility and Education in Britain. Research, Politics and Policy*. Cambridge University Press.

Chamberlain, M. (2006). *Family Love in the Diaspora*. Transaction Publishers.

Chamberlayne, P., Bornat, J., & Wengraf, T. (2000). Introduction: The Biographical Turn. In P. B. Chamberlayne, J. Bornat, & T. Wengraf (Eds.), *The Turn to Biographical Methods in Social Science Comparative Issues and Examples*. Routledge.

Cohler, B. (1988). The Human Studies and Life History: The Social Service Review Lecture. *Social Service Review, 62*(4), 552–575.

Crossley, M. (2000). *Introducing Narrative Psychology Self, Trauma and the Construction of Meaning*. The Open University Press.

Denzin, N. K. (1989). *Interpretive Biography*. Sage.

Dingwall, R. (1997). Accounts, Interviews and Observations. In G. Miller & R. Dingwall (Eds.), *Context and Method in Qualitative Research*. Sage.

Erben, M. (1998). *Biography and Education: A Reader*. Falmer Press.

Erel, U. (2009). *Migrant Women Transforming Citizenship: Life Stories from Britain and Germany*. Ashgate Publishing Limited.

Erikson, R., & Goldthorpe, J. H. (1993). *The Constant Flux: A Study of Class Mobility in Industrial Societies*. Clarendon Press.

Goldthorpe, J. H. (2003). The Myth of Education-Based Meritocracy. Why the Theory Isn't Working. *New Economy, 10*(4), 234–239.

Goode, J. (2019). *Clever Girls. Autoethnographies of Class, Gender and Ethnicity*. Palgrave Macmillan/Springer Nature.

Goodson, I., & Sikes, P. (2001). *Life History Research in Educational Settings Learning from Lives*. The Open University Press.

Halsey, A. H. (1977). Towards Meritocracy? In J. Karabel & A. H. Halsey (Eds.), *Power and Ideology in Education*. Oxford University Press.

Halsey, A. H., Heath, A. F., & Ridge, J. M. (1980). *Origins and Destinations Family, Class, and Education in Modern Britain*. Clarendon Press.

Hammersley, M. (2003). Recent Radical Criticism of Interview Studies: Any Implications for the Sociology of Education? *British Journal of Sociology of Education, 24*(1), 119–126.

Hammersley, M. (2008). *Questioning Qualitative Inquiry: Critical Essays*. Sage.

Hammersley, M. (2011). *Methodology: Who Needs It?* Sage.

Hanley, L. (2016). *Respectable: The Experience of Class*. Allen Lane.

Heath, A., Mills, C., & Roberts, J. (1992). Towards Meritocracy? Recent Evidence of an Old Problem. In A. Heath & C. Crouch (Eds.), *Social Research and Social Reform*. Clarendon Press.

Jewkes, Y., & Letherby, G. (2001). Insiders and Outsiders: Complex Issues of Identification and Difference in Social Research. *Auto/Biography, 9*(1/2), 41–50.

Josselson, R., & Lieblich, A. E. (1993). *The Narrative Study of Lives* (Vol. 1). Sage.

Klockars, C. (1974). *The Professional Fence*. Tavistock Publications.

Lewis, O. (1961). *The Children of Sanchez. Autobiography of a Mexican Family*. Random House.

Lewis, O. (1964). *Pedro Martinez*. Random House.

Liodakis, N. (2006). Review of 'Mobility and Inequality: Frontiers of Research in Sociology and Economics' by Morgan, S., Grusky, D., and Fields, G. *Canadian Journal of Sociology Online November–December*. http://www.cjonline.ca/reviews/mobility.html

McLeod, J., & Thomson, R. (2009). *Researching Social Change*. Sage.

Merton, R. K. (1972). Insiders and Outsiders: A Chapter in the Sociology of Knowledge. *American Journal of Sociology, 78*(1), 9–47.

Mishler, E. (1999). *Storylines: Craftartists' Narratives of Identity*. Harvard University Press.

Motzafi-Haller, P. (1997). Native Anthropologists and the Politics of Representation. In D. Reed-Danahay (Ed.), *Auto/Ethnography: Rewriting the Self and the Social* (pp. 169–195). Berg Publishers.

Oakley, A. (1982). Interviewing Women: A Contradiction in Terms. In H. Roberts (Ed.), *Doing Feminist Research*. Routledge.

Platt, L. (2011). *Understanding Inequalities Stratification and Difference*. Polity Press.

Plummer, K. (1983). *Documents of Life, an Introduction to the Problems and Literature of a Humanistic Method*. George Allen and Unwin.

Plummer, K. (2001). *Documents of Life 2 an Invitation to a Critical Humanism*. Sage.

PMG. (1982). Popular Memory: Theory, Politics, Method. In R. Johnson, G. McLennan, B. Schwarz, & D. Sutton (Eds.), *Making Histories Studies in History-Writing and Politics*. Hutchinson and the Centre for Contemporary Cultural Studies, University of Birmingham.

Potter, J., & Hepburn, A. (2005). Qualitative Interviews in Psychology: Problems and Possibilities. *Qualitative Research in Psychology, 2*(4), 281–307.

Probyn, E. (1993). *Sexing the Self: Gendered Positions in Cultural Studies*. Routledge.

Probyn, E. (2004). *Blush: Faces of Shame*. University of Minnesota Press.

Reed-Danahay, D. (1997). *Auto/Ethnography: Rewriting the Self and the Social*. Berg.

Riessman, K. (2008). *Narrative Methods for the Human Sciences*. Sage Publications Inc.

Roberts, B. (2002). *Biographical Research*. The Open University Press.

Salerno, R. (2007). *Sociology Noir Studies at the University of Chicago in Loneliness, Marginality and Deviance, 1915–1935*. McFarland and Company, Inc.

Scheurich, J. (1995). A Postmodernist Critique of Research Interviewing. *International Journal of Qualitative Studies in Education, 8*(3), 239–252.

Shaw, C. (1930). *The Jack Roller A Delinquent Boy's Own Story*. The University of Chicago.

Shostak, M. (1982). *Nisa, The Life and Words of a !Kung Woman*. Allen Lane.

Shostak, M. (1998). 'What the Wind Won't Take Away' The Genesis of Nisa – The Life and Words of a !Kung Woman. In R. Perks & A. Thomson (Eds.), *The Oral History Reader*. Routledge.

Shostak, M. (2000). *Return to Nisa*. Harvard University Press.

Skeggs, B. (1997). *Formations of Class and Gender: Becoming Respectable*. Sage.

Skeggs, B. (2002). Techniques for Telling the Reflexive Self. In T. May (Ed.), *Qualitative Research in Action*. Sage.

Stanley, L. (2008). Madness to the Method? Using a Narrative Methodology to Analyse Large-Scale Complex Social Phenomena. *Qualitative Research, 8*(3), 435–447.

Stanley, L. (2013). *Documents of Life Revisited: Narrative and Biographical Methodology for a 21st Century Critical Humanism*. Ashgate.

Strauss, A. L., & Corbin, J. (1998). *Basics of Qualitative Research. Second Edition. Techniques and Procedures for Developing Grounded Theory*. Sage.

Thomas, W. (1958). *The Polish Peasant in Europe and America* (Vol. II). Dover Publications.

Thompson, P. (1981). Life Histories and the Analysis of Social Change. In D. Bertaux (Ed.), *Biography and Society. The Life History Approach in the Social Sciences*. Sage.

Thompson, P. (2000). *The Voice of the Past*. Oxford University Press.

Thomson, A. (2007). Four Paradigm Transformations in Oral History. *Oral History Review, 34*(10), 49–71.

# 5

# An Overview of the Career Aspirations and Trajectories of My Informants

In this chapter I examine the career aspirations of my informants and provide an overview of their career trajectories. The word 'career' is used very broadly here to refer to a 'path through life', implying commitment and expectations about the future (Richardson, 1977). It includes both occupational careers, narrowly understood, and, for example, the career of housewife and mother. I shall begin by drawing on the literature to map out the range of options open to British Pakistani women from different generations within Milltown, and more widely.

## Generational Differences in Aspiration and Career

It is common to refer to British Pakistanis as first or second generation. First generation means those who originally migrated from Pakistan to Britain. Second, and subsequent, generations are British-born. It is important to distinguish this usage of 'generation' from those that peg its meaning to the distinctive experiences and outlooks associated with those who come of age in a particular historical period (Lovell, 2007). For



A. Saeed, *Education, Aspiration and Upward Social Mobility*,
https://doi.org/10.1007/978-3-030-82261-3_5

example, 'the 1960s generation' refers to those who became adults in that decade. 'First-generation British Pakistani' can thus refer not only to mothers who arrived in Britain in the 1960s, but also to more recently arrived transnational brides born in Pakistan. Nevertheless, in this usage as well, the focus is on significant differences in experience that generate distinct attitudes, capabilities and opportunities.

My informants reported that their mothers were housewives who had never worked outside the home in Britain, and this is representative of the experience of most first-generation British Pakistani women. They were expected to keep house, cook and look after the children and were dependent on their husbands, and in some cases on children, for financial support within the household (Becher, 2008). Dale et al. (2002) argues that the time taken up by their extensive homemaking responsibilities prevented them taking paid work outside the home. Purdah was another reason why they did not work outside the home. For this generation, the association between Pakistani women and the domain of the household and family has been documented in the academic literature. As noted earlier, Anwar (1979, pp. 130–135) reports that those Pakistani women in northern English towns who did enter the labour market characteristically worked from home, often as outworkers for the local garment industry (Allen & Wolkowitz, 1987; Brah & Shaw, 1992; Phizacklea & Wolkowitz, 1993).

First-generation British Pakistanis will have in common the experience of arriving in a strange country that has alien customs and a dominant language that may be unfamiliar. They chose, or are required, to follow the 'traditional' norms about the most suitable personal career for women within their families and for dress and public comportment. Moral law requires that women's work is in the home, including paid work as well as housework and the work of mothering. By contrast, across the country, a significant proportion of the second generation shows a different pattern, at the very least delaying marriage in order to pursue further education and occupational careers.

First-generation British Pakistani women largely conform to Pakistani traditions of virilocal residence. The relations they have with family members are shaped by traditional certainties, and individuals base their behaviour on moral precepts about how to behave 'as a wife and a mother'. For many of these women motherhood is seen as a source of personal fulfilment and a key aspect of personal identity (Becher, 2008, p. 102). Mothers are regarded as the child's first teacher, particularly of religious practices and values. Motherhood is therefore a continuing social relationship. Fathers are breadwinners, whose responsibility is to work outside the home, which makes fathers less visible in the home and family. So there is a particular family form assumed here, associated with this career trajectory. Fathers are the head of the household and reflect traditional notions of patriarchy. The work of British Pakistani mothers within the home keeps them fully occupied. Their workload is heavy and includes responsibility for the housework including cooking, cleaning and caring work such as 'nurture, physical maintenance, management and daily discipline' of the children (Becher, 2008, p. 97). Caring for their children involves mothers 'being there' (p. 101) all the time; women are thus expected to sacrifice their time to be available for their children. The emotional support that mothers provide by being gentle and loving is linked to religious prescriptions of idealised and proper conduct for mothers.

None of my informants were women who had arrived in the UK as transnational brides, but there are such women who are the same age as the informants in this study. The characteristics of this group are documented in Aston et al.'s (2007) research on 'Pakistani women's attitudes to work and family', carried out for the Department for Work and Pensions:

> Some women had come from abroad to marry and settle down in the UK, and they had rarely worked immediately following their marriage; partly due to a lack of English language skills, unfamiliarity with the new country, and sometimes their own and their husbands' and families' beliefs that men should be breadwinners. (Aston et al., 2007, p. 2)

So, transnational brides may be the same age as second-generation Pakistani women, but they are likely to have attitudes and aspirations that are more similar to the mothers of those women. First-generation mothers and transnational brides tend to have similar biographical experiences, particularly in terms of motherhood being the primary career from an early age and having grown up and been educated in another country. While transnational brides are similar to first-generation women migrants in many respects, they may engage in some local work outside the home and are perhaps more likely to attend language classes. They have not, however, had a full British education,[1] although they may have received a higher level of education in Pakistan than that of their mothers-in-law. Above all, they represent what is still widely seen as an idealised lifestyle for a British Pakistani woman, since they have married early and taken on the religiously sanctioned duty of motherhood, in line with a morally sanctioned discourse on appropriate roles for women.[2] Transnational brides are regarded as 'traditional' by my informants and with their typical career trajectories closely replicating those of their mothers-in-law.

At the same time, some common experiences are shared by transnational brides and British Pakistani women, such as the hostility they may have to face from some quarters towards Islam and its cultural manifestations, such as dress.

## Diverging Experiences Within the Second Generation

Previous research has documented the conflict within British Pakistani communities between parents and children as a result of their somewhat differing values (Anwar, 1998; McDermott & Ahsan, 1986; Saifullah-Khan, 1976). However such differences also exist within generational cohorts to some degree, as well as between them. Indeed, the values attributed to first-generation parents in the research literature may also be found among second and third generations.

---

[1] Funding to support them learning English has been cut.

[2] Tenvir's (2015) study in the south west of England showed how early marriage and lack of formal education can leave British-born Pakistani women vulnerable to patriarchal dominance.

So, within the generation of women that I am studying, a variety of aspirations and trajectories is found. For many the pattern, particularly in working-class communities of the kind from which my informants came, is still very similar to that of the first generation, with young women marrying men from Pakistan or having a marriage to a British Pakistani man arranged by parents before the age of 20 (see also Tenvir, 2015).

In this community it is a minority who have developed rather different aspirations, wishing to pursue advanced levels of education and achieve professional careers. As a result, they remained in education beyond the compulsory stage, rather than for example leaving to get married and have children. It can be argued that they are bonded with others on a similar trajectory by their exposure to education's 'destabilising' potential, which offers an alternative to 'traditional' British Pakistani womanhood (Pilcher, 1994).

British-born second-generation Pakistanis are likely to be more at home with the forms of the English language prevalent in British society and with British cultural life. Furthermore, their aspirations and ideas are more likely to be influenced by contact with non-Pakistani peers than is the case with the first generation. However, it is clear that the effects of this are not uniform, as British Pakistani girls respond in various ways to these experiences. None of the young women in this study have followed family tradition in leaving school as early as possible and marrying almost straight away. For some of them, education has created new experiences, outlets and opportunities that their mothers did not have. Dale et al. (2002) argue that it is 'unsurprising' that the experience of a British education, the acquisition of the English language, exposure to Western cultural values and educational qualifications means that many younger British Pakistani women would expect to do jobs which their mothers did not do (p. 943). As British-born citizens they have learned about Britain 'from the inside' and become aware of the aspirations and orientations of peers from a variety of backgrounds. From this perspective, what is surprising is that so many second-generation Pakistani women do *not* develop these aspirations. The role of social class inequalities is at least part of the explanation.

## The Segment of the Second Generation My Informants Represent

All of the women I interviewed in this study had embarked on educational courses post-16 and aspired to obtaining a degree. While in part this reflects differences in their aspirations and orientations from those of their mothers, changes in mainstream society have also widened educational opportunities and career expectations for women over time, and some Pakistani women have capitalised on these (as explained in Chap. 2). Archer (2003) argues that the final third of the twentieth century was a significant period of gender equality in higher education participation, but of stagnation in redressing class inequalities, and with only sporadic attempts to address ethnic inequalities. These rather contradictory trends represent both opportunities and barriers for working-class British Pakistani women.

Policy documents relating to higher education, such as the *Dearing Report* (Dearing, 1996) and the document *The Future of Higher Education* (Clarke, 2003) from the Department for Education and Skills, reveal the Government's commitment at that time to extend higher education provision to social groups that had not previously participated. British Pakistanis as an under-represented group in higher education were encouraged to take up these opportunities. In Chap. 2 I showed the remarkable increase in the numbers of British Pakistani women embarking on degree-level qualifications, paralleling the increase in the number of university places. However, I also showed how some writers raise concerns about low attainment levels. As regards translating qualifications into professional-level jobs, the non-traditional routes British Pakistanis are more likely to take, and the types of courses they study, can add to the difficulties they face.

The depressed labour market conditions in former mill towns constitute a yet further challenge for British Pakistanis living there. For my informants the way out of this was to aspire to professional jobs requiring advanced qualifications and skills.

## Professional Aspirations

In the following discussion I present the distinctive aspirations of my informants and what distinguishes them from first-generation British Pakistanis.

An aspiration can be viewed as a projection into the future, based on a present reality, which is itself partly defined by the past. Ambitions can be broad and general in scope, for example, to embark on degree-level study or to have a professional career, or more specific, such as to enter a particular profession.

Aspirations can vary in other respects too. For example, what is involved may be nothing more than a vague hope without much commitment to bringing it about, or it may involve great determination and systematic planning. An aspiration is a fantasy until a pathway has been found to the opportunities which may enable it to be realised. Aspirations therefore have different prospects of becoming reality. The genesis of an aspiration can also vary in temporal terms. Some aspirations are present from childhood, while others develop later, as new insights and opportunities become available.

The aspirations of my informants differed too in the strength of their underlying motivation. Generally speaking though, they were underpinned by a belief that a professional career would bring financial rewards, but also by the idea that education would result in a more interesting life.

## Aspirations to Do Something Interesting, Appropriate and Worthwhile

There is a strong momentum among some second-generation Pakistani women to acquire qualifications to achieve higher-status jobs in spite of depressed local economic conditions. Dale et al.'s (2002) work in Oldham reported that 'Asian women getting higher qualifications are unusual and therefore likely to display other characteristics—for example, considerable determination and strength of character' (p. 8). My informants did have strong aspirations to do interesting work that they deemed at the same time to be 'appropriate' and worthwhile. This represented part of a distinctive outlook among second-generation British Pakistani women.

Robina, discussing her cousin who was academically able but abandoned her degree course and embarked on having a family instead, comments: 'She doesn't do anything now. She got medium results like me, she's got married and had a kid and not bothered with getting herself a career'. This route amounts to a passive option from Robina's point of view because a home-based career is regarded as something that has happened to her cousin, rather than something she actively sought and achieved by her own efforts. Robina views her cousin's trajectory as not worthwhile, because she is no longer engaging with the educational opportunities available, eschewing the active alternative of making a career outside the home. Thus for Robina there is a specific notion of the ideal personal trajectory that is appropriate for 'a person like me' or 'people like us'. She regards this as a possibility for British Pakistani women, in a historically evolving situation:

> To me education is everything. … My mum really really had a passion and wanted to be a nurse … but as soon as she was 16 she got married … she wanted to get an education … In my family, education is important. It's always education. That's what I say to the Asian girls in education—you've got to push yourself. And they're sat there putting their lip liner on. I look at them and think, I wish I had the same opportunities that you have now. The world's so much more modernised than what we had. They've got so much more freedom. Not taking advantage of the education you've been given. (Robina)

In aspirational terms, reflection on the future is characterised by emotional engagement, something to be 'passionate' about. It is important to care about what will happen to you in the future. There is an active ideological perspective reflected here, echoed in Beck and Beck-Gernsheim's (2008) ideas about the contemporary opportunities and motivations to 'make oneself'. Robina's emphasis at this stage is on the responsibility that the individual bears for her own career project. The individual should work hard on 'producing' herself, through engaging in the right habitual practices. Robina assumes that through education one can make oneself, and in doing so she echoes dominant narratives about higher education as a route to career success (Hart, 2013). She reflects the view too that the improvement in educational opportunities enables women to create their own biographies. From Robina's perspective, this has become easier with time.

The centrality of her occupational career for Robina explains her strong commitment to her education. Having a career outside the home is part of her vision of the good life. In this respect her orientation matches 'the project of the self':

> Careers have a particular role to play in such choices, with a focus on the career as an organising and regulative principle—how and why is a career pursued, and how the career is part of the project of the self. The project of self-management links home and work, leisure, dreams and daydreams (Grey, 1994, p. 481) and in this climate of individualisation, agency is more important than social structure (Giddens, 1991). (Hardill, 2002, p. 13)

When Robina highlights the need *to push yourself*, her emphasis is on the *individual* self making choices, seizing opportunities and taking responsibility for thought, action and behaviour (Giddens, 1991, p. 75; Berlant, 2011; Spohrer et al., 2018). She does not ignore social structures providing new opportunities that need to be accessed by the 'entrepreneurial self', which takes the initiative in order to achieve a new and original outcome (Rose, 1998, p. 151). A particular agentic personality is indicated, one that works to seize new opportunities to bring about a transformation in careers for women like herself. It is a fusion of imagination with the commitment involved in doing the necessary work to make it real.

Others among my informants show a similar commitment to exercising their own agency, linking this to the pursuit of occupations outside the home. An important element of this is achieving independence:

> I wanted to open up my own business because I wanted to be independent. (Nasreen)

For Nasreen a career as a businesswoman would serve her aspiration to become a proactive individual. She envisages that such a career would have positive outcomes for her, thus making it worthwhile. Meanwhile, Shamila emphasises the other side of this commitment—rejection of the more conventional trajectory for Pakistani women from this community:

> I'd be bored out of my mind if I was a housewife. I'd probably kill myself. (Shamila)

Here Shamila projects an imagined scenario based on her taking the same role as her mother. She engages emotionally with that possible future self. She pithily and figuratively makes clear that if she took on that role, she would find it unbearable.

However, what is involved here is not just rejection of the role of housewife, my informants are also operating with a status hierarchy of jobs:

> I thought, right, I want to do something proper. I don't just want to work in a shop. (Ayesha)

Ayesha identified the type of work that she wanted to avoid as lower-skilled shop or administrative occupations. Whilst she was not explicit about it lacking interest, she wanted to avoid it because such work could not 'make you'. A more skilled job was deemed 'proper'. This echoes the view that a career must offer a vehicle for the self to 'become' (Grey, 1994, p. 481). Ayesha aspired to a job that was deemed appropriate for someone like her, because of its potential to fulfil a career ideal related to professional status.

*Interviewer*: What other big decisions did you make in college?

*Ayesha*: I suppose I can jump on, because in college I've done a few courses which didn't really make me, they didn't really stand out. I've done like hotel office and reception which was quite good … that was an NVQ and after I had done it I thought ummmmh [uncertain] and ok I can work in reception but it's not like really something major that I wanted to do in my life. It was just kind of a job I've done, that I thought it was a waste of time doing it, but anyway I got my qualification. And then I got into beauty quite a lot. I got a couple of beauty qualifications and I'm still interested in that, but I wanted to do something more academic … and I suppose from then the big educational thing was planning to get to uni. I went on an access course to do that.

Expecting to do personally fulfilling work was therefore deemed important. She regarded the NVQ courses she had done in hotel office and reception as a 'waste of time' and implies that the beauty course was too, instead she wanted to do 'something major' with her life. The implication is that work identity is salient to one's sense of self and affects self-esteem. Work is not just a job, but a vocation that ought to have a deeper purpose. It contributes to defining the self because of its continuous and dominant presence.

In these terms, then, a professional career is seen as providing a deeper level of experience, based on interest and job satisfaction. Nasreen explains that one of her reasons for aspiring to take a degree stemmed from the pragmatic desire 'to keep your brain active so you might as well go back and learn new things'. She could then apply this new learning to her work. Here intellectual stimulus is seen as a form of enjoyment, as well as forming part of a strategy to live a more worthwhile life.

Of course, aspirations are not always pursued effectively or successfully, but this does not necessarily mean that they are abandoned:

> I knew I wanted to be a teacher. Even now I would have liked to have become a teacher but I never went into it because I thought I won't be able to. I wouldn't be able to cope with the work. I knew I wanted to work with children. So from that point of view I wanted to do it, but educationally I didn't do anything about it until I started college, when I decided to do the health and social care course. In my record of achievement it said that I enjoyed working with children. I was good at relating with children. I worked with children for years after that. When I first started the course I really loved it. I was working with babies and children. But now I think differently. I think I'm delayed in my decisions and I feel that I should have made them before. It feels like I'm doing everything too late. But I'm still doing it though. (Ayesha)

Similarly, whilst Shamila asserted that she wanted to avoid the boredom of being a housewife, she nevertheless did not embark on higher-level study and describes the disappointment she now feels working as a low-skilled administrator.[3] Her emotional response to the lack of challenge and tedium of her work is convincing:

[3] Recent work by Islam (2020) among lower-class women in New Delhi captured a similar sentiment. Her informants regarded only working outside the home as productive, and working in the home as non-work giving rise to feelings of inertia and boredom.

> The amount of times I've sat in her office and cried because I've not had enough work to do. … When I see my friends with degrees and a good job and that, I think ohh I wish I had done that. I wish I was somebody important, a professional or something. (Shamila)

She lives out her professional role in her mind, rather than in reality. One of the ways that she deals with the boredom of her job is to extend her role surreptitiously into being an unofficial social worker. She is inquisitive, organised and alert, and uses these strengths to bring interest to her work. However her low self-esteem regarding her abilities has prevented her from applying for higher grade jobs, even when her boss is supportive. Since the subjective and the objective aspects of life are interrelated, aspirations based just on personal desires may not stand the test of real-life situations (Bourdieu, 1977, 1990; Giddens, 1984, 1991).

## Cosmopolitan Aspirations

For many of my informants, an interesting career would be one that brought them into regular contact with people from other backgrounds.[4] Raheela aspired to leave home for the new experience of interacting with people from different cultural backgrounds and varied social and political interests. Nasreen's aspiration was to open her own nursery serving a wider range of people than just the Pakistani community. She felt this would be more interesting than opening an Asian beauty parlour, because the clientele of the latter would be restricted to the local Pakistani community. She values her independence in forging her career:

> It was either doing a beauty parlour and doing hair and beauty and stuff or childcare. Hair and beauty is opened everywhere. Your customers tend to

[4] For George Herbert Mead (1934) social interaction with other groups is significant in overcoming the tendency to perceive them only in a generalised way. Through interaction they can become 'significant others' who influence one's sense of self. Positive communication and other forms of interaction are based on perceiving positive universal values in the other, which generate reciprocal sentiments in the relationship. For Mead this can give rise to intense emotional experiences, since there is a fusion between the 'I' and the 'Me', the biological or core (perhaps even spiritual) self and the socially constructed self or selves.

> be Asian as well and I thought that's being too Asian, whereas if you do childcare you get a mix of people coming in and everything. (Nasreen)

What is evidenced here is a cosmopolitan outlook (Merton, 1968). Despite being brought up in a Pakistani community, my informants had had opportunities at school to form friendships with people from mainstream backgrounds. In contrast, their parents had had few opportunities to engage socially with non-Pakistanis. In Chap. 1 I noted how Pakistanis in northern English towns in the 1960s and 1970s lived together in slum housing which had been vacated by the upwardly mobile mainstream population. Fathers' social contacts through factory work were minimal because their limited competence in English was a barrier and because factory work was organised on ethnic lines, with Pakistanis doing different shifts from Whites or working on different floors. Meanwhile, mothers were largely limited to their homes and the immediate local community.

The situation for second-generation Pakistanis was somewhat different: there was more contact with mainstream society, and thereby scope for the development of a more cosmopolitan orientation that is closely associated with the development of aspiration for educational success and pursuit of a professional career. By contrast, wanting to get married early and have children effectively located a woman in the locality, and rendered locals as her most significant others. The aspiration to go to university and obtain a professional job involved stepping into a more cosmopolitan world, in which one meets a much wider variety of people in terms of ethnicity, religion and social class. At the same time of course there are some potentially difficult negotiations involved in learning how to behave with new types of people and in new contexts. This was helped by informants' early experiences of cross-cultural contact.

Nasreen talks about a strong friendship she had with an English girl at school. Her friend came to her house, which was a rare occurrence and therefore created a new situation for Nasreen. She explains how she naturalises a point of difference into an everyday routine:

> My gori [White[5]] friend, when I took her home, my mum was like, she wasn't shocked, but well my mum went to throw the bin out and I told my friend to go upstairs and that I'd come up in a minute. My mum was thinking who is she? There was no communication because my mum doesn't speak English. But now my friends are all gorian, who come. At college all my class is full of gorian. It doesn't bother me. They're nice to you. That's all that matters. (Nasreen)

Nasreen's mother was not 'shocked' by the presence of an English girl accompanying her daughter into their home, but Nasreen implies that there was something implicitly unexpected and possibly risky in having a 'gori' friend, a 'stranger', come to her house (Schuetz, 1944). Nasreen exercises agency in not just imagining but creating this new situation. However, it gives rise to ambiguity for her mother. Although Nasreen does recognise her mother's apprehension, she leads the way in defining this new situation, and it becomes part of her biography, a sign of a cosmopolitan orientation. For her mother it might have seemed out of place to have a non-Pakistani in the intimate space of the home. An English girl would represent particular, unfamiliar, patterns of behaviour or habitus that would be seen as incompatible with a Pakistani Muslim way of life. Perhaps that is the reason why Nasreen mentions this story. It reveals something about her mother's knowledge and lack of understanding of Nasreen's friend. It also reflects a pivotal moment—the first in a series of routine encounters between English friends and her family at home.

These strong early relationships help to explain the ease with which Nasreen interacts with 'gorian' in the future. The condition upon which her relationships with non-Pakistanis are based is for them 'to be nice to you', suggesting a minimum level of respect and civility to make those relationships routine. Appreciating these universally accepted principles of conduct in the ways that people engage becomes a way of accepting and overcoming cultural manifestations of difference.

[5] The literal meaning of gori is White and its usage implies English, and also '*gorian*' is the feminine plural.

Some of the other informants similarly explored new friendships with English people. They showed courage when they invited them to their homes, challenging tacit parental boundaries that this might be inappropriate or clarifying what the act meant socially for them. One effect of this was to help the field of family evolve in the light of their own more rapidly evolving habitus. Another was to facilitate the development of a cosmopolitan perspective and the social skills that this demanded.

Ghazala also talks about how early (teenage) friendships and shared activities with non-Pakistanis meant that she felt at ease with them, to the point where she did not see them as different from her. What they discovered was that ethnicity was not a defining boundary in the acquisition of skills and pursuit of joint activities, such as music:[6]

> I feel that I had a different upbringing to my Pakistani friends. I did something that none of my Pakistani friends have done. They didn't have an extra-curricular activity, where they'd played in a band or where they'd mixed with White people in the way that I did. So I think that because I was the only Pakistani person there and I was the only Pakistani person who played a musical instrument. And so perhaps how I relate to White people is different to how another Pakistani person that I know would relate to White people, because I've integrated with them more because of the types of things that I've done. Not just band, I'm talking about other extra-curricular activities, such as being part of the hockey team at school and being part of the basketball and the rounders team. You know, things like that. Being part of the school play. There have been a lot of times when I've taken part in things and I've been the only Pakistani person there. But that's never ever put me off, but it's something that I have and I look back and realize. I've only really started thinking about that when I experienced the racism at work, and I thought gosh. I became more aware that I was the only Pakistani person there at work. (Ghazala)

[6] Recent statistics show very few Pakistanis take part in extracurricular activities. Around 4% of British Pakistani youth take part in music classes compared to 28% of British Indian and 20% of White British youth (From Social Mobility Commission report 'Extra-curricular activities, soft skills and social mobility' published July 2019).

By contrast with her experience at work, Ghazala had had positive relations with White people. Referring to one of her friends who also participated in the music groups, she reports that:

> Her mum used to take me to band and drop me off. It was really kind of her. One thing I remember is that, I didn't realise that there was actually a cost to going to band and I came from quite a poor family and I found out that she had actually been paying for me to go to band, for two or three years. (Ghazala)

Similarly, one of Ghazala's friends from school did not live very far from her home, and her parents helped by taking Ghazala to orchestra every week for several weeks, whilst she was a teenager. So whilst Ghazala is aware of the restrictions of living in the locality, she regards herself as having experienced quite a cosmopolitan life in Milltown as a child. Ethnic differences did not represent a barrier to cross-cultural social engagement. She draws on the quality of contact that she had with English people when she was younger and the recreational identities she shared with them. It facilitated her access to cultural capital, though this was not the motive at the time. She realises how ethnically unselfconscious the contact was then. The acquisition of cultural capital is not always a purposeful and rational endeavour, but something acquired 'naturally' through enjoyable experiences.

## Aspiring to Take a Degree

Informants' aspirations to obtain a degree often resulted from their belief that it would lead to a professional career, though it was often valued in its own right as well, thus being treated both as an objective and as a stepping stone.

Qualifications were seen as entry tickets into particular sorts of job by this group of women; they were essential to a 'capital portfolio' (Hart, 2013, p. 56). Wrigley (2000, p. 3) emphasises that this is particularly important for young Asians, who may not have attendance at prestigious schools to aid them. Even those who did not embark on degree-level study, such as Shamila and Noreen, discussed their feelings about it unprompted, illustrating the perception of ideal career trajectories of this segment of second-generation Pakistani women, and their recognition of the cultural capital that qualifications provide. But they viewed a degree as meeting a deeply felt need for education. The two sorts of ambition were often closely linked:

> If you've got a degree then you'll get a lot better jobs than someone like me who hasn't got qualifications. I won't understand the deeper meaning of education because I've not been down that route. (Shamila)

While Noreen challenges the idea that a degree is a panacea for a fulfilling life, suggesting that life experience is more important, and though she herself did not take a degree, she typifies the views of the cohort in nevertheless retaining a commitment to a degree as a goal:

> I just have this notion in my head that when I do my degree, I don't know why I have to have one, but maybe it's something deep down I would want to do, but not till I'm 40. (Noreen)

There is uncertainty here about whether the actual content of the degree is intrinsically worthwhile or not, even though it is recognised as having social status and the potential to be personally fulfilling. For those who do not have a degree, secrets of fulfilment 'remain unknown' (Shamila), but attractive. Even Noreen, despite her questioning of the intrinsic value of a degree, feels that she ought to aspire to getting one, albeit later.

In summary, then, my informants combined an instrumental commitment to obtain a degree in order to obtain higher status and more financially rewarding occupational positions with a belief in the intrinsic value of higher-level education. For example, Robina conveys this in terms of '*having done well for myself*'. She regards herself as being 'the most educated in her family' and is 'proud that no one can take that away from me'. An ideology of social status enhancement and an anticipation of personal fulfilment were central to informants' aspirations to study for a degree.

## Early Aspiration to a Particular Profession

All of the informants initially left school with the idea that if they acquired qualifications they could get a better job and either become a professional or have an occupation which reflected that one 'had done well for oneself' (Robina). For some this was a matter of becoming generally well-educated with no specific career in mind initially: the aspiration was to do something interesting with their time, to have sufficient income to live comfortably and be financially independent, to work in mainstream contexts and to avoid early marriage to a cousin from Pakistan. However, others had an early commitment to obtaining a particular type of job:

> I just knew that that was what I wanted to do. I liked reading stories and books and things like that and I was always drawn to the nurse character. She was always kind and caring and I wanted to be that person [She smiles]. I wanted to be the heroine. (Raheela)

Here Raheela explains that she had a strong aspiration from the age of 13 to become a nurse, which would involve leaving home at 18 to complete her training. She regarded the idea of the nurse being a 'heroine' favourably. This reference beautifully captures the dream-like origins of some people's aspirations to follow a specific professional career.

Ghazala too held strong and specific career aspirations from the age of fourteen. Whilst at secondary school she knew she wanted to become a social worker. This was based on her school experience of 'being the agony aunt' to her friends. She was not a high-flying student, but obtained good enough grades for her to embark on A Levels and higher education. Ambition, hard work and drive underpinned pursuit of her aspirations. It was only after completing her A Levels and doing a gap year before university that she learned more about what social workers actually do. So what was originally an idea based on a fantasy and limited knowledge and experience, albeit a strong commitment, was reinforced by practical contact with social workers.

> I got a job within social services. It just so happened that it was in social services and was in the personnel department and I suppose that opened

> up a lot of opportunities for me ... during that year I was able to make a lot of contacts ... I'd got myself known with the service managers who provide the services. (Ghazala)

So, like Raheela, Ghazala too held ideas about a particular professional occupation, without having any practical experience or contact with that profession before she committed herself to a higher education course. For Ghazala, this practical contact with the world of social workers arose by accident. Since she needed to earn money to finance herself through university, she worked as an administrator for the local council during her gap year. This brought her into contact with social workers whose support helped her to focus her aspiration as a real possibility.

Nasreen had a strong early aspiration but of a different kind from the others since it did not involve obtaining a degree or entering a traditional profession. She aspired to run her own nursery business. Nevertheless, this too represented a break with the 'normal' trajectory laid down by first-generation Pakistani women, especially given her commitment to provide the service for people from different ethnic and religious communities.

## Later-Forming Aspirations

For some of my informants specific occupational and educational aspirations developed later on as a result of various contingent factors—doing well at school or in Tahira's case having a brother who went to university to do dentistry. Tahira had no strong aspiration initially but achievement at school served as a trigger. Then her aspiration became focused on dentistry as a result of her brother. She explains that at secondary school she was not aware how academically able she was until she obtained her first set of educational qualifications. She achieved nine A-grade GCSEs. Earlier, she had thought vaguely about going into teaching. However once she obtained her high GCSE grades, her older brother who was by then a dentist encouraged her to 'challenge herself'. The qualifications she obtained were seen as pointing to the kind of profession she should go into—a higher-status one. Dentistry or medicine are regarded more highly than teaching because they demand higher grades for entry:

> My brother … was the one that gave me the option. Your GCSEs are too good for you in a sense to go into teaching at this point, just push yourself a little bit more. So at that point I had a choice between whether I wanted to do dentistry or medicine. (Tahira)

The formation of aspirations was less well-defined in other cases. For example, Shamila had a vague and weak aspiration to become a professional because this would mean that she could 'become somebody … an important person'.

At the age of 16, Noreen did not have any strong educational or occupational aspirations. She left school with few GCSE qualifications and with little idea of what she wanted to do with her life. She enrolled on a travel and tourism course but did not attend. She had been given the freedom by her family to 'make something of herself', and there was no expectation to get married. She would have liked to have done an apprenticeship of some sort, but did not know what her options were, if any, regarding this and saw few career prospects open to her. The only appealing option was to seek paid work outside the home. Later, at the age of twenty four, she embarked on an e-learning access course, but she found the course difficult and decided that she would not return to studying until she had improved her writing skills 'in private'. Nevertheless, she still expresses a desire eventually to do a degree.

## Benefits of Obtaining a High-Status Job

There were two main benefits that my informants associated with obtaining a higher-status job: financial rewards and the style of life that these would support, and high personal status both in society in general and within their own families. My informants did not always find it easy to talk about the financial rewards and the lifestyle that this would make possible. Materialistic motivations for one's decisions could be seen as un-Islamic. However, Robina did talk about how the material benefits of education motivated her and her parents, so that they would never have to go back to her early experiences of living what she saw as a materially impoverished life. Education was part of a family strategy to improve their financial standing through the possession of certain material goods, such as a desirable car, and to be able to live away from the local community with its poor-quality housing:

> All my life I've had to struggle. As children we had to do without toys. I don't remember having toys, ... And now to be able to. If somebody would have said that I would be living in a detached house and driving an Audi A3 then I'd be like yes, ok [in disbelief]. Because we lived in a terraced house, in an Asian house, in an Asian area and you think you're never going to get out of that rut. But to be able to live in a nice house and to live in a nice area and to own a nice car, it's like a dream. When you've been struggling all your life. So yes, I think education has, yes it does buy you material goods so it's given me a lot in terms of material goods, but I've had to work hard to get there. It's been an uphill struggle. (Robina)

Robina viewed living in an Asian area as being in a 'rut' and a struggle. She used the term 'Asian house' to refer to the disrepair which other research have pointed out characterises houses in poor Pakistani communities (see Bowes et al., 2002). However, there is also a cultural dimension to her evaluation. When she entered my parents' front room where the interview were conducted, she commented on the way the room had been 'set' with a 'modern' eye, and with new furnishings. It was not what she regarded as an 'Asian house' because the furnishings were new and modern and the room spacious even though the house was in a Pakistani area of the town. What this suggested is that she regarded houses as sites for the display of taste, and as potential signs of social mobility and success.[7] Her symbolic insights reflected an aspirational upwardly mobile self.[8]

Ayesha too talked about the importance of living in the right area. She linked her current success on her teaching course with the aspirations she

[7] For a discussion on how home décor shows aesthetic literacy within the context of migrant homes see Pahl (2014) and Savas (2010).

[8] For Robina and her family, financial success is regarded as a way out of living in a Pakistani area and helping 'dreams' to be fulfilled. Her family do succeed in moving to the suburbs later in her life, although it is not the fantasy they imagined. The local police have had to instal surveillance cameras on their property to try to deal with the racial harassment the family have been subjected to by local White youths. They are clearly on the periphery of the community and feel unwelcome in that area.

had for the future. She had moved out of central Milltown, which was occupied by many Pakistani families, to live on a council estate on the outskirts of town. She regards living there less as a choice, but more as a decision that was made for her. This context provided an impetus for her strongly held aspiration to earn enough money to be able to live in a more affluent and safer area:

> I want to get a good degree grade and then a good job because I want to get a house. I don't want to live in this area. I want to give something better to my kid. I don't want my kid to grow up on council houses and stuff like that, I don't. I don't want him loafering around on the streets with kids who are on drugs and stuff.[9] (Ayesha)

So, participating in the labour market brought financial rewards which opened up choices, motivating my informants. Shamila worked full-time in administration during the week and in a clothes shop at the weekend. She explains what she is able to spend her money on. Her socialising options have increased and so has her independence. She is able to afford to go out for meals with her friends, to wear fashionable clothes and to help her parents pay some household bills. She did not talk explicitly about money being a primary motivator for her decisions to take on two jobs, but implied that she appreciated the financial rewards:

*Shamila*: I love where I work. I know I might not have the same sort of people somewhere else, maybe. So for now it pays my bills. I like getting up in the morning and going to work. The solicitors sounded great. I applied for it and I got it. It was pooh money. But it was great to have money. I could go shopping.

*Interviewer*: Do you make a contribution to help your parents at home?

*Shamila*: Mum and dad won't accept any money. No. I think my mum and dad are very proud. Obviously they don't have a lot of money, but there's no way they'd take money off me

[9] Not all the women interviewed would characterise the area of this research as drug-ridden, even though it includes council housing. One shopkeeper however whom I talked with did indeed lament the drug culture amongst a cohort of second-generation boys.

> for business and stuff. I pay the council tax and obviously I get the shopping and anything that's needed in the house, but they won't let me put any money towards the house and stuff.

She implies here that she pays for household items, and perhaps also the internal decoration, modernising the 'Asian home', as discussed above. Shamila appreciates the financial independence that regular paid work outside the house provides.

> But it would have been the same if I had gone towards education. The independence it's given me is that you make friends, and then you get to go out here, there, and everywhere. I haven't taken any money off my mum and dad since I was 17. So since I've had that job, mum and dad haven't even bought me a pair of shoes, because I wouldn't allow them to buy me a pair of shoes. So if I want something, I'll have it. But if I don't want anything, I won't have it. Now it's nice knowing that now my mum and dad can just concentrate on my little brothers and keeping the house and that's it. It's nice knowing that I can just fend for myself. If I do ever get married and have kids. … when I go out, there's no way I'd let other people pay for me. I have to be in control when it comes to money. I don't like to think that I depend on men. I like having that control. I like to know that I can pay for myself. (Shamila)

Being financially independent plays a large part in Shamila's sense of who she is now and could be in the future. She clearly enjoys exercising autonomy in pursuing the increased consumer and lifestyle options open to her.

## Social Status and Parental Pride

Some parents would be proud if their daughters had successful careers. This was a source of motivation for many of the young women and this reflected the binding power of their relations with their parents:

> I think another reason I feel like this about going to uni is because no one in my family has come out with a degree or anything. And I just kind of

want to make my parents feel proud that our kids have done something. But it's there mainly because I want to do it. (Ayesha)

Ayesha indicates that parents wanted their children to be successful in their education and careers, and to have 'done something' with their life.[10] Ayesha appreciates this aspiration in hindsight, as she reflects on the benefits that her foundation degree will confer. Her aspiration is reinforced by her thinking of the risks of a life without a degree and its consequences.

Robina also emphasised the significance of parental attitudes. Her mother's education had been thwarted by a patriarchal family ideology. The male head of the extended family, her mother's *thaia*, enforced a traditional naturalised gender order which required women to keep house and men to be the breadwinners. Since Robina has been released from the inflexible bonds of tradition that tied down her mother and grandmother, her mother expected her to have a successful career outside the home. This then underpinned Robina's career aspirations.

Ghazala, Tahira, Raheela and Robina managed to achieve professional careers as a social worker, dentist, senior nurse and teacher respectively. At the time of the interview, Shaheena, Nasreen and Ayesha were pursuing degree-level study with a view to becoming teachers or in one case a businesswoman. Noreen hoped to embark on degree-level study in a couple of years. Only Shamila was left with only a vague aspiration to complete a degree in the future, when the necessary support might be available.

## Conclusion

In this chapter I have shown how the career aspirations of my informants differed from those of other British Pakistani women, including women from the first generation, more recently arrived transnational brides, and others who had received a British education but had married early and

[10] See also Shahrokni (2018) for a discussion of the current generation wanting to give back to former generations whose migration stopped them achieving their dreams.

not continued into post-compulsory education. For all informants their career was central to their aspirations. They regarded forging a career outside the home as a key part of their strategy to 'make oneself'. They were strongly committed to cosmopolitan ideals and to obtaining a degree, and wanted professional work that was intrinsically demanding. They aspired to move into new social groups, both at and outside work. The financial rewards of participating fully in the labour market and particularly of having a professional career would allow them to improve the quality of their homes in terms of space and interior style, and even to move to a more affluent part of the town. Affluence would widen their lifestyle options generally. At the same time, academic and professional success were ways to generate parental pride and honour the sacrifices that migrating parents had made in order for their children to have better lives.

## References

Allen, S., & Wolkowitz, C. (1987). *Homeworking: Myths and Realities.* Macmillan Press.

Anwar, M. (1979). *Myth of Return: Pakistanis in Britain.* Heinemann Educational Publishers.

Anwar, M. (1998). *Continuity and Change in the Lives of Young Asians.* Routledge.

Archer, L. (2003). *Race, Masculinity and Schooling. Muslim Boys and Education.* The Open University Press.

Aston, J., Hooker, H., & Page, R. (2007). *Pakistani and Bangladeshi Women's Attitudes to Work and Family.*

Becher, H. (2008). *Family Practices in South Asian Muslim Families Parenting in a Multi-Faith Britain.* Palgrave Macmillan.

Beck, U., & Beck-Gernsheim, E. (2008). *Individualisation.* Sage.

Berlant, L. (2011). *Cruel Optimism.* Duke University Press.

Bourdieu, P. (1977). *Outline of a Theory of Practice* (R. Nice, Trans.). Cambridge University Press.

Bourdieu, P. (1990). *The Logic of Practice* (R. Nice, Trans.). Polity.

Bowes, A. M., Dar, N. S., & Sim, D. F. (2002). Differentiation in Housing Careers: The Case of Pakistanis in the UK. *Housing Studies, 17*(3), 381–399.

Brah, A., & Shaw, S. (1992). *Working Choices: South Asian Women and the Labour Market.* Department of Employment Research Paper, No 91.

Clarke, C. (2003). *The Future of Higher Education*. The Stationery Office Limited.
Dale, A., Shaheen, N., Kalra, V., & Fieldhouse, E. (2002). Routes into Education and Employment for Young Pakistani and Bangladeshi Women in the UK. *Ethnic and Racial Studies, 25*(6).
Dearing, R. (1996). *National Inquiry into Higher Education Department for Education and Employment*.
Giddens, A. (1984). *The Constitution of Society Outline of the Theory of Structuration*. Polity Press.
Giddens, A. (1991). Structuration Theory: Past, Present and Future. In C. Bryant & D. Jary (Eds.), *Giddens' Theory of Structuration: A Critical Appreciation*. Routledge.
Grey, C. (1994). Career as a Project of the Self and Labour Process Discipline. *Sociology, 28*(2), 479–497.
Hardill, I. (2002). *Gender, Migration and the Dual Career Household*. Routledge.
Hart, C. S. (2013). *Aspirations, Education and Social Justice Applying Sen and Bourdieu*. Bloomsbury.
Islam, A. (2020). 'It Gets Really Boring If You Stay at Home': Women, Work and Temporalities in Urban India. *Sociology, 54*(5), 867–882.
Lovell, S. (Ed.). (2007). *Generations in Twentieth-Century Europe*.
McDermott, M., & Ahsan, M. (1986). *The Muslim Guide*. The Islamic Foundation.
Mead, G. (1934). *Mind, Self and Society*. University of Chicago.
Merton, R. K. (1968). Patterns of Influence: Local and Cosmopolitan Influentials. In *Social Theory and Social Structure* (Enlarged Ed.). The Free Press.
Pahl, K. (2014). The Aesthetics of Everyday Literacies: Home Writing Practices in a British Asian Household. *Anthropology & Education Quarterly, 45*(3), 293–311.
Phizacklea, A., & Wolkowitz, C. (1993). *Homeworking Women: Gender, Racism and Class at Work*. Sage.
Pilcher, J. (1994). Mannheim's Sociology of Generations: An Undervalued Legacy. *British Journal of Sociology, 45*(3), 481–495.
Richardson, C. (1977). *Contemporary Social Mobility*. Frances Pinter.
Rose, N. (1998). Governing Enterprising Individuals. In N. Rose (Ed.), *Inventing Our Selves Psychology, Power and Personhood*. Cambridge University Press.
Saifullah-Khan, V. (1976). Purdah in the British Situation. In A. L. Barker & S. Allen (Eds.), *Dependence and Exploitation in Work and Marriage* (pp. 224–245). Longman.

Savas, O. (2010). The Collective Turkish Home in Vienna: Aesthetic Narratives of Migration and Belonging. *Home Cultures, 7*(3), 313–340.

Schuetz, A. (1944). The Stranger: An Essay in Social Psychology. *American Journal of Sociology, 49*(6), 1944.

Shahrokni, S. (2018). The Collective Roots and Rewards of Upward Educational Mobility. *The British Journal of Sociology, 69*(4), 1175–1193.

Spohrer, K., Stahl, G., & Bowers-Brown, T. (2018). Constituting Neo-Liberal Subjects? "Aspirations" as Technology of Government in UK Policy Discourse. *Journal of Education Policy, 33*(3), 327–342.

Tenvir, F. (2015). *The Educational Experiences and Life Choices of British Pakistani Muslim Women: An Ethnographic Study*. Unpublished PhD Thesis, University of Worcester.

Wrigley, T. (2000). *The Power to Learn. Stories of Success in the Education of Asian and Other Bilingual Pupils*. Trentham.

# 6

# The Influence of Families and the Local Community on Informants' Aspirations and Careers

In the previous chapter I examined the development of my informants' aspirations to stay on in education and to professional jobs. One of the main factors that shape children's aspirations, and facilitate (or obstruct) their pursuit of these, is their families and local communities. In the case of working-class Pakistani communities there is a stereotypical perspective that portrays them as socialising, and perhaps even forcing, girls into the traditional 'career' of wife and mother. While this certainly picks out an important feature of community and parental attitudes, I shall argue that the contexts faced by my informants were more subtle and varied than this stereotype implies.

Bourdieu (1977, 1990) and Giddens (1984) note that subjective and objective aspects of experience are not distinct, but operate in mutually constitutive ways. Structure can both constrain and enable particular kinds of action. The family habitus can be viewed as a place where people develop a set of pre-conscious expectations about the future, attitudes and forms of behaviour that are taken for granted and not articulated. At the same time, these must continually be 'strategically mobilised in accordance with the contingencies of particular empirical situations' (Emirbayer & Mische, 1998, p. 978), with the result that on occasion they can have unpredictable consequences.



A. Saeed, *Education, Aspiration and Upward Social Mobility*,
https://doi.org/10.1007/978-3-030-82261-3_6

In this chapter I want to examine the complex role that family played in the lives of my informants. I will begin with a brief discussion of the structure of the Pakistani family in this working-class community, before going on to examine parental attitudes towards the education of girls, the educational resources parents can offer and the consequences of these. Finally, I shall discuss the role that siblings and friends from the local community can play.

## Pakistani Families

There are variations in living arrangements of the Pakistani family in the British context. Some families live as a nuclear unit at one residential address, geographically distant from relatives. In other cases, members of the same extended family live in quite close proximity, so that some relationships characteristic of an extended family living in the same household still operate. This is a matter of degree of course. While only one of my informants lived as part of an extended household, and only one had relatives living on the same street, most had relatives living in the same area of town, or elsewhere in the North of England, and had regular contact with them:

> My grandad's brother, he was one of five brothers. He was seen as the king at the top. So he was the *thaiah* because he was the head of the family. He ruled everyone else underneath. Although everyone else lived in their own houses, he controlled them. He was at the top of the tree. (Robina)

Here specific terminology, '*thaiah*', is used to refer to the eldest male or patriarch in the extended family, who is described by Robina as wielding authority over everyone else. Moreover, this patriarch regarded traditional home-based careers as appropriate for the women, which restricted the opportunities for Robina's mother considerably.

For the most part, then, 'family' for my informants meant not just the nuclear family but included aunts and uncles, grandparents and in-laws or one's *biraderi*.[1] Moreover, their influence could extend from as far

[1] I noticed that people seemed to apply the term *biraderi* in different ways. Biraderi referred to all of the extended family and was also used by some people to refer to those people who are of the

away as the village in Pakistan where the family came from, indicating the transnational boundaries of the Pakistani community.[2] For my informants nevertheless, parents played the major role in education and career trajectories. However this very much took place in the context of the local community, which gave rise to many expectations. For example, Shamila noted that not many young women on her street went to university. Indeed:

> The majority are much younger than me and are married with kids. The woman that I overheard yesterday, she's 20 and she's married and got a little girl.

She went on to comment about the impact of this on her parents:

> In some ways it must be hard on them. They've got older daughters, I'm 27 and I've got a 26-year old sister. We're not married and my mum and dad don't put that sort of pressure on us, but it must be really hard for them.[3] You know how it is: 'my daughter's married, my daughter's got so many (children)'. Or 'are your kids not getting married?' Or 'how old are your daughters?' The usual stuff.

---

same caste, but not related consanguineously. The Pakistani caste system is based loosely on one's family's occupation, place of origin and one's language. Sometimes one of these criteria is given more emphasis than others. Mirpuris speak the dialect '*Mipuri*' and come from the area of Pakistan known as Mirpur. Jat are a landowning caste. Kashmiris come from Kashmir.

[2] My data did not support the widespread assumption that Mirpuris embraced more of a 'village culture' than Punjabis with regard to parental expectations and daughters' autonomy in educational decision-making. For this reason I do not define my informants in caste terms, because none of the three Mirpuri women had married early, and both Punjabi and Mirpuri women told stories about being asked to marry at 17. Although this difference in career aspirations was not evident in my data, Robina reported caste differences that would not necessarily show up in my small sample and in one interview. There were also ethical considerations with my raising it as an issue, given that a caste system is unacceptable in Islam and that I myself was a supposedly more educated Punjabi. Shaheena explained that the shift in community opinion over time meant that whilst as a Mirpuri woman she had not been allowed to continue into higher education at the age of 18, she was allowed to do so five years later. Perhaps this does indicate significant differences in attitudes towards women's education and changes experienced by different castes, which my data does not fully capture.

[3] Shamila's father did put pressure on her to marry a cousin from Pakistan when she left school. Shamila and her mother resisted.

A major factor shaping the lives of my informants, then, was the expectations and attitudes of their parents, in the context of the wider community.[4]

## Attitudes of Parents

Within the local community the predominant assumption was probably that at the end of compulsory schooling the next stage for daughters would generally be to get married and have children, and in many families arrangements began to be made for this when girls were 16 or 17. Many parents saw little purpose in their daughters continuing in post-compulsory education, not least because some saw this as potentially damaging their marriage prospects or at least delaying their realisation of their full worth from an Islamic perspective: if maternity is regarded as the most creative act and as an affirmation of love, then delaying it in order to pursue education could be regarded as undesirable (Syed, 2009, p. 442).

However, there was a diversity of attitudes among my informants' parents regarding their daughters' futures at the end of post-compulsory schooling. Some held, and sought to enforce, the traditional expectation that a daughter would not continue into further education and should marry soon after completing her compulsory schooling. This was true of the parents of Shaheena, Nasreen, Shamila and Raheela. However, at the other extreme, there were one or two parents who put pressure on their daughters to continue to higher education and a professional career. The attitudes of the other parents lay between these two extremes, and of course there could be differences in expectation between parents within the same family. Moreover, expectations were not usually entirely fixed but could change.

Early marriage is endorsed by traditional and religious expectations (Dale et al., 2002; Gilliat-Ray, 2010; Mohammad, 2005; Wilson, 2006).

---

[4] Dale et al. (2002, p. 953) report that Asian young people named parents and other family members as having a greater influence on their career choices than career advisers or teachers (Allen, 1998; Kalra et al., 1999).

A local imam explained to me that the Hadith[5] endorses early marriage because sexual relations outside marriage are forbidden, and early marriage reduces the risk of such contacts.[6] Many Pakistanis in the local community upheld religious expectations of early marriage for women which was reflected in the attitudes of many of my informants' parents. Raheela's early aspiration to become a nurse was ridiculed by her mother:

*Interviewer*: And did everyone around you know that you wanted to become a nurse?

*Raheela*: I remember having a conversation with my mum when I was about thirteen or fourteen and she just laughed about it. She thought it was highly amusing, I remember that.

In much the same way, Shaheena was expected to follow her sister's career trajectory, marrying soon after completing compulsory education. Shamila too explained that her father expected his daughters to marry kin from Pakistan and not go on to further education at all. Moreover, as I noted in Chap. 1, this was the predominant pattern in the local community, reinforced by a commitment to the institution of purdah.

Shaheena observed how common it was for young women she knew to marry rather than embark on higher education, because there was such an expectation within families that women should not be *too highly educated*. However, as this last phrase suggests, there was some scope for variation in how much education was acceptable. And the parents of most of my informants had a rather more flexible attitude towards their daughters' education than an insistence that it should end at the formal school-leaving age.

Indeed, often parents did not see education as incompatible with marriage and motherhood. There was an understanding within some families that since mothers are the primary carers of their children, it is important for them to be educated for the benefit of the next generation. This is captured in the repeated wisdom that *if you educate a woman you educate*

[5] The *Hadith* refers to the body of knowledge that conveys the narrations originating from the words and deeds of the prophet Muhammad.

[6] There is no pressure on men to marry young, although they may find themselves bound by other traditional expectations, such as to be the main breadwinner.

*a family*. This is a way in which traditional ideology served to justify educating daughters. The work of Haw (1998) in a Muslim girls' school in Bradford presented a complex picture of influences (and not just relations with teachers) on the changing moral framework of purdah. On the one hand, her research confirmed the view that parents saw motherhood as a natural career path for a girl as it was religiously sanctioned. It was an assumption that went unchallenged in this faith-based school. However, Haw also shows how parents fuse norms emanating from Islam with high educational expectations for their daughters, who have opportunities, unavailable to their mothers, to become well-educated in such a school. The academic results from Muslim schools show that they do succeed in helping students to achieve high levels of academic success, which could enhance their career opportunities.[7]

My research, however, revealed other ways in which post-compulsory education was sometimes seen as beneficial for daughters. Robina reports that:

> My parents understanding was that if we've got education we can stand on our own two feet and, come tomorrow, if something happens to them, then they know that we can still rely on ourselves. We don't have to rely on a man.

She revealed how her mother's expectations of the kind of marriage she might have are different from her mother's own experience of a monogamous, lifelong relationship. Traditional expectations for women's careers were changing irrespective of informants' own aspirations. In Robina's mother's opinion, since women might not be married all their lives, they would need the financial resources at least to 'stand on your own two feet'. Independence within marriage was therefore encouraged. The people studied by Dale et al. (2002) regarded education as a means of achieving independence within marriage. Thus education was not necessarily an alternative to marriage in every circumstance. Robina's comment suggests that where women might need to be independent or even have the lead career in their families, then education is a necessity. Ahmad (2001)

[7] See Ansari (2004) for a discussion of the history of campaigns for Muslim-only schools in the UK.

too reported that financial independence was seen as an insurance in case parents died or a marriage failed.

Some families thus agreed to or even supported their daughters' continuing education, but there was variation in the types and levels of education seen as appropriate or allowable. For example, Shaheena reported that:

> You know because nobody in my family went, even though my parents did want me to get educated, yet I don't think they wanted me to go to uni. At that time, I think they were quite backwards and I think they thought a girl should not be educated so much, she doesn't need to go to uni. Because at that time a lot of girls that age were getting married. A lot of them got married straight after school or straight after college.

So, for some families there were limits to the level of education that was acceptable: daughters might be permitted to go into further education, but not higher education. And yet there were also some pressures working to change this. Robina reports:

> My sister didn't want education. She thought she could live a life without education, but when she wanted to get married and stuff, she couldn't because people wanted a degree. She found it hard to get married.

Robina talked about the need for both men and women to obtain a degree if they wanted to marry someone from Britain, or even get married at all. A degree then could improve one's marriage prospects, and in this way too traditional ideas could be used to justify education (Ahmad, 2001; Singh, 1990).[8]

Another kind of limit on what sorts of education would be encouraged for daughters concerned what subjects could be studied, with a view to acceptable careers. Tahira reports: 'My mum wanted me to do, at this

---

[8] However, there is a risk involved here, and the strategy of obtaining a degree did not succeed in the case of Robina's sister. By the time she had completed her degree she was 30, an age considered old for marriage, and in the end she married a man from Pakistan rather than a British-born Pakistani.

point, teaching. You get good holidays and when you get kids, then you can have the holidays with them'

Robina's experience was similar:

> It was either that I go into social work or into teaching, so I went into social work and then thought I don't want to do it. I thought teaching, if I settle down kids-wise then it will be more convenient than anything.

Thus, ideas about what kinds of education and career were compatible with motherhood and with traditional expectations of the role of women shaped the sorts of education and jobs my informants aspired to. They did not aim at high-level jobs indiscriminately.

While most of my informants' parents offered fairly limited encouragement to their daughters to stay on in education and to aspire to professional jobs, the experience of one of them was quite different. Robina was subjected to relentless pressure from her parents to succeed in becoming a doctor. She had cousins who were also being pushed in this direction, with an equal amount of pressure. In Robina's case the pressure came from her mother, who was reacting against her own restricted educational opportunities.

## Parents and Their Educational Capital

Parental attitudes towards their daughter's education and future life were not the only important aspects of the role of family in shaping my informants' aspirations and educational careers. Also important was the extent to which parents could offer direct advice and support for the non-traditional educational and career trajectories to which my informants aspired.

An important aspect of this was variation in parents' own levels of education. Some had experienced little formal education:

> My mum and dad didn't go to school. My mum can't read and write. My dad, very basic. (Shamila)

Anwar (1979) has documented the educational level of first-generation Pakistani workers living in a Pakistani residential area in a town in the North of England in the 1960s. Twenty-two per cent were illiterate and had never been to school, and around 31% had either a limited knowledge of English or none at all.[9] He explains that most of the older and middle-aged Pakistanis did not get a chance to go to school in Pakistan, either because of their family's financial circumstances or because there was no school in the village.

Of course what is important here is not simply education per se, but education of a kind that would be relevant to life in Britain, most obviously the capacity to speak and write English adequately. Various factors affect the degree to which migrants acquire the knowledge and skills to participate in the new society they have joined. For example, early work by Modood et al. (1997) revealed that those people who lived in areas where there was a high concentration of their ethnic group were less likely to speak English and acquire other relevant skills than those who had more direct contact with members of other ethnic groups. For Li (2017) some first-generation Pakistanis experienced *declassment* in the British labour market, thus leaving their children in a disadvantaged starting position.

All of my informants' parents seem to have had very limited knowledge of the British education system. Abbas (2002, p. 75) has noted the importance of such knowledge for educational success. Wrigley (2000) has also hypothesised that negative experiences of officialdom in Pakistan may result in lack of institutional involvement and hence knowledge of schools in Britain. Equally, of course, limited knowledge and capability in English would reinforce lack of involvement, although not all of my informants' parents were uninvolved—Raheela's uncle had campaigned successfully to get halal meat available in schools and unsuccessfully for the establishment of an Islamic girls' school.

While lack of knowledge of the English education system prevented parents providing their daughters with much guidance about how to succeed in that system, for some of them, the lack of parents' engagement with their daughters' education gave them leeway to make their own way

[9] For a discussion of a wider definition of literacy, see Pahl (2014).

within it. In other words, daughters could make decisions relating to their education independent of parental advice.

Tahira provides an example in discussing the decision about which subjects to study at A Level:

*Interviewer*: And when you were making those decisions, who helped you to make those decisions?

*Tahira*: Myself. I made them completely by myself. … At the end of the day, the final decision was with myself. I didn't discuss it with my parents because my mum didn't really know the difference between a biology, a physics or a chemistry. It's not that she wasn't interested in my education but she didn't understand about the different topics that were involved.[10]

Tahira's parents did not know how academically gifted she was and how she could use science A Levels to go on to train as a dentist. Similarly, Tahira did not involve her parents in her decision to go to university and to choose one that would require her to live away from home:

*Interviewer*: And was it ok that you were going to be applying away-from home?

*Tahira*: I don't think my mum actually knew that I wasn't applying to Manchester. I don't think anyone actually knew.

The opportunity to side-step parental involvement then gave some women opportunities to do what they wanted. Lack of knowledge of the education system sometimes prevented parents from exerting direct or indirect influence on possible choices (Reay et al., 2005, p. 78).

However, lack of parental involvement could also cause problems, sometimes in surprising ways. Thus, while Shamila's parents' lack of knowledge about the world of education gave her the freedom to make her own decisions about her education, she later came to regret one of

[10] Placing an indefinite article erroneously before each subject is done to convey the complete lack of knowledge Tahira's mother had about the different science subjects. Each subject is caricatured as a material thing that is tangible rather than a separate discipline with its own internal vocabulary and tools of analysis (Hirst, 1974). The different windows onto the world that different disciplines offer are regarded as beyond the mental purview and understanding of Tahira's mother.

those decisions: since she found A Levels 'boring', she abandoned further study and sought work. She now wishes that she had completed a degree:

*Shamila*: I do regret going into work at 17. I wish my parents had been stricter with me when it came to education. My big sister's been [to university], my little sister's been and my little brother's moving out next month to go to university. And I just wish they'd been stricter with me.

*Interviewer*: Had they [your parents] been strict with them [i.e. her siblings]?

*Shamila*: No. No.

*Interviewer*: They decided themselves?

*Interviewer*: They decided themselves?

Shamila here expresses a wish that her parents had been able to help her make what she now believes would have been the right decision. This perhaps illustrates Beck and Beck-Gernsheim's (2008) view that the autonomy to make decisions independently is central to high modernity, creating a gulf between older and younger generations: young women find themselves operating in a terrain where parental expectations and attitudes towards women's life plans do not help them. In this sense they may have to operate as a generation without parents as role models in an important area of their life.[11]

Like Shamila, Ayesha also spoke of feeling adrift, expecting parental guidance that simply was not available:

> I think education-wise, I don't think we were really pushed that much for anything. I'm not blaming my mum or anything, because she's wonderful the way she is. But she had a hard time with us. But I think we were kind of left to it. She's quite soft my mum, and so I think we were never really pushed to anything. She never, I don't remember her asking us. Neither did my dad. So I didn't know what I wanted. I think it's good before the end of school age to know what you want, to know what you're good at. ... I feel if someone would have guided me a little in the times when I needed it, when I didn't necessarily know myself that I needed it, when I was a bit lost

[11] Sometimes siblings were able to act as role models. This will be discussed later in the chapter.

> and then someone would be there and say these are your choices. Even if it had been someone in your own family, but then at the end of the day the choice is yours. If my mum had said, go to uni, I would not have said, ok I'll go to uni. It's just that I need to understand myself what I'm good at and what I should be doing.

This reveals the tensions between the Beck and Beck-Gernsheim (2008) model of the self-autonomous individual creating a narrative of identity and the need for social and cultural guidance and support. Ayesha talks here about the interplay between independence and knowledge. She is not told what to do but at the same time regrets the lack of guidance and having someone helping her to know what she could become. This confirms Littler's (2018) argument that it is not enough to aspire. One also needs to be part of social contexts that enable aspiration to become reality.

For many of my informants, however, the situation was rather different: parents sought to exercise control, discouraging pursuit of their aspirations or, in Robina's case, pressurising her into pursuing an impossible path. As already noted, Robina is unusual in, effectively, having the aspiration to go to university and become a doctor forced upon her:

> If somebody was to ask me what my dream job would be, I don't think I could answer that question, because I think along the line I've lost it somewhere. I don't really have the answer because for so long I've been told what I'm supposed to do.

This is a poignant reflection on her own lack of control over her decisions. Robina's mother had internalised the view that schools with mainly White children were better schools: a large number of Asian children in a school would be less conducive to educational success. For this reason Robina was sent to a sixth form college where there were very few Asian children. This environment made her the target of endless racist name-calling and isolation. She regards these racist experiences as being the source of her putting on a substantial amount of weight, which she has never been able to lose. Her parents' limited knowledge of school cultures meant that Robina was not well-placed for flourishing in the sixth form. Not surprisingly, her parents' emotional investment in backing their daughter's success and their viewing a British education as the vehicle for achieving that success were met by severe disappointment when she failed to achieve the necessary grades. Her mother cried and her father remained silent in response to her failure. Robina was frightened to tell them her results: three B grades and not the A grades needed for studying medicine:

*Robina*: To me education is everything. My parents have always seen it as a must. My sister, she went to uni but she dropped out and so that came as a disappointment that a daughter dropped out.

*Interviewer*: When you told your parents that you got the GCSE or A Level results that you did, what did they say?

*Robina*: My mum started crying and stuff … I actually hid my GCSE results because I didn't want my mum to know. And I remember going to school that day and I thought please let there be a mistake in my results, I knew the disappointment she was going to have. The expectations, but I tried as hard as I could but no matter how hard I tried, they just weren't going to be good enough. All the pressure was on me because my older sister didn't do well. … When I told my dad my A Level results, he just drove home in silence. It felt like the longest 20 minutes' drive I had ever been on. I remember I took the phone line out of the socket. I didn't want anyone to know what I'd got.

For Robina the outcome of having controlling parents with limited knowledge of the education system was similar to Ayesha's, who did not have any parental guidance. Both felt 'lost' and did not know what they wanted to do or become. Also, whereas others exercised self-discipline to succeed in education, Robina describes home life as 'regimented' by her parents, with little scope for autonomy and self-direction. This has implications for her confidence to venture out to university, away from home, although her mother did give her permission to go, albeit without supporting the idea. But in Robina's account she lacked the independence of thought and sense of personhood required to make this decision. Furthermore, the parental pressure to succeed academically remained a prevalent negative force whether she was at home or away. This stress, together with the putative costs of going to university away from home, meant that she never left home to study for a degree. She did her degree whilst living at home. She talks about an independent spirit that she does not possess, but which she notices in English girls who are better equipped to apply practical wisdom when facing new situations. Yet there is an important sense in which Robina reveals independence of spirit through the determination and courage needed to complete her degree in the face of her parents' disappointment.

## The Role of Siblings and Friends

An important factor in achieving educational success, in addition to parental attitudes, was the presence or absence of siblings,[12] and the potential role model and encouragement (or discouragement) they provided. At the very least, older siblings sometimes performed the function of normalising the experience of going into higher education:

*Interviewer*: Was it acceptable for you to leave home and go to college?
*Raheela*: Yes because I wanted to study, but it was harder for my elder sister because she had the argument the previous year, because she went first.

For Nasreen, too, having an older sibling who had broken through the barrier meant that the possibility of pursuing a degree was opened up for her too, and in addition her sister could be a positive role model for, and influence on, her, as well as 'fighting the battle' for her younger sibling.

Not all informants had elder siblings of course or at least ones who had taken a non-traditional route. None of Shaheena's older siblings had gone to university, and they did not support the idea of Shaheena attending. If they had done so, Shaheena's mother might have given her permission to attend a local university:

> My brothers and sisters if they had stuck up for me then maybe, but my brother and sister were not sticking up for me. They were like, why do you need to go? Because they had never been I didn't have anyone to say to mum, let her go.

---

[12] This bonding capital is regarded as important in the work of Thapar-Bjorkert and Sanghera (2010), as it leads to significantly more Pakistanis going into higher education.

This indicates the important role that those older siblings who had already paved the way could play in helping younger siblings to forge their careers and conversely the difficulties if older siblings had not forged such a path and did not support it.

One informant reports that in her family it was common for older sisters to have the responsibility of being a child's second mother. In other families, even where this did not happen, older siblings played an important role in the formation of career trajectories of younger siblings. Nasreen reports that her older sister:

> brought me and my younger brother up. All the time we've always been with her. Obviously my mum is not educated and Shaheena is and so it's more her that has helped me with my education.

She also drew on the same source of advice later when thinking about her career:

> I thought I might do business because I thought I might open my own business one day and so I thought that might be a good thing to do and stuff like that. Obviously I asked my sisters to see what they said and did it that way.

Crucially, older siblings are part of the same generation and have had their own experience of the education system, so that they can provide foresight and even specific strategies of what to say in problem situations (see also Bok, 2010). They also often provided emotional support in the form of encouragement and reassurance. Older sisters, in particular, often gave general backing to decisions on education and careers. This was true even when they did not provide specific advice, as Ghazala reports:

> I did speak to my older sisters about it, and again it was always you do whatever you feel comfortable with, whichever one you want to do.

The salience given to a younger sibling's well-being, so that she is 'comfortable' and 'happy', is striking in this response. However, it was not always the eldest sibling that played this role:

*Interviewer*: So when you were younger, because you wanted to do different things, was there anyone in particular who influenced you?

*Nasreen*: It was actually my middle sister Shaheena. She does because she sits down and she talks to you. She says, would you be happy doing this? Or that? She sees the goods and the bads and says, it's up to you at the end of the day.

Here the older sibling creates a psychological space for the informant to imaginatively engage with future scenarios, momentarily allowing the self to distance itself in partial and exploratory ways from the schemas, habits and traditions that constrain social identities and institutions (Emirbayer & Mische, 1998, p. 984).

Nasreen suggested that parental support could seem too remote, as well as that parents lacked the capacity to advise. By contrast, older siblings could be more proactive, and their experiences offered a more convincing basis for advice:

> My mum just says do whatever keeps you happy. She won't pressure me to go to uni, for example. She says, if you want to go, go. Whereas Shaheena goes, go to uni, try it out, it's a different life. Because she's the only one who's gone to uni out of all of us. (Nasreen)

Older siblings' own experiences could also generate high expectations, which informants found encouraged them to aim for particular career trajectories over others:

> I always knew when I left school, I knew that I would go to sixth form and after that I would go on to university because that was the path that my siblings took. I was encouraged with that and I was always encouraged to do what I wanted to do. (Ghazala)

Tahira's brother was able to offer significant support to his sister, which was a key factor in her securing a place to study dentistry at university. In response to her high GCSE grades he encouraged her to think of career options other than teaching and to challenge her mother's ideas about what career would suit her:

> At that time I didn't have a clue what A Levels I was going to do. My mother wanted me to do, at this point, teaching. You get good holidays and when you have kids, then you can have the holidays with them. My brother was doing dentistry. He was the one that gave me the option, look your GCSEs are too good for you in a sense to go into teaching at this point, just push yourself a little bit more.

Tahira was the only girl in her family, and her brother's involvement in her decision-making allowed her to make decisions independently of considerations relating to her future role as mother. Her brother also helped in a practical way to navigate the pre-university process. He guided and advised her on the tacit requirements of the application process. For example, he advised her to do work experience and helped her with her application letter. This guidance did not compromise her autonomy to make a decision, but proved highly useful. It also helped her to focus her decision-making and demonstrated that at least one family member had substantial cultural capital. And he helped her to accumulate her own:

*Tahira*: I did work experience at a dentist's. That was in Kirkley. I did work experience at an orthodontist in Milltown. So yes. At that point I knew I wanted to do dentistry. Once I had chosen my A Level subjects, I knew I wanted to do dentistry. I did my work experience after that. Because my brother who is doing dentistry said the core aspect that they look at, at the interview stage, is have you done work experience.

*Interviewer*: So in terms of your work experience, your brother suggested that this is what you needed to do? In order to get onto the university course? He said that this would look good on your application?

*Tahira*: Yes

*Interviewer*: Did you get any support from anyone, when you were filling out your personal statement? Or…

*Tahira*: My brother helped me quite a lot. So yes.

*Interviewer*: Was there anyone at school that helped you?

*Tahira*: No. We had like a tutorial at sixth form where they gave you a template showing you how to write a statement, so you weren't completely left alone. Javed, my brother, helped me with what I should actually put into my statement and that's because he's actually done the course. Maybe I was at an advantage there.

Whilst she sought advice from her brother about how to secure a place at university, she was ultimately in control of the decision about which university she would attend. She did not want to go to university near Milltown and was keen to 'experience uni life' away from home.

In a similar way Nasreen's sister helped her with her studying at college:

> She [her older sister] helps me out quite a lot. Like I'm doing my Level Four at college, and they don't have many facilities. It's more geared for Level Three, and you can't use your Level Three books for Level Four. So, she's always going to uni and getting books for me and stuff. Helping me out and reading my work. So yes, it's mostly her.

When models or mentors were not available within the family, they could sometimes be found among school or college friends. Shaheena explained how her aspirations to go to university were influenced by her British Pakistani Punjabi-speaking friends at school. They helped her to realise that she too could shape her future, raising her expectations about what she was capable of doing. Her role models were therefore outside the family and outside the immediate Mirpuri community of her neighbourhood:

> I think it was my friends who made me decide that I might want to do something with my life. They were all different but they all wanted to do something. One of my friends wanted to be a pharmacist. And she was a really good friend of mine and there was one friend that wanted to be a social worker. There were like a few other ones. I thought, if they can do it, why can't I do something? Because in my family, nobody went to university or anything so when I went to sixth form that's when I really knew that I wanted to go to University. (Shaheena)

Others lacked sources of support and advice and were aware of their need for other people to stimulate them to act independently and embrace change in their lives:

> So one day maybe, when somebody puts a rocket up my backside I might try and do somehing different. (Shamila)

## Conclusion

The norms and values maintained by Pakistani families create a particular social and moral order. But the distinctive family habitus of each informant influenced the objective conditions of what was possible.[13] Parents' expectations about what their daughters would do at the end of compulsory schooling varied. Some sought to impose relatively traditional expectations, others left leeway for the women to make their own decisions. One or two parents actively encouraged staying on at college, going to university and aiming at a professional job, in one case pressurising their daughter, with unfortunate consequences. There was also variation in the knowledge and understanding that parents had about the English education system, which also had consequences for my informants' careers. In some cases, lack of parental knowledge and support was compensated for by siblings. They may have already forged a path to university, creating a precedent, and could also be a source of cultural capital. In some cases a similar role was played by friends made at school from outside the local community. In the next chapter I shall look more broadly at the role of schools in facilitating access to cultural capital.

## References

Abbas, T. (2002). Teacher Perceptions of South Asians in Birmingham Schools and Colleges. *Oxford Review of Education, 28*(4), 447–471.

Ahmad, F. (2001). Modern Traditions? British Muslim Women and Academic Achievement. *Gender and Education, 13*, 137–152.

Allen, A. (1998). What Are Ethnic Minorities Looking For? In T. Modood & T. Acland (Eds.), *Race and Higher Education* (pp. 51–73). PSI.

Ansari, H. (2004). *'The Infidel Within': Muslims in Britain*. Hurst & Company.

Anwar, M. (1979). *Myth of Return: Pakistanis in Britain*. Heinemann Educational Publishers.

Beck, U., & Beck-Gernsheim, E. (2008). *Individualisation*. Sage.

[13] I am using habitus in the sense that attitudes, expectations and ethics are embodied in a way of life, in a practice.

Bok, J. (2010). The Capacity to Aspire to Higher Education: 'It's Like Making Them Do a Play Without a Script'. *Critical Studies in Education, 51*(2), 163–178.
Bourdieu, P. (1977). *Outline of a Theory of Practice* (R. Nice, Trans.). Cambridge University Press.
Bourdieu, P. (1990). *The Logic of Practice* (R. Nice, Trans.). Polity.
Dale, A., Shaheen, N., Kalra, V., & Fieldhouse, E. (2002). Routes into Education and Employment for Young Pakistani and Bangladeshi Women in the UK. *Ethnic and Racial Studies, 25*(6).
Emirbayer, M., & Mische, A. (1998). What Is Agency? *American Journal of Sociology, 103*(4), 962–1023.
Giddens, A. (1984). *The Constitution of Society Outline of the Theory of Structuration*. Polity Press.
Gilliat-Ray, S. (2010). *Muslims in Britain: An Introduction*. Cambridge University Press.
Haw, K. (1998). *Educating Muslim Girls*. The Open University Press.
Hirst, P. (1974). The Nature and Structure of Curriculum Objectives. In P. Hirst (Ed.), *Knowledge and the Curriculum a Collection of Philosophical Papers*. Routledge.
Kalra, V., Hepburn, P., & Penhale, B. (1999). *Tackling Barriers into Employment for Pakistani and Bangladeshi Young People*. Oldham Metropolitan Borough Council.
Li, Y. (2017). Persisting Disadvantages: Barriers to Ethnic Social Mobility in the UK. In D. Khan & F. Shaheen (Eds.), *Race and Class in Post-Brexit Britain*. Runnymede.
Littler, J. (2018). *Against Meritocracy: Culture, Power & Myths of Mobility*. Routledge.
Modood, T., Berthoud, R., Lakely, R., Nazroo, J., Smith, J., & Beishon, S. (Eds.). (1997). *Ethnic Minorities in Britain: Diversity and Disadvantage*. Policy Studies Institute.
Mohammad, R. (2005). Negotiating Spaces of the Home, the Education System, and the Labour Market: The Case of Young Working-Class, British Pakistani Muslim Women. In G.-W. Falah & C. Nagel (Eds.), *Geographies of Muslim Women: Gender, Religion and Space* (pp. 178–200). Guildford Press.
Pahl, K. (2014). The Aesthetics of Everyday Literacies: Home Writing Practices in a British Asian Household. *Anthropology & Education Quarterly, 45*(3), 293–311.

Reay, D., David, M., & Ball, S. (2005). *Degrees of Choice: Class, Race, Gender and Higher Education*. Trentham Books Limited.

Singh, R. (1990). Ethnic Minority Experience in Higher Education. *Higher Education Quarterly, 44*(4), 344–359.

Syed, J. (2009). Reconstruction of Gender in Islamic Thought: Iqbal's Vision of Equal Opportunity. *Women's Studies International Forum, 32*(6), 435–444.

Thapar-Bjorkert, S., & Sanghera, G. S. (2010). Social Capital, Educational Aspirations and Young Pakistani Muslim Men and Women in Bradford, West Yorkshire. *The Sociological Review, 58*(2), 244–264.

Wilson, A. (2006). *Dreams, Questions, Struggles South Asian Women in Britain*. Pluto Press.

Wrigley, T. (2000). *The Power to Learn. Stories of Success in the Education of Asian and Other Bilingual Pupils*. Trentham.

# 7

# School and College Influences on the Formation of Careers

In Chap. 5 I discussed my informants' aspirations to pursue further and higher education and to obtain the kinds of job to which they saw this as providing a gateway. I examined the different forms these aspirations took, and what gave rise to them. The sources were personal, financial, familial and social. Wanting to have a worthwhile and interesting professional career based outside the home was a significant motivation to pursue further study but so also were avoiding poverty as adults, gaining independence, and making parents proud. In Chap. 6 I showed that while the women's families differed in the roles they played in shaping their aspirations and in providing cultural capital of the kinds needed to succeed in the UK education system, in most cases, as with other working-class families, there were severe limits on what they were able to offer. I shall argue that the educational system therefore took on a particularly important role for my informants in forming their aspirations and as a potential source of cultural capital. In this chapter I will explore their educational experiences in this light.



A. Saeed, *Education, Aspiration and Upward Social Mobility*,
https://doi.org/10.1007/978-3-030-82261-3_7

## The School System in Milltown

All of my informants were not only born in Milltown but attended schools in the area as well. However, their school careers only overlapped partially and, during the whole period covered in this research, the system changed from one involving primary, middle, and secondary schools to one where children moved straight from primary to secondary. Thus, Noreen moved from primary to middle school at the age of ten, and from middle to upper school at the age of 13, where she remained until the age of 16 (see Table 7.1 below and Appendix Schools in Milltown). Most of the others left primary school at 11 to move to secondary school, where they stayed until they were 16.

Noreen contrasts her experiences in two schools; the middle school Queensmead and the upper school Nofields, each about the same size. She attended these schools following her older brother and sister. Queensmead was a half-hour walk from her home, the upper school only five minutes away. Noreen's views echo a common pattern of student

**Table 7.1** The post-primary schools my informants attended

| Name of school | Name of informant |
|---|---|
| Queensmead Middle School 10–13 | Raheela |
| | Noreen |
| Summerfield Secondary School 11–16 | Ayesha |
| | Ghazala |
| | Nasreen |
| | Robina |
| | Shaheena |
| | Shamila |
| Grange Park Secondary School 11–16 | Tahira |
| Nofields Upper School | Raheela |
| | Noreen |
| Alderfield Upper School and Sixth Form | Raheela |
| Oldfields Sixth Form Centre | Ghazala |
| | Shaheena |
| | Shamila |
| | Nasreen |
| Ashwood College (local) | Ayesha |
| Ditchley College | Tahira |
| Kirkley High School (Sixth Form) | Robina |

accounts in which experience at secondary school is contrasted unfavourably with that at primary or middle school.

At the time when Noreen attended Queensmead, there were no Islamic faith-based schools in Milltown. This school had a strong Christian ethos, which manifested itself in daily school assemblies featuring Christian prayers and hymns. She speculates whether from her parents' point of view 'it was better to attend a school which had some religion in it, some appreciation of God, than none at all' (Noreen). However, other non-religious though equally symbolic features of the school were more important for her, not least the house system:

> I was the sports captain for my house. Everyone in [the house] voted. Everyone in the netball team was a captain [of one of the four houses] and … there were four or five of us who were in the same class and we were house captains. I was quite popular in Queensmead.

Here Noreen describes how her high status as the sports captain meant that she bonded with those people who were of a similar status to her. Relationships in this sense were clearly demarcated. Perhaps being sports captain of her house provided her with symbolic capital in the form of personal qualities such as charisma (Lamaison & Bourdieu, 1986).

Bernstein et al. (1966) usefully discusses the organizational cultures of schools as being made up of instrumental and expressive orders. The instrumental culture is centred on efforts to facilitate the acquisition of specific skills and bodies of knowledge. The expressive order refers to behaviour and activities to do with conduct, character and manner (Power et al., 2004). It is clear that at Queensmead Noreen enjoyed high status in terms of the expressive order of the school, in which the house system played a central role. For Bernstein et al. (1966), the rituals associated with such features of the expressive order:

> construct a framework of meaning over and beyond specific situational meanings. Here the symbolic function of ritual is to relate the individual through ritualistic acts to a social order, to heighten respect for that order, to revivify that order within the individual and, in particular, to deepen acceptance of the procedures used to maintain continuity, order and boundary which control ambivalence towards the social order. (Bernstein et al., 1966, p. 429)

Noreen's success in sport, and the status it gave her in the expressive order of the school, enabled her to develop cultural capital in other ways: 'I was on the (school) netball team. There were lots of events at school and after school and I used to read there'. As the sports captain of her house, she was committed to the values of working hard for the benefit of the house. Her motivation in this area seems to have had an effect on her attitude in other areas, such as her disposition towards reading and school work more generally. A specific aspiration in one area, sport, spread out into a desire to excel in other areas, such as reading for pleasure sponsored by the school. The concerns and values of the school, its 'expressive culture', gave her resources to succeed in terms of the instrumental order of the school as well. There was a lot of cultural capital in the form of sports skills and academic subject-based knowledge available to access, and her status in the expressive order opened the door to this for her, both psychologically and institutionally.

When she had to leave Queensmead and move on to Nofields, her upper school, the world changed for her. This was a very different place:

*Interviewer*: Was it a poor school?

*Noreen*: Yes extremely. There wasn't even a playground. There was a small courtyard, you couldn't even call it a courtyard. It had a fire escape, stairs made of metal the griddy type, and that led into the courtyard, and the teachers would park their cars. You couldn't use it, at break time. There was no school field, so you couldn't do any sport … And so at break times, you would literally hang around on the corridors. People would go and smoke in the toilets …. It was just a different environment. Queensmead was light, it had windows all the way around, the energy was different. Nofields was dark gloomy corridors. There was hardly any sunlight coming in. And at break time you were not even exposed to the sunlight. You had to stay on the corridors. You weren't getting any fresh air. It wasn't healthy. It wasn't a healthy environment. In your games lessons you were indoors again, you were in the gym. There was no track. You're not breathing in any fresh air.

She found the lack of suitable sports facilities at Nofields frustrating. Whilst at her previous school she had gained status through sport, at her upper school the opportunities for sports were minimal. There were no fields, no school matches and no enthusiastic peers. Thus material impoverishment at this school diminished her scope to develop physically and socially. Furthermore, at the upper school Noreen did not find a thriving official expressive culture in which she could participate. It seems that not only could she not capitalise on the reputation that she had built up at Queensmead (always a potential problem in moving schools) but also Nofields did not provide the environment where she could capitalise on the physical and social skills that she had developed in Queensmead.

In the different environment her priorities changed and she turned to participation in an anti-school peer culture. She was no longer committed to doing well in her school work, but concentrated instead on enjoying herself, 'having a laugh' with her friends, and joining in with the general scorning and ridiculing of poor teachers. She describes here what her physics lessons were usually like:

> When I look back now, I think it was just a laugh, that lesson was just a laugh. No one took a blind bit of notice, he [the teacher] had no control. It was just a laugh.

Disruptive behaviour, whilst satisfying at a day-to-day level, meant that she left school with few qualifications. Her involvement in the school was as a rebel: she flourished socially but not academically. She was not motivated to learn:

> Nofields, it was à dive. I made the most of it. I had a great time. I don't regret it. But if we're talking education, then I think the role of schools should be to provide some sort of direction, should prepare you for the outside world, for work, for apprenticeships.

'Flourishing socially' in this upper school did not mean acquiring social or cultural capital that could be used to gain educational qualifications and a professional job.

Indeed, according to Noreen's account very few students at Nofields obtained the qualifications necessary to go on to university, indicating the paucity of cultural capital available in the school. She left school with a handful of CSEs[1] and no O Levels, and a persistent feeling of a life-long deficit in being able to write academically. This has impeded her ability to be successful in further study:

*Noreen*: I still find the whole thing of writing an essay traumatic.
*Interviewer*: Why is that?
*Noreen*: I don't know. It's because at school we were never told. We were never told to write essays about anything …. When I read [now] I read lots of essays that interest me, whether it's Islamic philosophy or whatever and I'm learning, and am aware of the style of writing that I like and what's easier for me to understand and which writers I like. So I have a better idea of what writing is about. I write poems myself. So I have a better idea, so I'm hoping, inshallah [God willing] that the next course that I do, those skills will be apparent.

What we have here then is an illustration of the considerable variation that may be found in expressive and instrumental orders between schools operating in the same area, and the effects that these can have on children's school careers. Obviously, many other events were occurring in Noreen's life during her time at these two schools, and these may well have affected her. However, it seems clear that the change in socio-cultural context that she faced had important implications for the development of her aspirations and for what sorts of cultural capital were and were not available to her, and therefore for her future prospects.

[1] Before GCSEs were instituted as a common examination at age 16, GCE O-Levels were used for higher levels of achievement (a minority of pupils) and CSEs (Certificate of Secondary Education) for lower levels (the majority). The top grade for CSE counted as an O-level pass.

## The Shaping of Aspirations

In Chap. 5 I sketched the development of my informants' aspirations. Of course, one does not simply acquire an aspiration once and for all. Not only may aspirations vary in strength and degree of specificity but they must be sustained and developed if they are to be realized: school experience can support this process or undermine it. Teachers clearly play a potentially important role in this respect too. A local imam explained to me that in Islamic tradition a teacher is regarded as more important than, or at least of equal importance to, a parent. This reflects the moral seriousness attached to education and teachers by Pakistani families (Wrigley, 2000).

Some of my informants expected a good teacher to want the best for them, and even to take on a mentoring role. This would involve sharing complex understandings of the future pathways open to them. Jessica Bok (2010) argues that the demand to 'raise aspirations' is hollow if we do not attend to the knowledge young people and parents have about how to achieve their ambitions. She compares the difficulty of many working-class and ethnic minority students aiming for university as acting a play without a script or going on a journey without a road map. Ayesha explains what such a role might involve:

> I feel if someone would have guided me a little in the times when I needed it, when I didn't necessarily know myself that I needed it, when I was a bit lost and then someone would be there and say these are your choices.

Of course, even when provided, guidance was not always followed. Ayesha reports that her careers teacher *did* help her to understand the options for further education, but Ayesha was not then ready to respond to this positive input. She blames herself for not accessing this support:

> I remember once when I was in college and somebody in college got me in touch with a careers teacher. They would have given me my options but my mind wasn't set on it properly.

Of particular importance in shaping informants' aspirations were the expectations teachers communicated to students:

*Interviewer*: Which were the good teachers? Were there any that really stood out?

*Shaheena*: Oh I would say my high school English teacher. She had so much faith in me, it was unbelievable. I remember I got Es for my English language and literature mocks, because I didn't revise because I wasn't bothered at that time. And she predicted me a C for my English Language and literature! I said: 'Are you sure?' She goes 'Shaheena you are intelligent'. She just had so much faith in me. And I did end up with 2 Cs for my English .... Nobody had so much faith in me as her. It's unbelievable. I mean that even when I got bad results in my mocks, she would still say, 'I know you can do it'. She just said like, I was so shocked that she predicted me two Cs. I never even thought that I could get them. I wasn't that interested in education, it wasn't that I was naughty, it was just that it didn't interest me.

Shaheena explains here how one teacher's expectations of what she could achieve in English surpassed her own, and in doing so made her recognize the possibility of some mastery in that subject. This in turn gave her a sense of what she was capable of achieving, thus opening up new choices for her and developing her aspirations.

Peers at school could also play a crucial role in shaping aspirations, if only by presenting alternative possibilities:

> One of my friends wanted to be a pharmacist. And she was a really good friend of mine and there was one friend that wanted to be a social worker. There were like a few other ones. I thought, if they can do it, why can't I do something? Because in my family, nobody went to university or anything. (Shaheena)

> I think I only stuck to school because of my friends. (Shaheena)

For Ghazala, her relationship with her friends at school helped her to develop her early aspiration to become a social worker:

> I was quite fortunate because I knew that I wanted to be a social worker not really knowing what a social worker was. All I knew about being a social worker was that I wanted to help people. It was when I was at school and so I must have been about fourteen or fifteen, I was used to doing that. I was always helping people. I was the agony aunt at school with my friends. That's why I wanted to be a social worker.

## Teachers' Expectations and Ethnicity

Up to now I have examined the role of teachers' expectations, both as these related to my informants as students within predominantly working-class schools, and as individuals. Unsurprisingly perhaps, teachers' expectations of their students were also sometimes linked to ethnicity. There were two areas where this came to the fore in my informants' accounts; physical education and classes in Urdu.

PE would not normally be regarded as a subject crucial to cultural capital, but discussion about it did reveal the ways that labels can operate to perpetuate traditional gender ideas about appropriate conduct and careers at school.[2] I noted earlier how Noreen's sporting prowess in middle school had been an important element of her success there. However, Raheela's experience was very different. She found that, in PE lessons, some teachers tended to discriminate against Pakistani girls, on the grounds that they would follow a traditional path into marriage, and therefore would not benefit from wider opportunities such as participation in sport:

> She [the PE teacher] always used to make out it was a big effort teaching Asian girls, when at the end of the day they were going to get married anyway so what was the point of teaching them anything. (Raheela)

[2] Brah and Minhas (1985) argued that Asian girls were stereotyped in mainstream contexts as passive, shy, docile and timid. Also, Bhachu (1996) argues that it was common for White feminists to view Asian girls and women as oppressed by patriarchy, purdah and constraining and static home-cultural values.

Raheela regrets teachers' expectations that British Pakistani girls would become housewives and therefore would not benefit from wider opportunities, for example, sports. Such labelling is powerful because it can extend to limiting opportunities and academic success in other subjects. What this indicates is that my informants had to resist internalising these views about 'what Asian girls are like'. But it is clear from what she goes on to say that the teachers did not simply give up on the girls. She comments:

> I could run. I could play netball and stuff like that so I don't think I got as much stick [from the PE teachers] as some of the other girls did. (Raheela)

Here, the teachers can also be understood as trying to motivate 'Asian girls' to participate. In contrast to some of their peers, my informants were keen to embrace an active positioning, which ran counter to their teachers' expectations but was shown by their demands to take part in PE.

While in this case Pakistani girls were discouraged from taking up, or actually denied, some opportunities, a more complex case centred on the provision of Urdu as one of the languages that could be studied in school. This had arisen from multicultural and anti-racist policies and as a result of pressure from the local community.

> Multicultural education was an attempt to break down stereotypes by calling for 'greater tolerance'. It involved the school in creating an appropriate environment where respect would be given, for example, to dietary preferences, dress, customs, religions and cultural heritage, and sensibilities. (Figueroa, 1995; Abbas, 2004, p. 10)

Furthermore, there was pressure from the local community: Raheela's uncle had been a community elder who campaigned to have Urdu taught in schools. Basit (1997) has discussed at length how many parents valued their daughters' being able to study and take a GCSE in their heritage language. This tended to be part of a list of demands that related to respecting home culture, such as being able to wear shalwar kameez and wanting their daughters to retain their religion and other aspects of their culture. Speaking and writing Urdu opened up the possibility of transnational communication with people in Pakistan and other countries and carried prestige for the user within the local community.[3] Urdu is widely perceived by users as rich and an elegant language. However, it was unlikely to serve as cultural capital in the UK education system, except in very specialised ways.

Raheela describes her experience of studying Urdu at school:

| | |
|---|---|
| *Raheela*: | At that time there was a lot of campaigning going on with regards to, I remember there was a big hoo ha with regards to halal meals. So my uncle had campaigned for that quite a bit, as well as about Urdu being taught at schools. Being his niece, it was expected that I would be doing Urdu .... There were a lot of different tutors, coming and going, doing the same thing and it wasn't well organised. It was really rubbish. They weren't really ready to launch it as an exam really, as a subject to be taught, that year that I did it. |
| *Interviewer*: | In hindsight, are you pleased that you did it? |
| *Raheela*: | I don't think I've learnt anything. I don't think I use anything that I learnt from that course now. I can't read Urdu any better than I did then. It was a waste of time really. |
| *Interviewer*: | Do you wish you had done a different language? |
| *Raheela*: | Erm, yes. I wish I had done another language. Not necessarily French or German—those were the two that were being offered at the time. Maybe Spanish, or something that I would use now. Do you know what I mean? |

Whilst the struggle to have non-European languages recognised in English schools has been an important one, Raheela's experience shows that this was not always accomplished with adequate expertise and as a result Urdu was not useful or personally enriching for her, as community campaigners had intended.

Tahira explains how the school supported the community aspiration that Pakistani pupils should learn Urdu, but at the expense of their

[3] Urdu is spoken in Pakistan and India and within Pakistani diasporic communities. It is very similar in spoken form to Hindi.

studying other languages. Pupils would therefore *not* get the chance to study both Urdu and a European language. She now realizes that studying Urdu, a decision she regrets, was influenced by the narrower future that others envisaged for British Pakistani children. This vision was at odds with what Tahira went on to become:

> How it worked in our school, I don't know if I should be mentioning this though. The people that were in the higher sets, the top set, the *gorai* [White English people], they had the choice of doing French. But if you were not too, how can I put it without being politically incorrect, if you were not taking your education that seriously let us say, they would put the kids into Urdu. Or say that kids who could not speak English because say they've been in Pakistan a lot of years, they got put in Urdu. They never got the choice of doing French. And from the school's viewpoint they probably thought they've got a better chance of passing Urdu which is supposedly a language spoken at home, as opposed to doing French. So a lot of my friends, well I was in top subjects, but my friends whom I would see at lunch-time, they were all doing Urdu. And hence I wanted to do Urdu …. Looking back at it now it was probably not the wisest of decisions. I wish I had kept to French instead of Urdu.

Although Tahira could have studied French because she was regarded as bright enough, she chose Urdu over French so that she could avoid separation from her Pakistani friends. She mentions how pupils learning Urdu were viewed in deficit terms or stigmatised. Tahira's parents did not mind at all whether she studied Urdu or not since, as a Pashto speaker, Urdu GCSE was not a way to recognise and respect her home language. For some informants studying an alternative foreign language other than Urdu reflected a wish to travel to places other than Pakistan. For them, choosing to study a European language would have prepared them for their envisaged future lives, which would involve travelling the world, extending their social and cultural capital and having a fulfilling time. It fitted better: was consistent with a projected cosmopolitan image of themselves, one that learning just Urdu did not support.

However, Shaheena's view was different: she spoke favourably about being able to speak and read Urdu:

> It's been useful speaking Urdu because my mum can't speak English, and so when we have appointments and things, I can interpret for her. So when you're bilingual it does help your family because you can interpret something for them in Urdu. It's like whether you're Mirpuri, Punjabi or Urdu, you have similar words.[4] You can interpret then.[5] I used to go with my mum to hospital appointments, because at that time they didn't have hospital interpreters. And I also read letters to her and tell my mum what the bill is.

Shaheena had initially learnt some Urdu at mosque, as all the women did, and continued studying it at school where she obtained a good grade in it. For a Mirpuri speaker, Urdu represented a higher social status language because it was the language of the elite in Pakistan and acted as a lingua franca with other non-Mirpuri-speaking Pakistanis. It was useful when she needed to interpret for her mother. She thus emphasised the practical value of speaking Urdu whilst navigating within the locality.[6]

Ghazala both identifies with and dissociates herself from her mother tongue Punjabi, and Urdu. She acknowledges that speaking Urdu can be a useful skill and act as linguistic capital, but it should not be used to define people solely in narrow ethnic terms within mainstream contexts:

> But I did make it clear to them, when I used to hear people, colleagues, say to me that it's fascinating that you're going to go on to do your social work degree, there's a shortage of Asian social workers. I was very erm conscious that I needed to get across to them that I wasn't going into any job including social work just because I could speak a specific language. Ok, yes, I was fortunate that I did bring my language skills and my cultural skills but it wasn't just about that. It was about who I was as a worker and the other skills, not just that I could speak a specific language.

[4] Shaheena regards different home languages as significant markers of identity.

[5] There has been a recent change which forbids relatives to translate for those who cannot speak English in medical contexts. An official interpreter is required, if one is needed.

[6] Work by Saeed (2016) draws attention to elitist judgements held by overseas Pakistanis towards working-class British Pakistanis. In this context, speaking Urdu can bring cultural capital rewards for the latter.

The example of Ghazala illustrates how speaking Urdu could operate as cultural capital within the mainstream culture, but at the same time she also felt that it was limiting.

## Schools and Career Choices

Closely associated with variation in teachers' expectations about students' likely levels of academic achievement and their future careers were judgments about their probable occupational destinations. Some informants found that their schools expected that they would go into relatively low-level jobs, and this constituted a barrier to their own more ambitious aspirations.

Tahira explains that there was a generally held belief in her secondary school that the majority of pupils would go into manual or routine non-manual jobs. Indeed, the school was not able to cater for those students whose exam results eventually showed them to be above average. This became a problem for her when she unexpectedly obtained exceptionally good GCSE results. The work experience available to pupils at Tahira's local comprehensive school was in manual jobs. According to her, the careers advice did not recognise many other options:[7]

> The careers teachers give you options of working in Asda, working in Tesco, they didn't really push you. I think at my school, I don't think they actually thought that somebody would actually be able to do dentistry, somebody would be able to do medicine. So it was more general and broad. Like working in a shop or you know, nothing at a professional level. And that's why at GCSE level I didn't think I got that. In our R.E. subjects, one of the subjects was to fill in an application form. It was filling in an application form for a store. They didn't give you an application form for filling in for a university or anything of that sort. So it was very much like that. That was the case for all students. I don't think the school thought that they had students who could push themselves to a certain level.

[7] Brah and Minhas (1985) reported that careers guidance teachers would frequently dismiss the aspirations of Asian girls as 'too high'.

For Reay et al. (2005) class cultures are constituted partly by the types of schools attended and partly by one's family milieu. And these cultures can explain the later choices that people make in terms of whether or not to aim at higher education, to what institution they apply, and for what course. Tahira's comments also highlight the specific class barriers that needed to be overcome by students from her school if they were to achieve social mobility.

However, Tahira did manage to obtain work experience for herself at the beginning of sixth form to support her university application to study dentistry. Her brother advised her that this would be necessary, and she arranged it by approaching dentists directly, independently of her college:

*Tahira*: I did work experience at a dentist's. That was in Kirkley. I did work experience at an orthodontist in Milltown. So yes. At that point I knew I wanted to do dentistry. Once I had chosen my A Level subjects, I knew I wanted to do dentistry. I did my work experience after that. Because my brother, who is doing dentistry, said the core aspect that they look for at the interview stage is have you done work experience

*Interviewer*: How did you get in touch with them? Did anyone help you?

*Tahira*: I just rang around. I said I want to do dentistry and can I come and have a look and they said, yes, sure.

In this way Tahira was able to overcome her school's low expectations of students' occupational prospects. As noted in the previous chapter, being able to rely on the support of her brother was very significant for Tahira.

Raheela had a similar experience of being given little support in pursuing her career aspirations. She explains that her teachers played no part in helping her decide what, as a young working-class Pakistani woman, she might become:

*Interviewer*: Did you get any help from teachers or careers teachers?

*Raheela*: No, but that's because it was me that wanted it. It was up to me. I can't remember anyone particularly wanting to help.

Clearly, then, there was considerable variation even within educational institutions of the same kind as regards careers advice and levels of expectations. This seems to have largely reflected differences in the social class composition of the schools. However, schools and teachers were not simply important in the expectations that they projected about students but also in what access they could provide to cultural capital.

## Bridging Opportunities

It has often been noted that there is a significant cultural gap between working-class homes and schools, highlighted by Bourdieu in his discussion of cultural capital (see Chap. 3). In the case of my informants this was true despite their access to some ethnic capital at home. In particular, my informants' parents had very little experience of the British education system and were also rarely able to provide their children with much help in academic skills and learning subject knowledge. As a result informants were particularly dependent upon the extent to which teachers were able and willing to provide a bridge for them between the worlds of home and school.

It is clear that ineffectual teachers often represented barriers to my informants' efforts to learn skills and subject knowledge, in order to achieve qualifications. However, their accounts also made clear how good teachers had created opportunities for them:

> There was an ICT teacher who was on the same level as you and you could talk to him like a friend. There were strict teachers. He was funny. He influenced me to do ICT. You felt like asking him more because he was at your level. With the strict teachers you wouldn't ask them. If you asked him, he would show you. He was a better teacher than all these strict teachers. You're not going to learn anything if you can't ask them questions. (Nasreen)

Ayesha had a more broadly favourable experience of teachers:

*Interviewer*: Do you remember anything about the teachers?
*Ayesha*: They were just really nice. They were helpful. You could go up to them and ask them something. And most of the time they were quite good.

So like many students, Nasreen judged her teachers in terms of their strictness, while especially valuing those who would respond helpfully to questions (Furlong, 1976; Gannaway, 1976). For both her and Ayesha, feeling comfortable enough to ask questions helped to define a good teacher and a fruitful learning environment. This was particularly important for students, like them, who aspired to do well at school but who lacked much of the cultural capital needed to do so, making them dependent on teachers being willing and able to explain what they could not understand.

There were also other ways in which teachers could provide bridging opportunities for their students. As we have seen, Noreen was educationally successful in her middle school. She speaks passionately about a particular pedagogic style that she found motivating and enriching:

> I remember doing something at Queensmead about going up to Haworth on a school trip for a day and then when we got back we had to write, not just an essay, but a project on what it was about and what we saw there, who was in the family and what was going on etc etc. I put my heart into it and did it really well. I think I did really well and got second prize.

Here Noreen talks about an educational experience that fully engaged her and had a lasting impact. It was an experience involving real-context learning, which inspired her to explore a new world under her own steam. The experience can be regarded as motivating her and helping her to access school knowledge.

By contrast, Shaheena explains a time when favourable teaching styles and learning environments were not available to her. The experience had lasting repercussions:

> And I remember one of the business studies teachers, she was quite nasty as well. I remember asking her for help for something and I remember she embarrassed me in front of the whole class. She went 'I am not here to do it for you!' [Shaheena spoke aggressively here], and I thought: I never asked you to do it, I just asked you a question. After that I never asked her again for help. I thought, why did she take that approach? She just seemed so mean.

Shaheena is referring here to a painful experience at school. The teacher is endowed with pedagogic authority and decides how pupils should comport themselves as learners. In this case asking a question about the subject matter is deemed inappropriate and is met by a sharp rebuke. The consequences of this disparagement are significant because Shaheena deals with it by excluding herself from any future dialogue with this teacher, and perhaps with others. An emotional barrier is created.

Whether or not bridging opportunities are created and sustained by teachers seems likely to be an important factor in determining whether or not working-class ethnic minority students can acquire the cultural capital that they need to succeed at school. This was certainly the experience of many of my informants.

## Post-compulsory Institutions

So far I have looked at variations across primary, middle, and upper schools in the support they provided for high aspirations, and in the opportunities they offered to acquire the cultural capital needed to pursue those aspirations. Similar variations were to be found between institutions providing post-compulsory education. For example, when Raheela moved into the sixth form she found the environment academically much more challenging than that of her previous school. She was unable to access the necessary support in the unfamiliar milieu and did not succeed in passing her A Levels. The contrast between success as a learner in her upper school and this subsequent failure at sixth form perhaps reflects the respective organizational cultures, these giving rise to different learning experiences:

*Raheela*: I felt that a lot of the work we were given at school was quite easy and it was more like cruising. I felt like I cruised a lot when I did my O Levels and so when it came to doing my A Levels, I struggled. I think when I was at the school doing my O Levels, because everyone else was at a lower academic level, it appeared that I was intelligent and very bright academically, but when I went to do my A Levels—I went to another school to do my A Levels—everyone else was already quite ahead and quite developed because they had gone to a different school. By the end of my second year, in my second year, I didn't used to attend my lectures. For anyone that knows me, they'd know that that's not me. I'd take the afternoons off and stuff like that.

*Interviewer*: Could the school not help?

*Raheela*: They tried to help me when the problem was identified, but it was too late because I had too much work on. And I failed all my A Levels. But it's ok.

Other informants also found that they could not cope with the new environment in the sixth form:

> I went to Oldfields because I passed all of my GCSEs. … I love history. I love knowing what's gone on in the past. I love writing. … Sixth form was just too strict for me. I wanted to be in a college environment. I just couldn't be bothered. (Shamila)

Shamila claims that whilst she did not have a studious disposition she began sixth form with a passion for most of her A Level subjects. But she found the lessons at the school sixth form centre 'boring', resulting in a loss of motivation. She disliked the distance created by hierarchical relations between staff and pupils, as 'too strict'. In an unrecorded discussion she explained that she preferred more equal and respectful relations as a source of motivation. Robina had a similar experience:

*Interviewer*: Were there any teachers that you liked?

*Robina*: No. They were like not really bothered. It was all left to you to get on with it. I got on well with my Psychology teacher. She was very young and new into the profession. The Chemistry and Biology teachers were very strict with me. They were old. You would walk in and there'd be no communication. You did your notes and then you'd go.

Here Robina depicts an absence of dialogue with most of the teachers. For a lot of my informants this was common with older teachers: they seemed to exude distance and lack of care or interest. The sixth form that Robina attended had been selected by her mother, who held high expectations for her daughter but had been greatly disappointed by her GCSE results. Her mother insisted that she attend the best 'type' of sixth form—one where she would not be distracted by her friends. In fact, no other Pakistani students attended it and this put her in a vulnerable position. There she was subjected to racial harassment. She ascribes her disappointing A Level results to racist bullying by peers and feeling unable to talk to her mother about this:

> No it was because my mum didn't want me to go to college with my friends. Because she felt that I didn't get the GCSE grades that I should have got because of my friends. The college that I wanted to go to, my friends were all going to that college. She wanted me to go to a college where I didn't know anyone, so she made me go to a White college. That was quite hard for me, because I was getting abused for racism and stuff. I was having to put up with that and my mum wanted me to become a doctor and so there was that added pressure. They used to call me Paki and stuff and spit at me. They wouldn't talk to me and left me out. Even my mates, weren't really my mates. They would talk about me. And say names behind my back, say that I was a Paki. I didn't want to go there at all. I was really bullied. I was really slim when I started college and then I put on weight because I was getting bullied, and I couldn't talk to my mum. So I turned to chocolate. I put on loads and loads of weight. So I didn't have a good time.

There were clearly insurmountable challenges posed by being the only student from a Pakistani background in the college. How then did others with cosmopolitan aspirations try to manage social bridging with peers from different cultural backgrounds?

## Exploring University Away from Home: Choosing Change

For Tahira the field of university was predominantly middle class. She became attuned to the nuances of class differences between herself and most of the other people on her course, which also overlapped with ethnic differences. In doing so, her experiences at university revealed the heterogeneity of the mainstream community:

*Tahira*: Out of my year there were sixty nine people and out of those people I could probably name about seven people. No more than seven that had gone through the same education as me and got in to do dentistry. The rest of them were from a different education background completely … I was friends with everyone. But you just knew and they knew what people had gone through. The people, it was quite obvious really to be honest. Just when you talked about things. When we talked about the things that they did and the things that we did. It was completely different. I can't explain it but it was obvious. Even parents and how, for example you [referring to the interviewer] said did you discuss it with your parents, or what you did in the evening or what have you, or how you did at university. It was the same as that. We just kind of kept it to ourselves. And we did our studies ourselves. But other students might have rang back home and said we did this or did that.

*Interviewer*: What was college life like—did you make the most of it in terms of doing other stuff?

*Tahira*: Yes. I definitely made the most of it. … I went to New York, Hawaii and Los Angeles. Las Vegas and in between I went to Spain and Germany. That was good.

Tahira represents university as allowing her to make a life of her own, interacting in new social fields (e.g., international holidays), and engaging with diverse people and their web of cultural meanings (Rozbicki & Ndege, 2012). The making of the self clearly involves other people.

However, among her friends she did form particularly close friendships with British Pakistanis from state schools in the North of England who shared her home background. This echoes Hussain's and Bagguley's (2007) finding about Asian pupils feeling less isolated if the university is ethnically diverse.[8] Shared background can make the social capital they provide sustaining.[9]

## Conclusion

As I explained in Chap. 6, my informants' parents often chose not, or were unable, to support their aspirations, and frequently lacked many of the resources that could serve as cultural capital within the UK education system. This was because, in almost all cases, the parents themselves had no formal educational qualifications and relevant experience. Furthermore, culturally, my informants were generally raised in families with traditional views of women's roles. Given this, schools played a potentially important function for my informants in engendering and supporting alternative aspirations, and providing opportunities to acquire cultural capital. However, while all informants attended state schools and colleges, in more or less the same area, there was considerable variation in how these institutions shaped aspirations and in what resources they could supply. This was not as simple as variation in what Smith and Tomlinson (1989) and others refer to as 'the school effect'. It partly reflected differences in the social class composition of the student body within each school, and how this affected teachers' expectations and the school ethos. Furthermore, in some cases there was a homology between economic and symbolic capital reflected in the material impoverishment

[8] There are also parallels with Jackson and Marsden's early study (1986) of working-class grammar school boys. Some boys would retain links with their neighbourhoods through youth organisations, which the schools would not always favour. Despite this, they reported that the 'easiest relations were only with those in a like position' at school (Jackson & Marsden, 1986, p. 127).

[9] Slootman (2019) explores how socially mobile young people from ethnic minority backgrounds who are integrated in mainstream cultures are still drawn to people from their own ethnic minority group. At university they are able to provide 'soulmate' spaces for each other. These relationships are supportive because they share similar attitudes and outlooks.

of particular schools, with the result that they were unable to provide institutional capital, in the form of high-level qualifications for most of their students. More broadly, there was an expectation that students from working-class backgrounds would go into working-class kinds of job. Such assumptions constituted a major barrier for those, such as my informants, who aspired to professional careers.

Moreover, informants also sometimes experienced significant changes in institutional environment over time as they moved between schools, both within compulsory schooling and in post-compulsory education. Sometimes new sources of support and cultural capital appeared, at other times they disappeared or were closed off.

Whilst schools' organizational cultures presented both barriers and opportunities to educational achievement, the attitudes and practices of individual teachers were particularly important and had far-reaching consequences.[10] Some motivated students and raised their educational aspirations. Others did the opposite. Generally speaking, teachers who were open to pupil questioning enabled cultural capital to be acquired, while those who were not so left students like some of my informants struggling. In addition, some teachers seemed to uphold traditional values in terms of career expectations for Pakistani girls, reflecting those prevailing in the local community. Two areas where this emerged, in somewhat different ways, were physical education lessons and the provision of Urdu as a language option. Equally important were expectations about future careers and the sort of careers advice provided.

In all these ways, schools played a complex role in the careers of my informants. In some cases, and in some respects, they offered important support and resources. In others they represented barriers, because most Pakistani girls from the local community who had developed ambitious educational and occupational aspirations, like my informants, were not able to source the necessary support and cultural capital from their families. This applied at all levels of the education system, from primary schools through to sixth forms and colleges.

[10] There is a growing literature on educational institutions and how they can be transformed for social justice (see Arshad et al., 2020; Smyth & Wrigley, 2013; Treanor, 2020).

## References

Abbas, T. (2004). *The Education of British South Asians Ethnicity, Capital and Class Structure*. Palgrave Macmillan.

Arshad, R., Wrigley, T., & Pratt, L. (2020). *Social Justice Re-Examined: Dilemmas and Solutions for the Classroom Teacher*. UCL IOE Press.

Basit, T. (1997). *Eastern Values, Western Milieu*. Ashgate.

Bernstein, B., Elvin, L., & Peters, R. (1966). Ritual in Education. *Philosophical Transactions of the Royal Society of London B, 251*(*B*), 429–436.

Bhachu, P. (1996). Identities Constructed and Reconstructed: Representations of Asian Women in Britain. In G. Buijs (Ed.), *Migrant Women Crossing Boundaries and Changing Identities*. Berg.

Bok, J. (2010). The Capacity to Aspire to Higher Education: 'It's Like Making Them Do a Play Without a Script'. *Critical Studies in Education, 51*(2), 163–178.

Brah, A., & Minhas, R. (1985). Structural Racism or Cultural Difference: Schooling for Asian Girls. In G. Weiner (Ed.), *Just a Bunch of Girls*. The Open University Press.

Figueroa, P. (1995). Multicultural Education in the United Kingdom: Historical Development and Current Status. In J. Banks & C. Banks (Eds.), *Handbook of Research on Multicultural Education* (pp. 778–800). Macmillan.

Furlong, V. (1976). Interaction Sets in the Classroom: Towards a Study of Pupil Knowledge. In M. Stubbs & S. Delamont (Eds.), *Explorations in Classroom Observation*. John Wiley and Sons.

Gannaway, H. (1976). Making Sense of School. In M. Stubbs & S. Delamont (Eds.), *Explorations in Classroom Observation*. Wiley.

Hussain, Y., & Bagguley, P. (2007). *Moving on Up. South Asian Women and Higher Education*. Trentham Books Limited.

Jackson, B., & Marsden, D. (1986). *Education and the Working-Class*. Ark Paperbacks.

Lamaison, P., & Bourdieu, P. (1986). From Rules to Strategies: An Interview with Pierre Bourdieu. *Cultural Anthropology, 1*(1), 110–120.

Power, S., Whitty, G., Edwards, T., & Wigfall, V. (2004). Schools, Families and Academically able Students Contrasting Modes of Involvement in Secondary Education. In S. J. Ball (Ed.), *The RoutledgeFalmer Reader in Sociology of Education*. Routledge.

Reay, D., David, M., & Ball, S. (2005). *Degrees of Choice: Class, Race, Gender and Higher Education*. Trentham Books Limited.

Rozbicki, M., & Ndege, G. (2012). *Cross-Cultural History and the Domestication of Otherness*. Palgrave Macmillan.
Saeed, T. (2016). *Islamophobia and Securitization. Religion, Ethnicity and the Female Voice*. Palgrave Macmillan.
Slootman, M. (2019). Ethnic Minority Climbers: Evaluating 'Minority Cultures of Mobility' as a Lens to Study Dutch Minority Student Organisations. *Ethnic and Racial Studies, 42*(5), 838–856.
Smith, D. J., & Tomlinson, S. (1989). *The School Effect: A Study of Multi-Racial Comprehensives*. Policy Studies Institute.
Smyth, J., & Wrigley, T. (2013). *Living on the Edge: Rethinking Poverty, Class and Schooling*. Peter Lang.
Treanor, M. (2020). *Child Poverty: Aspiring to Survive*. Policy Press.
Wrigley, T. (2000). *The Power to Learn. Stories of Success in the Education of Asian and Other Bilingual Pupils*. Trentham.

# 8

# Career Building and Cultural Navigation

As previous chapters have made clear, my informants developed different aspirations and career paths from those of their mothers and many of their second-generation peers. I discussed the various barriers to, and opportunities for, pursuing these aspirations that they met in their homes, communities, and school careers. Some aspects of their environment supported the development of aspirations for higher levels of education and upward social mobility and provided the cultural capital required to realise them. Yet there were many obstacles and limitations to be overcome.

For Bourdieu the social landscapes, or *fields*, that people pass through interact with their habitus, or habits of behaviour and the principles which underlie them (Maton, 2010, p. 53). Primary socialisation within the family is deeply formative of unconscious habits of bodily and linguistic comportment. The family's habitus can constrain its members' understandings of possible future courses of action. Entering a new field, or inhabiting a familiar one in new ways, can give rise to disjuncture, as if one were operating like a 'fish out of water' (Grenfell et al., 1998, p. 14). However, since the habitus and fields of social action are evolving, their interaction can give rise to new outcomes. This change comes about



A. Saeed, *Education, Aspiration and Upward Social Mobility*,
https://doi.org/10.1007/978-3-030-82261-3_8

because an individual's habitus and fields of practice have their own internal logics and histories and interact in contingent and sometimes unpredictable ways, opening up new opportunities for agency. In this chapter I want to emphasise the active role that my informants played in shaping their lives: in finding ways around barriers and in exploiting opportunities.

The concept of navigation seems a particularly appropriate metaphor for understanding the active construction by my informants of what were seen as culturally deviant careers. It implies an envisaged destination, but also the need to find a way towards it, working around obstacles and taking advantage of whatever opportunities present themselves, while avoiding various mistakes and dangers. My informants were often the first in the family to pursue higher education, so they did not necessarily have tried and tested procedures to draw on, but had to acquire the necessary information and skills and discover their own path. Navigation is also a process in which advice may prove particularly valuable, as with the pilot who takes a ship into harbour, who knows the local rocks, currents and other dangers well. Some of my informants were able to call on such advice, enabling them to work towards their goal; others were not, making their navigation more perilous.

For those following an already mapped out, traditional career path, navigation involves, at most, following some fixed route—analogous to travelling along a river or canal or, in the sea, following a safe passageway marked on a map. Whilst autonomy and individual piloting are required, this will be minimal. Often, in relation to such traditional careers, parents, as significant others, will be the navigators of the journey, for children, young people and even young adults. By contrast, my informants chose to navigate and forge their own career paths, ones of which most of their parents knew very little. They did not have a pre-established map they could follow to realise their aspirations. For Bok (2010) educational success is the outcome of one's capability to aspire and the circumstances in which this aspiration must be realised. She argues that the educational aspirations of poor pupils are restricted because of the limited resources available to them to navigate the education system and higher-status career pathways successfully. It is as if they have to perform a play without a script.

Based on the discussion in Chap. 5, people may navigate towards a very specific destination, for example, becoming a nurse, or alternatively their aspirations may simply point in a general direction, towards taking a degree or a professional job. The goal can be understood in terms of entering a chosen profession and an identity destination in terms of a new career subjectivity having been constituted (McLeod & Thomson, 2009).

Achieving a non-standard aspiration required my informants to engage in bodily navigation in contexts in which they would not otherwise have found themselves. In these new spaces, both in the mainstream and the Pakistani community, they would face obstacles and opportunities. Informants' presence and comportment within those spaces could trigger a redefinition of normative conceptualisations of British Pakistani women. Informants would have to exercise discursive agency if they were to engage with and contribute to those new definitions. Discursive agency is discussed explicitly and implicitly in the work of various social theorists (Mead, 1934; Youdell, 2006), who locate it in different theoretical frameworks. For Butler (1997) discursive agency can manifest itself in language and in performances such as bodily gestures, adornments and acts (Youdell, 2006, p. 36). Both discourse and its performative effects offer political potential, exceeding the intent or free will of the agent. This perspective on discursive agency incorporates the way different aspects of our identities, such as gender, ethnicity and career, become socially constituted, with an individual's control over the process varying. For Bourdieu, people are able to bring about changes to their embodied practices in part through discursive agency. This is because dialogue and persuasion reflect a profound engagement with common values, interests and purposes (Maton, 2010).

These young women's journeys were influenced by emotional currents, arising from interactions in their new environments. Informants needed to manifest emotional agency in their confidence, drive and resilience in exploring unmapped possibilities and managing counterflows. The relevant information necessary to avoid navigation errors on the voyage includes emotional feedback from informants' interactions. Navigating has emotional consequences, which become internal points of reference that contribute to one's understanding of routes. This emotional dead reckoning may be crucial to navigation in these women's narratives. These experiences in career building are linked to the wider emotional journey of finding meaning in one's life.

Agency therefore seems crucial to successful navigation in three dimensions of experience: physical, interactional and social and emotional. The work of Ballard (1994) is interesting in its suggestion that British South Asians employ a dominant social strategy to navigate between their home and mainstream cultures. He refers to second-generation Asians as 'skilled navigators' between their home and mainstream cultures: they 'code-switch' between two culturally contradictory value systems, which he describes as enclaves that are kept insulated from each other. 'Skilled navigators' succeed in reconciling these two cultures (Ballard, 1994, p. 30). This experience of two very different cultures is shared by Hanley (2016) when she writes that:

> changing class is like emigrating from one side of the world to the other, where you have to rescind your old passport, learn a new language and make gargantuan efforts if you are not to lose touch completely with the people and habits of your old life. (Page X, Introduction)

Here, the gulf between different class cultures is emphasised. My own research uses the metaphor of navigating between cultures in a systematic way to understand women's cultural navigation on their career-building journeys.[1] In doing so, it questions the assumption underlying Ballard's assertions that the interactions between mainstream and home cultures are based predominantly on separation and insulation from, or contradiction with, each other. For my informants, intersections of class, gender and ethnicity added further complexity to their journey as they navigated towards upward mobility. In this chapter I shall consider the strategies that these young women used when navigating within spaces that were predominantly Pakistani and in those that were mainstream.

[1] Ballard (1994) does suggest at one point that second-generation Asians will find a third way in the future, based on bridging and reconciling the value systems of mainstream and home cultures.

## Overcoming Barriers of Purdah

A deep involvement with the norms of a mainstream secular culture could be problematic for some Pakistani families. There was a vulnerability to and fear of losing religious and ethnic identity through assimilation into the mainstream. It was believed that too deep an involvement in mainstream secular society could have the corrupting effect of lowering one's moral standards. Informants had to navigate around these fears by remaining guardians of their own proper moral conduct. A particular focus here was purdah. However, what this navigation required here could be interpreted in various ways, and it was up to informants to gain some recognition from within their communities and families of what constituted proper conduct for them.

Shaheena talked about a running club that she joined for a short time, but had to give up because of perceived communal disapproval of undertaking physical activity in public, because it was an immodest thing to do.

*Shaheena*: I like to keep fit and healthy. I joined the Falcons in Milltown because they're quite popular and they've got long-distance runners. You get prizes and all sorts for country running. I joined, but then guess what? They do running up Mainland Road. You run to Summerfield Park and up the road and all the way to Mainland and back. And I thought all these Pakistanis that are going to drive past and see me, … they're gonna go and tell my mum and dad. I left. But I really enjoyed it but I couldn't do it because it's not common for an Asian girl to run on the main road. Does that make sense? Because of all these Asians that were gonna, they would have told my mum and dad and they would have shouted. 'Why are you doing it, you know what people are like. They'll talk. Why are you doing it?' I left, but I really enjoyed it, but I couldn't carry on with it. They were really good to you, they were really motivating you. They were really good runners as well. I remember … that they had different stages, you went in different groups, so if you were a beginner you'd go with the beginners, if you were more advanced, you'd go with them. But I couldn't go. It limits you at times, you know when you can do things, but you can't. … It's because we were running on the main road, on the pavement obviously, and there are too many cars going past. It's all right in the winter because you can put a hood on, but when it's light people know who you are. But sometimes even when you've got a hood on, people just need to be able to get a glimpse of your face and they know who you are anyway.

*Interviewer*: So people would have recognised you?

*Shaheena*: Yes. You know it's because my dad is quite well known in the Mirpuri community. And I even look like my dad and so that doesn't help. When people see me they automatically ask me if I am Aslam's daughter, which I am.

She wanted to participate in the running club but she decided she could not continue with it because it involved running in public: she would be recognised, and this would lead to problems with her parents because of what other people in the community would say, especially given her father's leading role. It was not her own commitment to Islam or her Pakistani heritage that prevented her participating, but rather the community's perception of what is appropriate conduct for a woman in public and the effects of this on her parents. A tactical withdrawal was required.

Shaheena understands her movement in the local space from her own perspective. She regards what she does as being healthy and values having a fit body and uses the language of sports science to talk about improving her body's fitness in stages.[2] Through sport she is able to identify herself as an achiever in the terms of the wider, mainstream society. The family field in which she finds herself is evolving at a 'slower' rate in terms of health education than, and is different from, the structure of her developing habitus (Maton, 2010). She is also aware of the power that the community's

[2] Diabetes is a widespread health problem in the South Asian community in Britain. Exercise and eating healthily are essential to minimise its incidence.

social norms have over her and her parents. Her parents view her physicality from a different perspective—how others in the Pakistani community would see her. Norms are often enforced not so much because people are attached to them but because they are afraid of others' reactions, which are often used as justification for imposing sanctions.

Although Shaheena faced constraints on her participation in this mainstream activity, she developed various strategies to deal with these. One was bending the rules: employing a strategy that reduces her public visibility vis-à-vis other Pakistanis and yet at the same time allows her to participate in sport. She like Ghazala and Raheela started to use a private gym, in effect segregating different parts of her life, keeping them insulated from one another.[3] The gym becomes a safe space for some of my informants, tacitly accepted by their families, but away from the glare of the conservative elements of the community. It represents a contemporary mainstream recreational activity, in an ethnically mixed space and is achieved independently through one's own financial means. Participating in sport, in the gym or elsewhere, offers control over one's body, the pleasure of participating in exercise classes and the feeling of being 'at one' with one's body, rather than separated from it. This is significant in the light of the stories told about the appropriateness of Pakistani women actively participating at all in sport at school, discussed in Chap. 7. There, some PE teachers complained about implicit community discourses resisted by informants that discouraged women's active participation in sport. As adults they embraced contemporary mainstream lifestyle choices without flouting community norms.

## Participating in Mainstream Organisations and Groups

The young women I met experienced regular contact over many years with people from mainstream backgrounds. This contact could be sustained by participating in ethnically mixed recreational groups and by

---

[3] Hiding as a strategy with which to negotiate Pakistani women's identities vis-à-vis their family and community is discussed in Dwyer (1998) and Qureshi and Moores (1991).

friendships where people understood each other's home cultures through everyday experiences at school or the gym. This affected informants' aspirations and guided their negotiations within their families and the Pakistani community.

Informants' navigation experiences could help them to develop as 'authentic' cosmopolitans (Hannerz, 1996) from their own point of view, where mainstream cultures come to co-exist and intertwine in their lives through organic relationships. I shall consider here how deep involvement with contrasting cultures manifests itself. Shamila lives in the Pakistani community, yet almost all of her friends in Milltown were English and working class. It is not always possible to insulate these two cultural worlds from each other, so strategies are required for dealing with this:

*Shamila*: All my friends are White. It doesn't bother me. They accept me for who I am. It doesn't bother me. They know my do's and don'ts. And I'm really honest about it. I'm not one of those that says I'm not going out clubbing because I don't want to. They know that I would love to, but they know I can't and they accept me for what I am. I'm not pretentious and neither are they. And all my friends are White. Not that I'm comparing them to Pakistani people but they don't care about what I can and can't do, and vice versa. They are no different to Pakistani people apart from their skin colour. The last two Christmases I've been to people's houses and spent whole days with them. They'll get halal meat for me when they cook for me and stuff. I don't see them as any different. … They don't treat me any different to how they would if I had been a White girl. I love it. Because I'm Asian, I don't think they judge me. Some Pakistani girls must look at me and think, look at the way she's dressed. But my White friends don't judge me at all. They just accept me for what I am.

*Interviewer*: Have you ever experienced racism?

*Shamila*: Never, ever ever ever. Never. No one has ever said anything to me. I don't know why. Nobody's ever treated me differently because of my skin colour. Never. I've always got on well with everybody at work. I've never had that.

Here, Shamila is allowing herself to 'become' a new person through her friendships. She does not challenge the worth of those durable aspects of her home culture that she cannot change (Taylor, 1994). In taking this approach she remains loyal to aspects of her home culture and thus achieves stability in her changing world. Her navigation paths here seem familiar and much traversed, so that strategies for avoiding obstacles are part and parcel of her customary stock of knowledge:

> Your sister said to me, did you come out dressed like that? Did your mum and dad not say anything? I said no. They're dead chilled out. She knows that we're good girls—that we won't do anything. Obviously I won't come out with my boobs hanging out. My mum likes nice clothes. When she sees me in nice English clothes, she won't bat an eyelid. So in lots of ways I've got it easier than my friends. I'm not bothered about the things that I can't do. What's the point, what's it going to achieve? And I'm not rebellious. You've just got to make the best of what you've got. (Shamila)

Whilst community members may disapprove of her dress, Shamila has negotiated her attire with her mother.[4] Through dialogue the values, interests and purposes that underpin her conduct and presentation are affirmed between herself and her mother. With her, Shamila has shared the logic of her evolving habitus. In doing this she had in effect created an ally. Shamila does not regard her clothes as reflecting a morally suspect interior and associates parental permission to dress like this in her everyday public life as reflecting a relaxed interpretation of religious culture. Her mother is willing to share her interest in wearing 'nice clothes'. She explains her parents' lack of obsession with her outward appearance, when she states that they are 'dead chilled out', an attitude not shared by the community at large. It is of interest that the phrasing comes precisely from the discourse that would deny that wearing these clothes suggests immorality. Shamila is therefore caught in a contradiction: she is still a dutiful daughter, but this is not how it seems to the wider community. She claims her conduct is not challenging the interests of the household, yet it could be interpreted differently. Her navigational performance is therefore daring.

---

[4] Shamila came to the interview wearing laced-up high boots, a mid-length skirt and thick black tights.

In some fields feminine habitus can produce gender capital for women, because they bring returns in terms of social approval. However, fields vary in the rules of the game or the 'logic of practice' that operate there, and informants' positions within the gender sub-fields can therefore bring them different capital returns. Since notions of what is masculine and feminine are deeply entrenched as if they reflected what was natural, rather than what was socially constructed, Shamila had to resist depictions of being deeply threatening or even immoral (Krais, 2006).

Shamila's evolving habitus is influenced by her wider social experiences. She is familiar with her dress style through her work as a weekend manager at a high street fashion retailer in Ditchley; for this work there are distinctive dress requirements. She does not want to dress differently in different contexts. However, she does not regard this knowledge as supplanting her understanding of religiously sanctioned, modest attire. Her weekend job does however provide her with the knowledge to appear fashionable and embrace a hyper-heterosexual femininity.[5]

Drawing attention to her role as a shop manager allows her partly to sidestep the sexualised rhetoric that deemed her clothes inappropriate. Shamila draws on a different line of argument when she refers to the quality of her clothes. In doing so, she is positioning herself in a different reference structure in order to strengthen the capital value of her behaviour. She does, however, use other means of indicating that she is 'morally proper', when she states that she covers her décolletage in public. Not to do so would be an explicit challenge to a morally appropriate presentation from a traditional perspective.

She is working hard through such micro-level attention to her appearance to obtain gender capital returns in all the contexts in which she is active. This poses the challenge of trying to change aspects of some contexts, swim with the current in others, remain 'unpretentious' and not 'lose herself'. It also involves confidently, if not boldly, trying to engage others with her *broad* range of experiences. This involves the skills of

[5] For Archer et al. (2007) working-class women's investment in their heterosexual appearance constitutes one of the few available sites for the generation of symbolic capital (see also Skeggs, 1997). Young women can gain a sense of power and agency from their performances of heterosexual femininities.

physical, social and discursive agency to resolve the dilemmas that arise from her appearance and conduct.

For those informants who attended university away from home, there was a greater scope for insulating the different worlds in which they lived from one another. Cosmopolitan aspirations could be given more or less free rein:

*Interviewer*: Why did you want to leave Milltown?

*Raheela*: I wanted to see what else was going on. I wanted to see how other people lived their lives. And I felt I knew what was going on in Milltown and I wanted to see what everybody else was doing. I went to Liverpool when I was 18, to do my nursing and become a nurse. I experienced a different culture almost, because everyone was White and I never met another Asian nurse when I was there. I met Asian doctors but not nurses and I was quite friendly with a nurse who was half Caribbean. But there weren't any Asians for me to like socialise with.

*Interviewer*: How did you find being in that environment?

*Raheela*: It was quite exciting. I was quite homesick to begin with, but it was exciting to be away from home and to be living my own life. It was good.

Raheela describes socialising with non-Pakistanis when she lived away from the locality. Opportunities to be independent in more of one's decisions in life were exhilarating, although the familiarity of home was a source of comfort. What she was particularly skilled at doing was managing the changes that this university experience created in her, when she returned home:

> I think I used to go home every two weeks and how I behaved, I remained respectful and didn't show that I'd lost all my marbles and my morals by going away from home, because I hadn't. (Raheela)

Her success in managing this new situation is as a result of her sharp awareness of the 'expressive responsibility' she bears (Goffman, 1956).

Clearly Raheela has this awareness of the consequences of particular ways of behaving. She avoids dissonance by cooperating with her family on their terms, upholding a 'polite appearance of consensus' (Goffman, 1956, p. 133), reaping the benefits of being a loyal group member and avoiding family disunity. This successful impression management, requiring a strong purpose, indicates her high level of continued engagement with her home culture. If she is unable to do this, conflict can ensue. In fact she talks in a way that suggests pragmatic manoeuvring and a high degree of competence in achieving career success and ethnic belonging. She does not feel like a 'fish out of water',[6] since her (new) habitus and the (old) social world in which she finds herself are insulated from one another. She does not feel torn between the requirements of the two cultures. Raheela does indicate that she has achieved an emotional balance in her life, across her different fields of experience, helped by the fact that for her they are not fundamentally in opposition.

## Attending Post-compulsory Educational Institutions

Within education it seems to have been a matter of luck whether the secondary school my informants went to was a good school or not. However, after compulsory education they exercised rather more agency, tempering the effect of luck. Generally speaking, they sought to find ways to avoid ineffectual institutions, trying to attend sixth forms that had greater positive transformational potential than others and showing resilience when learning the skills of how to comport themselves as successful students within the further education environment. However they were not always free to do this, as we saw in the case of Robina, whose mother prevented her from going to college with her friends insisting instead that she went to a sixth form where there were no Asian students, with unfortunate consequences.

There were two types of post-compulsory educational institution that informants attended: traditional school sixth forms offering A Levels and

[6] '[W]hen habitus encounters a social world of which it is the product, it finds itself 'as a fish in water', it does not feel the weight of the water and takes the world about itself for granted' (Bourdieu interviewed by Wacquant (Wacquant, 1989, p. 43) in Grenfell et al. (1998, p. 14).

colleges offering A Level and vocational courses. Six informants attended sixth forms at Kirkley, Oldfields and Alderfield schools. Two of the informants, Ayesha and Shaheena, went to the further education college in Milltown. Tahira attended a college out of town that had a reputation for being academically successful.

This section examines how the women I interviewed negotiated the system in choosing particular institutions. One aspect of this was that they sought to avoid ineffectual educational institutions. Tahira's discursive knowledge of the greater positive transformational potential of some sixth forms over others, and her determination to act on that knowledge, is significant in explaining her educational success. The strength of Tahira's resistance to the tacit expectation to join the local sixth form that other Pakistani girls attended is reinforced by her brother's experience. He had already blazed the trail at the more academic sixth form:

> A lot of my friends who did their GCSEs in high school, a lot of them did not pass their A Levels. They went to Ashwood. And I knew if I went to Ashwood College, I would not pass my A Levels. And it's what has happened. A lot of the girls that passed their GCSEs when they went to Ashwood, they didn't come out with the A Levels that they should have, probably.[7] That was the reason why I trekked it all the way. I used to catch a bus and a tram and then a fifteen minute walk to get to college. It's paid off in the long run. I don't regret it. It was the best decision I ever made that. (Tahira)

What was involved here was not only going to a college that would provide better teaching but also increasing the cosmopolitanism, that is class and ethnicity, of her contacts. She met people who had had very different educational experiences from her, and she was able to build bridges with them because they were on the same courses and shared the same sorts of career aspirations. At the new sixth form college she embraced and in turn was accepted by a particularly academic learning culture, with people from backgrounds other than British Pakistani, but who were all high achievers:

[7] This was not recognised as a failing sixth form at the time, but became so later.

> It was a kind of college where people were generally there to study. There were obviously some people who did want to doss, but generally they worked. And at that college you had to have a pretty good grade in, say I wanted to do chemistry, you had to have a C or above in chemistry GCSE to do chemistry there. They had tutors who would review how you were getting on. It was good. It wasn't like they let you into this college, they looked at your GCSEs before they let you in. So it was a good college. (Tahira)

For other informants too, those colleges that were closer to home attracted students of varying abilities and were non-selective. Some other students would be attending college as an opportunity to socialise with friends, and they were the reason some colleges would get a 'bad reputation' as being a place for 'dossers' and not for people who were serious about their work (Ghazala). This was important because my informants had to prove to their families that they were serious about their studies and distance themselves from other people from within the British Pakistani group who might not be sufficiently studious.

My discussion here reveals that a discursive understanding of one's situation, specifically in terms of what type of further education institution to go to, underpinned skilful action and a determined independence—and hence a particular bodily comportment and lifestyle choice. However, informants' experiences of such institutions were not the same, and their degree of success consequently varied.

Going to a 'better' rather than a 'worse' further education institution was not necessarily beneficial however, in terms of the pedagogic style experienced there. For example, while at the time Shaheena began sixth form she held high aspirations to succeed academically, she found the environment in the sixth form oppressive and in response additionally decided to take an evening A Level course at the local college. Here she found the teachers less authoritarian but still holding high expectations of their students; it was in this environment that Shaheena flourished academically.

She refers to different rituals for cooperative and democratic learning at the college, such as teachers being called by their first names, students being treated as equal to each other and the culture not being authoritarian or patronising. At college there was more room for cooperation on her terms. She valued being able to connect with her teachers and was not alone in what she thought and felt:

> It shouldn't be but you could tell the difference between a college and a sixth form … because in college, everyone was new. There was no favouritism. You didn't call them sir or miss, whereas in sixth form you felt like you were still in school. (Shaheena)

Shaheena contrasts the different institutional cultures, preferring the one that respects her and holds high expectations of her, and which does indeed help her to obtain good exam results. By attending the college, she resists the school's view of her as not being able to successfully complete the course. She goes beyond notions of what is appropriate for 'people like her'. In the college she is able to acquire institutional capital, but in an environment that she feels is not discriminatory. Thus the social space as a learner is also a symbolic space where she acquires cultural capital.

Ayesha took a series of vocational courses at a local FE college, together with some full-time work, over the course of five years. She experimented with various courses at NVQ level in hotel office and reception, beauty courses and hairdressing, but with 'none having made her'. After five years she embarked on an access course. This permitted her entry to university to do a foundation degree in teaching, which she began, but dropped out of in the first year because of emotional upset:

> And then I just let things get on top of me—like emotional things going on in your own head, it affects how you work and it affects everything that you do. It held me back. I wish that I had stuck it out.

She has re-embarked on this course but with a different perspective on how to ensure she is successful in obtaining the necessary institutional capital. This is related to re-orienting the way that she comports herself—her habitus within the field in new ways. Her description of a new awareness of what is required to succeed as a student reflects a growing embeddedness in that field, supporting her endeavour to obtain her degree:

> I've just been to the lit service in the library. They help you with references and stuff like that, because I was quite stuck with referencing. Every day from 12 to 1 you can go in and get a fifteen-minute slot. And I think this year, I'm being more aware what's out there. And I'm getting all the help that I can get, because at the end of the day I'm paying for the course. You want to do well in it and so you've got to get all you can to help you get there, don't you? So now I just try to stay with it and not go off track, and focus on what I'm doing. (Ayesha)

## Building Professional Networks of Support

Developing social capital was often an important part of the process of navigation. For Bourdieu, social capital derives from membership of a group and from the concomitant norms of reciprocity, trust, support and cooperation between the members. It is a resource that has value among group members. The acquisition of social capital is important because it increases the accrual of other forms of capital, particularly economic and cultural capital (Bourdieu, 1996, p. 293). Social capital operates functionally in relation to a particular goal. Who has capital can vary within different fields. How did my informants experience accessing social capital that facilitates educational and occupational achievement within the field of mainstream society (rather than the Pakistani community)? How did their ethnicity position them within the field of the workplace?

For Ballard (1994), British Pakistanis are vulnerable in their membership of mainstream society because they lack the power and privilege of being able to 'insist that all one's interactions should be ordered on one's terms' (Ballard, 1994, p. 32). Furthermore, their parents' employment experiences within the UK mean that informants are dependent upon links with outsiders to achieve social mobility. How then did my informants experience trying to become part of professional networks of support, and did they succeed?

Whilst Chap. 6 focused on how older siblings could be a source of support throughout the respondents' educational careers, some of those without older siblings to help them, such as Shaheena, could rely on friends or networks of professional support once they began to focus on a particular career. But this required a much more active approach:

identifying sources of potential assistance and negotiating access to them. For instance, in wishing to pursue a career as a nursery teacher Shaheena quickly realised the importance of building a convincing curriculum vitae, for example, by gaining work experience to support her application to university and for future jobs. Since she did not have any insider links to help her she used other, informal means. She contacted schools directly, using chutzpah and persistence to secure placements:

> Oh no, I just rang them or I'd go in. … I didn't rely on anyone else to ring up, I wanted to do it so I took the initiative and spoke to the headteachers or to the receptionists to make an appointment with the headteacher or whatever. Even when I went to Sure Start, first the lady was not too happy about wanting to take me on because they had had a really bad experience with another student and she said 'we don't really take people on as volunteers'. And I said 'you give me this opportunity and I will prove to you that you won't regret it'. So when she did take me on, she said I was one of the best placements they had had. It was really good … I knew she wouldn't regret it because I've done previous placements and I never had a problem and I understand that it doesn't matter, even if you're not getting paid, you have to be just like you were a real employee of that place. So I just did what I did in every other place. I worked hard and got on, and didn't have a problem with the staff. If I had any problems I would just ask them, and I would go as if I was a real employee and I worked just as hard as them. I didn't have the attitude, why should I work hard, I'm not getting paid. I thought I'm going there, I'm going to work hard and hopefully they're going to like me, because I did get a reference from them for university as well. (Shaheena)

This success in impressing upon others a definition of herself as a potential professional helped her to secure a place at university. By making herself and others socially comfortable in this new situation, she is able to demonstrate becoming the ideal employee (see also Exley, 2019, p. 151). It required emotional labour, as described by Colley; see also Colley, 2006 in terms of vocational capital).

> Vocational habitus refers to idealised and adopted dispositions necessary in order to become the 'right person for the job. … It (vocational habitus)

> operates in disciplinary ways to dictate how one should properly feel, look and act, as well as the values, attitudes and beliefs that one should espouse'.

Tahira employed a similar navigational strategy in seeking a place at university to study dentistry. Her brother had advised her that work experience was necessary to support her university application. But how was this to be obtained?

| | |
|---|---|
| *Tahira*: | I just went to a dentist's in Kirkley and just shadowed, just sat and watched him. And then I did the same in the orthodontist's. I did it for about a week. |
| *Interviewer*: | How did you get in touch with them? Did anyone help you? |
| *Tahira*: | I just rang around. I said I want to do dentistry and can I come and have a look and they said, yes, sure |

Tahira's proactive approach and subsequent skills as a dentist brought opportunities that surpassed her own expectations. She had worked for six months in a practice run by an English dentist in a nearby town. He offered to sell his practice to her at an affordable price before he retired. This provided her with a once-in-a-lifetime opportunity:

> I applied for jobs in Greathampton. There was a place, where I am now, where the owner was going to retire. He was sixty-seven years old. He said to me, if you work here, if you like it, buy it off me … it was a massive decision. So I just did it … and I think that was the best decision [I made]. (Tahira)

This opportunity extended her influence among non-Pakistanis as an expert with specialist knowledge and alters the type of influence she will have within the locality as a well-off, enterprising professional woman.

In these ways, some informants created their own opportunities by showing initiative and being persistent when forming links with people who were related to the professions that they were interested in entering. Obtaining this foothold was crucial if they were to succeed in becoming professionals, since it could familiarise them with the habitus of professional work cultures and provide capital they could employ to secure their careers.

It was almost by chance that Ghazala was able to access a network of people that later supported her in her success as a social worker, but she made good use of it. She was unable to finance a degree course initially so took a year out to earn some money. She got a job as an administrator for the local council in the personnel department. It brought her into contact with social workers with whom she was able to make lasting links:

*Interviewer*: Did you realize that from the very beginning, before you got a job as an administrator, or was that something you realized later?

*Ghazala*: No I realized it once I got the job. It was an admin. post and it wasn't until after I did the job that I familiarized myself with the different services and with the different areas that I could work in as a social worker. So doing this admin. job sort of helped me. … On reflection it was definitely the best thing that I did and it was all because I was able to get employment whilst I was at university in the field that I wanted to. Because I always knew that I wanted to work in social work and that's why I was doing a social work degree. I was able to make the contacts and then get the employment in the area that I wanted to be.

Ghazala got the administrative job during her gap year, the year before she began her social work degree course, and continued working there during the holidays throughout this course. Her colleagues supported her endeavour to become a social worker. They helped her to gain a placement whilst doing her degree and to deepen her understanding of what her future role would be. She learned about the way that the work of different social workers was categorised, so that she would then get an idea of the 'expert knowledge' that was needed for her professional role. She was thus able to build relevant cultural capital through these contacts. Moreover, in one way her ethnic background assisted this:

> Colleagues within the team would say oh we need Asian social workers, it's really good that you're going to become a social worker, there's a national shortage of Pakistani BME social workers. They were very encouraging and they wanted me to go off to university and were very encouraging, so yes. (Ghazala)

The process of navigation involved creating a capacity to deal with a wide variety of people from different cultural backgrounds. As I noted earlier however, a certain sort of cosmopolitanism was also a key element of the outlook of my informants, closely related to the nature of their aspirations. This is displayed quite clearly by the case of Nasreen, where the option of working within her own community arose. She had secured work in nurseries and her goal was to open her own nursery. However, there was a proposal from the local mosque to open a nursery for Muslim children. She did not find this appealing: it would be to behave in a way that was 'too Asian'. Instead, she wanted to respond to the preferences of Muslim parents in a context where children from many backgrounds were catered for:

> If you have Asian children coming in you have to give them Quorn or something like that in most nurseries. I've noticed that some parents are like no, I'd rather have them having meat and so since that nursery's got halal, they'll send their kids there. They'd attract more people to come won't they? (Nasreen)

Nasreen recognises and intends to meet the minority community's different 'cultural needs', for example, in terms of halal food being available. But she would prefer to work with people from varied cultural and religious backgrounds. She would provide halal meat for Muslim children rather than vegetarian protein substitutes because she knows from experience that this is what parents prefer and thinks that it would make good business sense. It tends not to be available to Muslim children in nurseries at present. Her insights into the nursery world reflect her bicultural sensitivity, increasing knowledge of parental wishes and business acumen. She makes active use of a considerable range of cultural knowledge:

> You need experience don't you? You need to know how it's run and stuff like that. And so if I do this level of work then hopefully it will get me into being able to work at deputy or managerial level. I'll have experience in how the nursery is run. I'll be familiar with all the policies, how they're implemented and everything like that. Because you need experience before opening your own nursery. (Nasreen)

The idea of a 'professional standard' is at the heart of Nasreen's learning and ambitions. It represents a universal code that appeals to her. She is not rejecting Islamic principles by not wanting to work in a nursery run by the mosque, but is embracing what she sees as the high standards offered in a professional environment that are not incompatible with her religious beliefs. There is thus a overlap between cosmopolitanism and professionalism, and this provides the basis for navigating towards realising her aspirations.

George Herbert Mead characterises people who reach out to a wider group than their own as having pioneering qualities such as leadership:

> Occasionally a person arises who is able to take in more than others of an act in process, who can put himself into relation with whole groups in the community whose attitudes have not entered into the lives of the others in the community. He becomes a leader. (Mead, 1934, p. 256)

What Mead means here is what might be called a 'trail-blazer', in other words someone who forges a new path, irrespective of whether anyone follows them—which is exactly the case with many of my informants.

However this process was inherently risky, and sometimes serious obstacles would be encountered, including racism. This was significant in Ghazala's experiences in the workplace:

> I had experienced some racism within my work which left me quite saddened and quite upset about things really. I had one particular colleague that I worked with who would often make certain remarks. One day he asked me how life was in Islamland which he found quite amusing, and I didn't, but he couldn't understand why I couldn't find it funny. And another time I was asking another colleague if I could have some plastic sleeves to

> put some work in and this colleague said to me, why do you need all these? And this other colleague said, oh she's going to send them all to Pakistan. (Ghazala)

One thing that this shows is how Ghazala's ethnic and religious identities were conflated as a locus for ridicule. This echoes earlier work on ethnic stereotyping within racially mixed workplaces or neighbourhoods in the work of Jackson (1972) and Seabrook (1971). This problem continued for her:

> A couple of months down the line I remember he had a new laptop on his desk and I said oh where did you get that from? And he said oh you can't use it, it's not Urdu-compatible. And I was completely shocked to the extent that I cried in work. I had never ever done that before. So, it left me feeling so distant from the team. I thought, gosh, I always put in 110% into my work and I've got someone here who does not appreciate me as a colleague and he feels that he can say whatever he wants to me. And I have approached him about it and he's continued to do it. At that time I'd been asked to do the ASW [Approved Social Work] training and I thought, no, why should I do that training. I don't feel part of this team. Why should I go off and do this extra training and bring this back to this team, when they don't appreciate all the hard work that I put in? Then I spoke to my manager about it and I felt that the situation was resolved, because I didn't put in a formal complaint but I documented everything that had happened. I spoke to the manager about it and he gave the person a warning about it and he was sent on anti-racism training. I wanted them to do something positive about it. But I was very close to not going ahead with the ASW training. … If I hadn't then I suppose I would have felt really disappointed with myself in some sort of way he would have won, and I would have been giving up. It's not that I haven't experienced racism before, because I have, but not from a professional, who I thought should know better. (Ghazala)

Here Ghazala is faced with a challenge to her identity as a professional social worker, one that strikes directly at her ethnic and religious identity. How to deal with this? She could withdraw from the physical space of the workplace with people who do not accept her as an equal part of their team. She considered refusing to engage in training that would provide skills to the team. Or she could seek help from her boss. This would be an uncertain strategy, because she does not know how such an approach will turn out. However, she does do this and the matter is resolved,[8] even if the effects on her remain.

Chamberlayne (2002) argues that overcoming divides and the hurt caused by racism is necessary for ethnic minority citizens if they are to achieve a sense of personal fulfilment and purpose (to live one's life from within). Reflexivity is necessary to understand the nature of racist situations and becomes part of a strategy for herself and others to transform them.[9] Ghazala finds a way to remain attached to her work team, rather than withdrawing into only having home attachments.

Unfortunately, by contrast, Robina's experiences of racism in the workplace offered no opportunity for negotiation or even resistance. It is the religious aspect of her identity that is problematized, against the background of her ethnic identity. Robina first talks about her experiences of applying for a permanent job as an IT teacher in a Catholic state school where she had been working as a supply teacher:

*Robina*: I worked in a Roman Catholic school, and I went for an interview there. In the interview they're supposed to ask you questions that are the same. I was asked questions about my race and religion. How would I fit into a White school? They talked about the Virgin Mary, would I be uncomfortable because of my religion and stuff.

*Interviewer*: How did you react to it?

*Robina*: I just told them that if they actually understood the religion, then the Virgin Mary is part of my religion[10] and so

[8] There is of course no guarantee that short-term interventions such as diversity training eliminate racist thought patterns.

[9] Members of a group can have a racist habitus because of the attitudes they hold and that have become familiar, consciously or not, to them. Attitudes may reflect how Pakistanis were conceptualised in the past, supported by enduring traces of earlier social structures and arrangements. Racism as a cultural trait can become institutionalised. If it goes unchallenged, then every day it remains conceivable, even if only implied.

[10] There is scope within Islam for Mary to be accepted in Christian terms, experiencing an immaculate conception and Jesus being her (and God's) son. Muslims however believe that Jesus was not the Son of God. There is no dissonance here, but rather a relativistic acceptance of the belief system of the other, as part of the Islamic belief system. The latter seems to be central to Robina's understanding of the Virgin Mary.

then why would I feel uncomfortable explaining part of my own religion? Then they asked me questions about me being an Asian and whether I would fit into a White school, which I didn't really like. I was working as a supply teacher there already and the kids yes, I did get abuse, the whole Paki this and that. But that's something that you get wherever you go. I just took it on the chin and took it as kids are going to be like that if that's what's been instilled into them. But for a grown man in education to say that to me, that was the person who I least expected to say that to me.

*Interviewer*: Did you say anything?

*Robina*: I said if the kids had any issues with it, then we could talk around it. But he didn't seem to think so because it was a Roman Catholic school.

Furthermore, the job interview became even more personally challenging:

*Robina*: When I got feedback from the interview from the head-teacher, she said that it's also because I had an Asian twang. But I don't think I have.

*Interviewer*: She said that?

*Robina*: Yes, which I don't think I've got personally

*Interviewer*: What, she fed that back to you as being a problem?

*Robina*: Yes. She said you don't realise it but sometimes you come across as having an Asian twang, which I found pretty offensive, but what could I do?

Of course, this is a faith school, and they prefer teachers who are 'of the faith'. Since she has worked in the school as a supply teacher, she does not regard her faith as being an obvious obstacle. But her liberal cosmopolitanism is not reflected in the ways that faith schools recruit their staff. However, insult was added to injury:

*Robina*: They didn't actually tell me that I hadn't got the job. I had to ring the school a few times to try. The next day when I was in the car park, this lady stopped me and said I'm sorry to hear you didn't get the job. And I said I didn't even know that I hadn't got the job. And she said, there was a staff meeting and we all got told that you didn't get the job and that the other guy got the job. And then this lady went in and told the deputy head—why haven't you told her that she didn't get it? And the headteacher called me into the office and apologised and made some lame excuses and stuff.

The deputy head was rude to me as well. He was upset that one of the teachers had come back to him to tell him that he had not told me that I had not got the post. I asked him about feedback for the lesson [interview lesson] and he said that I could come and see him the next day. He was pretty rude. In the interview feedback the deputy head never apologised that I was asked different questions from all the other White candidates. Even though you're supposed to ask the same questions to the candidates. He was talking about my lesson plan and stuff. And he talked about the starter activity and I said I'm sorry but I never did the starter activity you said I did. And he goes you did. And I said I didn't. He said I had done a word search that I hadn't. I said I didn't do a wordsearch, I did a question and answer session. So he got me mixed up with one of the other candidates, which he didn't agree to. I said I'll show you my lesson plan to show you what I did. Then he talked about the activity. I think because we never hit off to a good start I didn't bother and then he said 'don't just sit there and nod like an idiot'. He was so rude to me. As an Asian I think I have faced a lot of obstacles.

*Interviewer*: Why did he say that?

*Robina*: I don't know. He just said 'don't nod like an idiot. If you've got any questions, don't just nod like an idiot and say yes'. I said 'I haven't even got any questions. So why am I going to ask you?'

Whereas Ghazala managed to navigate her way around the problem of racism in the work setting to some extent at least, the obstacles confronting Robina were more difficult to deal with. She lacks the cultural capital necessary, in terms of correct comportment, accent and religious identity, to succeed in changing the relations in that field. Her failure reinforces her sense of powerlessness and as a result she suffers a loss of self-esteem.

Robina's confidence in winning a permanent contract in a secondary school has ebbed over her four years of trying.

*Interviewer*: How long have you done supply for?
*Robina*: This is my fourth year.
*Interviewer*: You've been looking for a permanent contract?
*Robina*: I've been looking but because I get a bit nervous and stuff and so I find it a bit harder. And a lot of schools around Greathampton are predominantly White, apart from Milltown. I tick the right boxes, being a woman and being Asian. Sometimes I think I'm just being called because I'm Asian.
*Interviewer*: Have you applied for many permanent jobs?
*Robina*: Yes, but last year I gave up, I thought I'm not going to get a permanent job. So I went back to supply teaching. I really don't want to be a supply teacher, because it's tough.

High-level academic qualifications at master's degree level have not guaranteed professional success for Robina. Racism has damaged her confidence, and this is a key condition for occupational success. She has no strategy in place to re-build her confidence and win a permanent job.[11] She now no longer applies for permanent jobs, because she does not expect to be successful in securing them. She views herself as insecurely positioned as an 'Asian' woman, who is only interviewed 'to tick boxes', and feels that she will never be taken on in a permanent role. Navigation is not always successful.

[11] For a detailed discussion of micro-aggressions experienced by black women, see Adegoke and Uviebinene (2018).

## Conclusion

In this chapter I have argued that my informants had to play a proactive role in building their educational and occupational careers, to try to achieve their aspirations. This involved navigating their way around conservative perspectives within the Pakistani community, such as those surrounding purdah, making and capitalising on contacts in mainstream society and coping with racism in the workplace. This required boldness and determination, since the strategies required were often risky, and were not always successful. Unfortunately, in a few cases the obstacles led to disillusionment and demoralisation, undermining the navigational capacity required and resulting in failure to progress towards realising aspirations.

For Ballard (1994), British Pakistanis are skilled navigators because they succeed in code-switching between two cultural value systems. They are able to insulate two cultures from each other. Segmenting one's life into Pakistani and mainstream elements was however only one navigation strategy employed by informants. They also integrated the values of each culture into the other. They used physical, discursive, social and emotional strategies, through which they often combined aspects of these two sometimes contradictory cultures, to try to prevent their own isolation from either cultural context. In this way their own habitus and the fields of their homes and workplaces were changed to varying degrees.

## References

Adegoke, Y., & Uviebinene, E. (2018). *Slay in Your Lane the Black Girl Bible*. 4th Estate.

Archer, L., Halsall, A., & Hollingworth, S. (2007). Class, Gender, (Hetero) sexuality and Schooling: Paradoxes Within Working-Class Girls' Engagement with Education and Post-16 Aspirations. *British Journal of Sociology of Education, 28*(2), 165–180.

Ballard, R. (1994). Introduction: The Emergence of Desh Pradesh. In R. Ballard (Ed.), *Desh Pradesh: The South Asian Presence in Britain*. Hurst & Company.

Bok, J. (2010). The Capacity to Aspire to Higher Education: 'It's Like Making Them Do a Play Without a Script'. *Critical Studies in Education, 51*(2), 163–178.

Bourdieu, P. (1996). *The State Nobility: Elite Schools in the Field of Power*. Polity.

Butler, J. (1997). *Excitable Speech: A Politics of the Performative*. Routledge.

Chamberlayne, P. (2002). Second-Generation Transcultural Lives. In P. Chamberlayne, M. Rustin, & T. Wengraf (Eds.), *Biography and Social Exclusion in Europe Experiences and Life Journeys*. Policy Press.

Colley, H. (2006). Learning to Labour with Feeling: Class, Gender and Emotion in Childcare Education and Training. *Contemporary Issues in Early Childhood, 7*(1), 15–29.

Dwyer, C. (1998). Contested Identities: Challenging Dominant Representations of Young British Muslim Women. In T. Skelton & G. Valentine (Eds.), *Cool Places: Geographies of Youth Cultures* (pp. 50–64). Routledge.

Exley, D. (2019). *The End of Aspiration? Social Mobility and Our Children's Fading Prospects*. Policy Press.

Goffman, I. (1956). *The Presentation of Self in Everyday Life*. University of Edinburgh Social Sciences Research Centre.

Grenfell, M., James, D., Hodkinson, P., Reay, D., & Robbinds, D. (1998). *Bourdieu and Education Acts of Practical Theory*. Falmer Press Taylor and Francis Group.

Hanley, L. (2016). *Respectable: The Experience of Class*. Allen Lane.

Hannerz, U. (1996). Cosmopolitans and Locals in World Culture. In *From Transnational Connections Culture, People, Places* (pp. 102–111). Routledge.

Jackson, B. (1972). *Working-Class Community; Some General Notions Raised by a Series of Studies in Northern England*. Pelican Books.

Krais, B. (2006). Gender, Sociological Theory and Bourdieu's Sociology of Practice. *Theory, Culture and Society, 23*(6), 119–134.

Maton, K. (2010). Habitus. In M. Grenfell (Ed.), *Pierre Bourdieu Key Concepts*. Acumen Publishing.

McLeod, J., & Thomson, R. (2009). *Researching Social Change*. Sage.

Mead, G. (1934). *Mind, Self and Society*. University of Chicago.

Qureshi, K., & Moores, S. (1991). Identity and Remix: Tradition and Translation in the Lives of Young Pakistani Scots. *European Journal of Cultural Studies, 1999*(2), 311.

Seabrook, J. (1971). *City Close Up*. Allen Lane.

Skeggs, B. (1997). *Formations of Class and Gender: Becoming Respectable*. Sage.

Taylor, C. (1994). *Multiculturalism: Examining the Politics of Recognition*. Ed. and Introduced by A. Gutman. Princeton University Press.

Wacquant, L. J. D. (1989). Towards a Reflexive Sociology: A Workshop with Pierre Bourdieu. *Sociological Theory, 7*, 26–63.

Youdell, D. (2006). Subjectivational and Performative Politics – Butler Thinking Althusser and Foucault: Intelligibility, Agency and the Race-Nationed-Religioned Subjects of Education. *British Journal of Sociology of Education, 27*(4), 511–528.

# 9

# Conclusion

## Summary

In this research my focus has been on the ways in which some women who grew up in a working-class British Pakistani community in Northern England developed aspirations to higher education and professional occupations, and how they were able to navigate their way towards these goals. My overall purpose, therefore, has been on explaining upward mobility, rather than the more usual concern with educational under-achievement and the lack of such mobility. Whereas much early research concerned with explaining social mobility has relied on survey method, I instead followed the example of a growing body of qualitative work, employing life history interviewing (see, e.g., Bertaux & Thompson, 2007) and personal stories (Exley, 2019; Goode, 2019; Hanley, 2016; Mohamed, 2020). Through in-depth interviews with informants I sought to document their experiences in depth, looking at how their lives were shaped by home, community and schooling; the barriers and opportunities they faced; and the personal agency they exercised in achieving upward mobility.

 
A. Saeed, *Education, Aspiration and Upward Social Mobility*,
https://doi.org/10.1007/978-3-030-82261-3_9

The main theoretical resources I have used are key concepts developed by Pierre Bourdieu, in particular 'cultural capital'. This term refers to those dispositions and artefacts that facilitate people gaining qualifications within the education system, thereby attaining higher-status positions in the occupational structure. These are often part of children's cultural inheritance, though they may also be generated by a process of investment, for example, through home tutoring, or the provision of extracurricular activities (Lareau, 1989). It is important to recognise that what counts as cultural capital depends on the nature of the field in which people are competing: different fields place different requirements on participants, and therefore different sorts of disposition and artefact are advantageous. Bourdieu does not suggest that higher-class culture is necessarily superior, but focuses on what is publicly *recognised* and granted higher status by institutions such as schools. My main focus in this research has been on the education field in the UK, though I have also given some attention to the workplace.

The main theme of Bourdieu's work is the way in which the class-structured distribution and (mis)recognition of cultural capital leads to the reproduction of social class differences in educational and occupational achievement. In the field of education, Bourdieu argued that the home culture of the dominant class infuses the school, setting the criteria by which achievement is judged and qualifications awarded. As a result, the kinds of disposition, knowledge and skills that are passed on in dominant class homes are those that facilitate success within the education system. Other cultural assets may go unrecognised by schools, and therefore cannot become 'capital'. In addition, the books and other artefacts that are available in these homes represent objectified forms of cultural capital that also enhance educational performance (Bourdieu & Passeron, 1977).

In the UK education system a range of things can serve as cultural capital: prior knowledge and skills (e.g., entering primary school already knowing letters and numbers in the English language and perhaps even already being able to read); relevant general knowledge and experience provided in the family and local community that may shape learning throughout a child's school career; and strong commitment to educational success, embracing personal characteristics like self-discipline and readiness to learn. Bourdieu uses the term 'habitus' to refer to dispositions and ways of thinking and behaving that are conditioned by our cultural backgrounds and which may facilitate or obstruct achievement within a field. He, and most subsequent researchers, have focused on social class differences in habitus and the consequences of these for the possession of cultural capital within the field of education, and therefore for social reproduction, though there has also been some work looking at gender and ethnicity.

Bourdieu has argued that what serves as cultural capital within the sphere of education is inherited by children of the dominant class as part of family habitus. By contrast, for working-class students there is a disparity between their home habitus and the dominant culture they face at school, making school an alienating, challenging, and therefore symbolically violent, experience for them. Their intellectual qualities may go unrecognised in the school environment. For Bourdieu, working-class pupils generally adapt to the objective probability of their lack of educational success and curtail 'unrealistic' expectations. Their career aspirations are therefore lower than those of dominant class children. A number of researchers studying education and class in Britain have endorsed this view of the working class as having very different expectations and resources from middle-class children (Ball, 2003; Reay et al., 2005).

From the point of view of this theory, girls from a working-class British Pakistani community would be very unlikely to aspire to high levels of educational achievement and to obtain professional jobs. They would be at a disadvantage within the education system because, comparatively speaking, they would lack the cultural capital necessary for success. This prompts the question which forms the focus of this study: how did my informants acquire their high aspirations and the cultural capital necessary to pursue them?

## My Informants' Backgrounds: The Role of Family

My informants were bought up in and around a working-class British Pakistani community in the North of England. The boundaries of any community are marked physically, materially, socially and psychologically. This community is indicated by a cluster of Pakistani shops and the surrounding terraced houses. Living here, for the most part, are people who have migrated to the UK since the 1960s, mainly from the Punjab. While they had been attracted to the area by the prospect of employment in the local textile industry, this declined in the 1970s, leading to depressed local labour market conditions. Socially, the area has some of the traits of what Tönnies referred to as *Gemeinschaft*, because the community is based largely on face-to-face contacts and personal relationships, and these are regulated by traditional social rules. Furthermore, people have similar backgrounds and experiences of migration. Even people unrelated by blood are referred to in kinship terms, creating a community of spirit. Psychologically, religion provides a moral and social framework that contributes to making a familiar, meaningful and enduring life for people. In this sense the community is an extension of the household and is internalised in people's minds, as a living organism with its own ways of thinking. Living there generates memories that create further emotional ties among its members. As a result, the community has its own 'local structure of feeling' (Williams, 1979). The influence of the local Pakistani community, whether nurturing or limiting, was evident in all of my informants' stories. The cultural patterns that informants' stories articulate also resonate, to one degree or another, with those of British Pakistani women living in similar communities in other parts of the UK (Ahmad, 2001; Mohammad, 2005).

Within this community, the families of my informants lacked many of the resources that could serve as cultural capital within the UK education system. Their parents had little schooling, rarely extending for their mothers beyond the equivalent of primary stage at best. Parents had little knowledge of the British education system and so could not directly help daughters with school or homework. For some of the women I interviewed this lack of parental cultural capital reduced their confidence in making educational decisions. Furthermore, generally speaking, parents generally were unable to provide financial support whilst their daughters went through post-compulsory education. In these terms, my informants were educationally disadvantaged (Bok, 2010).

Culturally, my informants were raised in families with traditional views of women's roles. Their parents came from rural backgrounds in

Pakistan, and they brought with them a pattern of life based on women being housewives, whose responsibilities were cooking, cleaning and looking after children. Women were economically dependent on their husbands (Becher, 2008; Oakley, 1974). Indeed, many of the girls in the same age group as my informants followed this traditional pattern, marrying soon after the end of compulsory schooling and having a family.

My informants, however, took a different path. There were a number of reasons for this. One was that they were influenced by the wider range of roles for women in mainstream British society. There had been fundamental changes in attitudes towards women's position in society since World War Two, challenging the idea that their proper place was in the home. It became normal for women to do paid work outside the home, including professional jobs, and this shaped the attitudes of the generation of British women to which my informants belong. New ideals and opportunities emerged. I suggest this is one reason why informants displayed a commitment to using education to 'make something of themselves' in a way that had been neither possible for, nor for the most part conceived of, by the earlier generation of Pakistani women in Britain. Although their behaviour did not show radical discontinuity in the sense of rejecting motherhood, they did want to delay having children so as first to establish a professional career. In this sense, they were pioneers of an emergent culture within their home community (Williams, 1980).

Unlike their mothers, my informants had opportunities to develop cross-cultural friendships through routine encounters within mainstream society, such as at school and college. Mainstream values relating to women's education influenced their individual career aspirations and became part of their habitus. Such experiences, in combination with a cosmopolitan outlook, enabled them to develop aspirations different from those of their parents.

My informants had high aspirations, which involved studying at degree level, and held quite specific attitudes relating to appropriate and worthwhile careers for them. They regarded it as their responsibility to try to achieve such futures. But they generally did not look to high-flying careers, such as becoming bankers, hospital managers or company directors, for example, directing their aspirations towards rather more modest professional roles such as teaching and social work, ones that were somewhat less distant from community views about the proper role of women and more compatible with motherhood. They saw both intrinsic and instrumental benefits in pursuing education and such professional careers. Raising self-esteem and providing personal fulfilment were seen as intrinsic benefits of education, but securing professional positions or non-professional paid work outside the home would also provide material benefits, such as improved housing and even relocation to a more desirable locality. In addition, in two cases, informants were motivated to secure professional work as a way of honouring parents, by giving them pride in their daughters' achievements. For some parents this would come as an unexpected surprise. Shahrokni (2018) sees first-generation migrants' sacrifices being reciprocated by subsequent generations through their educational achievements and social mobility, thereby representing intergenerational continuity rather than causing rupture between them. However, for my informants these goals of education and social mobility were not always shared by parents, such sharing being something informants had to work towards.

Whilst informants' high aspirations could bring symbolic gender rewards in the field of mainstream society, such career choices could be risky within the field of the Pakistani community. My informants' trajectories involved seeking to maximise the capital returns in both fields—in mainstream society and within the Pakistani community. They did not envisage their lives as being dominated by childcare and domestic duties, as their mothers' lives were, and yet they were committed to living within the spirit of Islam. It is through bridging between the worlds of home and local community, school and wider society, that they developed a specific femininity.

It is important to emphasise that there were some resources available within the community to pursue these career goals. Changing norms relating to marriage, and parental understanding of the changed position of their daughters as women brought up and educated in Britain, were cultural resources within the home which helped their career aspirations. For example, sometimes parents shared aspirations with their daughters and thus became a source of career support. One mother rejected a traditional option for her daughter—that of marriage to kin in Pakistan—and supported her in an alternative trajectory, involving participation in mainstream British society. Generally speaking, my informants wanted to avoid early marriages and other traditional arrangements, such as living with a husband's parents as part of an extended family. They saw such arrangements as incongruent with their own aspirations. Some parents appreciated their daughters' aspirations and orientations even when these were very different from those they had had themselves at the same age.

These parents were able to appreciate that daughters were in a different position with different resources, options and capabilities as a result of being born and brought up in Britain. For example, they recognised that higher education would enhance a daughter's marriage prospects, increasing the likelihood of her marrying someone from Britain in a professional occupation and thereby providing for a better life in terms of income and educational knowledge to pass on to children.[1] Furthermore, higher education could provide financial autonomy for the woman should the marriage fail.

Another source of cultural capital within families that served to support informants' non-traditional career aspirations came from siblings who had themselves already started on non-standard career trajectories. Tahira, for example, followed the same career path into dentistry as her brother, and Raheela, Ghazala and Nasreen followed their sisters in pursuing professional jobs. Very often this also meant that academic books were present within the home, which could act as a stimulus to developing non-traditional aspirations. Moreover, older siblings going on to higher education opened up the possibility that younger siblings could do so too. This was true for five of the women I interviewed. Older siblings also took on responsibilities towards younger ones and could mediate relations between parents and daughters. These older siblings could guide sisters in their specific career paths, providing both cultural and social capital that would facilitate career success. This could include the details of practical requirements to secure a place on a university course beyond just obtaining qualifications and helping to prepare the younger sibling for the new cultural milieu she would find herself in. They could provide crucial emotional support by creating a space for younger

[1] However, Fauzia Ahmad's (2012) work on Muslim marriages found that too much education can disadvantage women in the marriage market.

siblings to explore alternative options and make independent decisions. For three informants, older siblings provided day-to-day support, acting as mentors or guides. They might share resources or objectified capital, such as books or ideas, to help orientate a younger sibling in the new milieu. In this way, ideas that were different from those of informants' parents sometimes existed within the working-class Pakistani home. However, by contrast, where a girl was the first wanting to go into higher education, other siblings could actively discourage her participation, creating a barrier.

There were sometimes resources available to my informants within the home which facilitated their development of alternative aspirations and which they could actively work up into cultural capital that might enable them to gain qualifications and pursue careers. Moreover, there were personal qualities encouraged by a traditional Islamic upbringing in their home community that also served them well, such as moral seriousness, stamina and self-discipline. Paradoxically, the relative lack of cultural capital in their homes reinforced these qualities and the development of resilience. This can be understood in terms of spiritual capital, an intergenerational resource inspired by Islam and the experience of migration.[2] Nevertheless, because there was much that they lacked in the way of cultural capital that would have been available to their middle-class, White peers, they were more dependent than many such peers on what the British education system could offer.

Interestingly, the dispositions acquired within the home were not developed as part of an explicit investment strategy to help children with their educational careers. They were resources that were simply given rather than being the product of specific investment decisions designed to achieve specific future rewards. Resources can arise independently of any investment and be incidental. The terminology of capital implies conscious investment practices. If Bourdieu's work were understood only

[2] For a discussion of how Islam can be viewed in terms of capital generated within families, see Franceschelli and O'Brien (2014). Also, for a discussion of how cultural capital can exist within homes of disadvantaged people in the US, see Yosso (2005). Using the term 'funds of knowledge ', Luis Moll and colleagues explore similar issues among Mexicans in the USA, including what schools can do to give greater recognition to community-based skills and knowledge (Gonzalez et al., 2005; Moll & Greenberg, 1990). See also Pat Thomson's (2006) examples from Australia in *Miners, diggers, ferals and show-men*.

in terms of this rational model, it would not explain how people acquired most of the resources they possess. Bourdieu's concept of habitus however does highlight the unconscious aspects of behaviour that bring educational advantage and disadvantage to different groups of people. My research highlighted the ways that capital was exchanged too as a conscious and unconscious resource by British Pakistani working-class women within their relationships.

## The Role of the Education System

The relative lack of cultural capital in the home had consequences for family-school relations. Because parents were limited in their academic competence and knowledge of the education system, they did not usually attend parents' evenings and had minimal knowledge of the content of learning and the processes of their daughters' schooling. There was, in short, a gulf between home and school. This can be understood in terms of parents' migrant and class status, as well as religiously inspired notions that teachers should be entrusted with responsibility for one's children's formal education. In much the same way, working-class parents in Lareau's (1989) study of parent-school relations in California also granted teachers professional autonomy in academic matters, much more than did the upper-middle-class parents. This can be understood in terms of both social and cultural capital.

In addition, relative lack of cultural capital available in the home and community left my informants vulnerable to any deficiencies in schools as to what capital these could provide and to any barriers they introduced, for example, schools could obstruct the educational success of children from working-class ethnic minority communities through having low expectations of them. For instance, in one school Pakistani girls had to contend with the attitude of some teachers that there was no point in their receiving a broad-based education because of the likelihood of their following traditional careers as housewives. This expectation would of course have been endorsed by many other Pakistani parents. Schools also made assumptions about the types of jobs their students would take. Thus, a shared 'common sense' among parents and teachers co-produces low expectations. Tahira merely learned how to fill out an application for work experience in a supermarket, because there was no expectation that pupils from her school would ever apply for professional jobs. She mentioned this to show how she felt that her own aspirations went far beyond the collective aspiration the school held for its pupils. Whilst it may be regarded as understandable for teachers to expect pupils to lower their sights according to their surroundings, this posed another challenge for Tahira to overcome. Brah and Minhas (1985) reinforce this, noting that sometimes careers guidance teachers dismiss the aspirations of Asian girls as too high.

While schools engaged in selection processes that to a large extent differentiated on the basis of prior knowledge and skills, they did also have a positive capacity to encourage aspirations and facilitate the acquisition of cultural capital. Through their organisational cultures schools could be inclusive, non-alienating environments where informants could flourish. In addition, the distinct worlds of home and school could be effectively bridged by teachers, through the quality of the relationships they developed with their students (see also the ten schools used as case studies in Wrigley, 2000).

My informants usually went to their local primary school, which was attended mainly by Pakistani children from the school's catchment area. However, they attended different secondary schools, sometimes with very different organisational cultures. Whilst there was some scope for choice of school, families did not have the resources to judge which would be best or the financial resources to allow travel to more distant schools. As a result, it was largely a question of luck whether informants found themselves in schools which would help them to secure educational qualifications or not. Different schools transmitted different values and provided opportunities for the acquisition of different skills and bodies of knowledge and each informant attended at least two schools during the course of compulsory schooling. One informant, Noreen, attended a middle school which was able to support her and open up opportunities. It enabled her to develop sporting prowess, which had a beneficial effect on her learning more generally. By contrast, her upper school was materially impoverished and intellectually uninspiring, and she found it impossible to flourish there academically.

The attitudes of individual teachers were important in motivating informants and raising their educational aspirations. Teachers who were open towards pupil questioning evinced a positive dynamism that some informants found encouraging. Their views and concerns were listened to, and they were granted some power in the relationship. In short, many of my informants valued personalised adult engagement, and this is noteworthy since it suggests that they wished to engage with adults in less hierarchical ways than they generally experienced at home or in the community or mosque.[3] They had been brought up to respect and defer to adults.

Traditional teachers, in comparison, did not encourage this kind of pupil-teacher interaction, reprimanding pupils who 'talked back' to the teacher, treating such behaviour as inappropriate, disrespectful and undermining. Here, no bridge was available, and accessing the necessary cultural capital became very difficult.

For my informants, new ways of envisaging their futures and how to realise them were encouraged by some teachers' high expectations of their students' educational ability. This helped to develop aspirations to pursue careers outside the home, when the women were uncertain whether they would actually be able to achieve this. Such contacts boosted their confidence to explore unmapped possibilities and helped them to acquire cultural capital and, eventually, qualifications.

All my informants, except Noreen, achieved sufficient grades at GCSE to embark on A Level courses or further education courses of a similar level. Seven took this route. Participating in extended education strengthened and focused their aspirations for professional careers in mainstream society, even though some found themselves in unfamiliar and challenging environments.

By the time they came to participating in post-compulsory education, my informants did have some knowledge of the organisational cultures of

[3] The parents of my informants did ensure that their children received a formal Islamic education. All informants attended a local mosque daily after school from the age of seven until the teenage years. There they learned the Quran and Islamic rituals in a disciplined environment. In the process, they were expected to defer to and obey their teachers. This probably reinforced some of the personal qualities, mentioned earlier, that served them well in higher education and pursuit of a career. At the mosque school they also developed a positive and respectful attitude to (religious) literacy and knowledge generally.

the further educational institutions in Milltown, though this was not always accurate. They generally expected the sixth forms, attached to secondary schools they had not attended, to be better places to pursue A Level study than the local college with its much more vocational focus. However, informants came to realise that sixth forms often involved traditional pedagogic approaches characterised by distant and hierarchical relations with teachers and that this could make the experience alienating.

Some informants were able to benefit from the widening of access to higher education through foundation degrees, designed for social groups that had not previously participated (Archer et al., 2003). Three informants pursued this route, two of them as mature students in their early twenties. In spite of the barriers of traditional pedagogic approaches in some post-16 courses, four informants succeeded in taking and completing degrees through a traditional route, and three were still in the process of completing foundation degrees at the time of the interviews (Ayesha, Shaheena and Nasreen). Three of my informants had secured permanent professional jobs—as a dentist, a senior nurse and a social worker (Tahira, Raheela and Ghazala)—and one had a more precarious position as a supply teacher (Robina). Two had abandoned their initial aspirations, at least temporarily (Noreen and Shamila). However, even these two had nevertheless met other social and financial goals: they were financially independent and did paid work with responsibility outside the home (local government administration and retail management respectively), representing a degree of upward social mobility.

As members of the professional workforce, all these informants benefitted from good incomes which gave them a high degree of independence. Some could acquire their own cars and homes, pay for parents' home improvements and distance themselves from their childhood poverty. Their independence was exercised in the new lifestyle choices they made, such as eating out at restaurants and following new leisure pursuits with friends from different ethnic backgrounds. They could embrace a new femininity based on being more worldly and leading lives they found worthwhile and interesting, without rejecting wholly the idea of eventually wanting to become mothers.

What my research shows is that whilst there are 'objective probabilities' faced by working-class British Pakistani students, some of them manage, against the odds, to develop high aspirations and to acquire the necessary cultural capital for pursuing them. My analysis also reveals the range of socio-historical factors that can facilitate this, from changes within working-class Pakistani communities and in the broader society to various features of family life in such communities and of schools that can serve to facilitate the development of cultural capital. These factors do not of course guarantee success, but they improve the odds for those born into circumstances that could be judged objectively to offer little hope of upward social mobility.

## Navigation, Determinism and Agency

An important criticism that is sometimes aimed at Bourdieu's work is that it is deterministic (Certeau, 1984; Sayer, 2005). Whilst this may be unfair in some aspects, it is true that the main emphasis of much of his early work on education and culture was on how social divisions are reproduced and therefore on how those born into lower social positions are fated to remain in them, despite the shift to 'meritocratic' recruitment via the education system (Bourdieu & Passeron, 1977). This emphasis contrasts sharply with those accounts of the nature of postmodern society that downplay the significance of social class differences and emphasise how people actively construct themselves and their social lives (Giddens, 1990, 1992). I suggest that the concept of navigation which I explored in Chap. 8 provides a way of overcoming the tensions between these two viewpoints.

The metaphor of navigation was used there as a tool to analyse career building, both within the education system and beyond. 'Navigating' implies accepting the landscape as it is and finding a way through and around obstacles in order to reach one's goal. The concept of navigation captures those experiences that require problems to be resolved, thus revealing the strategies informants use. Rather than simply playing a passive role, in many respects my informants actively worked at finding their way towards achieving their aspirations. They employed a variety of navigational tactics: sometimes complying, sometimes negotiating, with others, finding ways round obstacles, taking risks, seizing and creating opportunities, challenging negative labelling and remaining resilient.

Within the home, there were some benefits in being brought up as part of a strongly defined local community. One of these was that life had a predictability that eased navigation within it: there were clear social rules that underlay relations between parents and their children. Moreover, for the young women to be given permission to continue into further and higher education, and for the repertoire of choices to be widened, it was necessary for them to conform to parental notions of proper conduct. Informants showed that they were serious about studying by avoiding illicit conduct. The consequence of this was to build up trust with parents that would allow new options to be explored.

Informants maintained stability in their changing world by remaining loyal to their home culture and not challenging those aspects they could not alter. They observed the rules of modesty in dress and comportment to some degree, whilst many also wore high street fashions, thereby seeking to avoid threatening their insider status as publicly accepted members of an Islamic community. This could be done because there was some leeway within the community about what was proper attire for women, and norms were changing. Sometimes, this required creating an alliance with one parent or with a sibling in order to challenge narrow notions of what was appropriate. Since the power of the Pakistani community's group norms could be very strong, negotiation sometimes involved tailoring what was asked for and the way that it was requested to what would be possible in the circumstances.

While my informants resisted conforming to any family expectations of an early marriage, and took advantage of community changes in expectation about women's careers, negotiations with parents would involve recognising that some courses and jobs would be regarded as much more appropriate than others. Particularly acceptable would be those that involved working with children. Sometimes informants had to involve parents in their decision-making or chose without parental pressure to do so. Sometimes the separation between home and school created a space for my informants to make decisions independently of their parents. They could, to a degree, compartmentalise their lives, so that parents and the local community would not know all of what they were doing. This could ease navigation by allowing them to sidestep parental and community perspectives, and it was often experienced as liberating. However, sometimes where there were no parents or siblings who could offer support and encouragement, informants could feel alone and adrift. They had to manage the emotional challenge of making decisions and face uncertainties about which route to take, on their own. Navigation was greatly eased by having siblings with whom informants could discuss their experiences.

Navigating in schools with poor resources and large numbers of working-class and ethnic minority students was found challenging by some informants, but also confidence-boosting for those who succeeded in such establishments. Pupils could take on different learner identities within the same school environments so that their exam outcomes varied. Individual personality and family circumstances underlay these differences, but also sheer contingency.

When it came to choosing subjects, since careers teachers did not know their students individually, it was necessary to prevent low expectations circumscribing options and to avoid pathways that some teachers deemed realistic for Pakistani women to pursue. Part of my informants' navigational strategies was to ignore these pre-conceptualisations, refusing to allow them to diminish self-esteem. Even so, they did not explicitly challenge their teachers, any more than they did their parents or the local community. There were limits on what they could do and they had to comply with much that hampered progress towards their goals. But this did not permanently discourage them for the most part or prevent them from finding a way forward.

There was considerable scope for navigation in the educational environments that followed compulsory education. It was possible to try to improve prospects of educational success by using their discursive knowledge of the education system to choose suitable colleges. Informants tried to choose academic sixth forms where the right learner dispositions would be cultivated. This also allayed parental fears of daughters not studying and engaging in unacceptable behaviour, even though it might require the effort of travelling out of town. However, there was a risk involved since there was no guarantee that a more traditional academic sixth form was better than the college. Some informants discovered that the new educational environment was unsatisfactory because the pedagogic approach was too didactic and teacher-student relations too hierarchical.

Informants needed the flexibility to change course if they did not flourish academically in a particular environment. Some informants were able to sidestep teachers' 'traditional' perceptions, for example, by ignoring their low expectations or by removing themselves from those classroom situations where teachers behaved too negatively towards students.

Where they did not succeed in doing this, the result tended to be examination failure, or a process of drift from one unrelated short course to another. Sometimes this amounted to navigating alone, without a script or 'road map' (Bok, 2010). Resilience was required to continue pursuing one's career aspirations after such set-backs, but often there was the flexibility to find a vocational route into higher education.

Those of my informants who attended university found an exhilarating space where young people were given the opportunity to forge new identities and make new links with people. However, when they returned from university, fitting back into being an insider within the family required a show of compliance. Conforming to home life was made easier for informants because the two life worlds were insulated from each other and not psychologically in opposition. Sometimes the price to pay though was feelings of discomfort or boredom. This indicated that the way in which my informants' developing habitus related to home life was changing more rapidly than the family habitus itself, each having its own internal logic and history (Maton, 2010). Generally though informants' good relationships within the family and community helped to avoid their being ostracised. The feeling of coming back into the in-group as a new person indicated that personal growth had occurred and that the aspiration to an interesting and different life had been met.

An important advantage in the process of navigating was that from childhood informants found ways to orientate themselves successfully within cross-cultural friendships. All of my informants developed these at school, college and university. At the same time, informants saw themselves as guardians of those enduring aspects of home culture that were sacred and of value. Through 'points of affinity' (Appiah, 1992, p. pix) with different cultural worlds, they progressed in their career navigation and developed a unique habitus that linked their past, present and future.

Being responsive to new opportunities facilitated informants' navigation. Since employment prospects within Milltown were poor, they travelled out to nearby towns for training and work. In this way, those with qualifications avoided the penalty of unemployment. Travelling and working outside their immediate locality reflected their energetic commitment to their career aspirations.

Gaining access to career support networks required informants to seek help from mainstream colleagues, since this resource was not generally available within the Pakistani community. They therefore tried to obtain work experience placements, voluntary work or low-paid work within a particular profession in order to build up the knowledge and skills they needed. Through such experiences, they learned about the routes to particular professions and the ways to comport themselves within the workplace. In addition, all of my informants were committed to forging good relationships with colleagues and to being accepted as equal members of a team. They tried to engage in the workplace as equals rather than as stereotypes based on the heavily scripted pattern of such interactions showing Pakistani women in a negative or limited light.

Cosmopolitanism was a key aspect of my informants' aspirations. It can be understood as an essential quality of mobile people. It involves learning how to behave in relation to new types of people and new contexts and valuing them. However, the freedom to be cosmopolitan is a negotiated process: informants were vulnerable to policing by some dominant others in the mainstream workplace. This made cross-cultural contact there risky. Two informants showed how negative dominant ideas relating to Muslims and their lack of shared values with mainstream society made them vulnerable to being deemed outsiders within the workplace. This was jarring because they were wholly committed to a life in Britain where they were born and therefore had no reason not to see themselves as legitimate rational citizens with dispositions that were open to a liberal society and thus well-adapted to their workplace (see Beck, 1998, 2003).

My informants sometimes found themselves in workplace situations where their presence was seen as incongruous. Part of their struggle was to normalise their roles as both professionals and British Pakistani women. This required the capability to exercise discursive agency to challenge depictions of themselves as an extreme 'other' or a 'stranger within' and to clarify ambiguities about or distortions of their aspirations. Where possible, they responded to those who tried to police their behaviour by explicitly challenging such negative labelling and through soliciting support from colleagues. Where this was not possible the journey became much more challenging.

## Final Reflections

As I indicated at the beginning of this chapter, there is a tension between the main thrust of Bourdieu's account of the way in which class-cultural differences and the education system serve social reproduction, and the focus of my analysis on how some women from a deprived working-class Pakistani community managed to achieve educational success and upward social mobility. Bourdieu's work has sometimes been criticised as deterministic, for failing to take account of the autonomy, albeit limited, available even to those in subordinated positions.

Bourdieu (1977, 1986) drew attention to the way that class inequalities affect the processes of 'choice', describing the ways in which choices and aspirations are embedded in common sense or tacit knowledge of 'what is appropriate for people like us'. For Bourdieu, unequal patterns of choice between different social groups reflect the particular social relations and location from which they are asserted, and mirror unequal opportunities in access to privileged forms of cultural, social, economic and symbolic capital. His work is deterministic because the past is seen to play a large part in determining people's future capabilities, particularly the ability to transform their lives.

For Bourdieu, whilst people do not act as automatons within fields, in most circumstances they act in socially regular and predictable ways, based on what is expected of them in their particular position (Maton, 2010). For example, in *The Inheritors* (1979) and *Reproduction* (1977) Bourdieu and Passeron address the reasons why people from middle-class backgrounds are more likely, and those from the working-class less likely, to attend university. They explain how innumerable stimuli during upbringing shape the outlooks, beliefs and practices of people in ways that impact upon their educational careers. Rather than the educational system blocking access to people from non-traditional backgrounds, these social agents take themselves out of the system, seeing university as 'not for the likes of me'.

For this reason, Hussain and Bagguley (2007) questioned the usefulness of applying Bourdieu's theoretical ideas in understanding the relative success of British Pakistani women in higher education. They argued that the theory of cultural capital is not able to explain how the community built on individual experiences of higher education in order to allow large numbers of Asian women to participate in higher education. However, in this research I have tried to show that Bourdieu's work does provide some important resources for understanding how those in subordinated groups can nevertheless succeed in the education system and in gaining upward mobility.

A very different perspective was provided by some contemporary social theory (Beck & Beck-Gernsheim, 1995; 2008; Giddens, 1990, 1992). This claimed to identify a cultural trend that emphasises the exercise of autonomy in creating particular desired futures. These authors claim that career formation relies on the self creating a biographical narrative and working to realise that narrative. According to Giddens (2007, p. 57), the modern self is able to ask the question 'How shall I live?' and then construct that self in a sustained and coherent way.[4] Beck and Beck-Gernsheim (2008) argue that women are now able to answer this question in a way that they have not been able to do in the past: that there are new contemporary opportunities and motivations open to women to 'make themselves'. In particular, the improvement of educational opportunities has meant that women can create their own biographies, because they 'may develop a new private and political self-awareness' (p. 58) and be in a better position to 'actively confront their own situation' (p. 59). Rather than relying on tradition, and following the same trajectory as previous generations, there is an impetus 'to make their own projects and actions, to work out their own ideas about the future, with little support from any model or tradition'. Indeed, it is claimed that 'The choosing, deciding, shaping human being who aspires to be the author of his or her own life,

[4] There are questions about just how modern this is. After all, Augustine's *Confessions* written in 397–400 CE is precisely about this question.

the creator of an individual identity, is the central character of our time' (p. 59)

While there may be a great deal of truth in this, these writers can reasonably be criticised for presenting this type of autonomy as universal, whereas not everyone is able to create themselves and realise the biographical narrative as they would wish. This mode of operating may only be available to well-resourced people. My informants did show personal qualities such as having a high moral character, playing by the rules, as well as having ability and a capacity for hard work. What they did not have much control over was how much they would be rewarded for these qualities in the workplace (McNamee, 2018). Spohrer et al. (2018) show how the discourse of 'raising aspirations' represents a neo-liberal technology of the self, individualising educational 'failure' as a lack of the right kind of ambition when the economic and educational resources necessary for success have not been provided. Similarly, Berlant (2011) views this discourse as demanding that young working-class people work on themselves to raise their expectations even in the face of a status quo that disadvantages them and remains unchanging. Whilst my informants saw it as their own responsibility to put in the necessary effort to 'make something of themselves' this could not be achieved independently of the contexts they found themselves in and the particular pattern of resources available to them. As Littler (2018) argues, it is not enough to have an aspiration, one needs a social context that helps turn aspiration into reality. Whilst Giddens' work points out that agency and reflexivity are exercised in real social contexts, his work does not explore or theorise the ways in which structural inequalities can affect this project of self-actualisation.

More recent authors have discussed the social and emotional challenges facing people from working-class backgrounds when they strive for upward social mobility (Exley, 2019; Mohamed, 2020). Others have noted the painful experiences and costs of social mobility (Hanley, 2016). And some have suggested the futility of contemporary social mobility projects, given that they are underpinned by neo-liberal narratives that ignore social class, ethnic and gender inequalities (Littler, 2018). Friedman and Laurison (2020) also reflect on how class cultures operate socially to channel already privileged people into elite occupations.

Whilst the mobility journeys in these studies can be described as long range, they follow the early work of Hoggart (1957) which explored the degree of alienation experienced by working-class children who went to grammar schools.

Even amongst my informants, navigating was often a long and arduous journey, marked by uncertainty and sometimes feeling lost. In the process, some lost the high degree of self-belief required to succeed (e.g., Shamila's experience reported in Chap. 5). The road was frequently uncertain and long in the absence of support. I would not want to underestimate the significant moments of alienation some informants experienced on their career journeys. A biographical approach did capture those moments and attend to the ways that racial micro-aggressions could serve to undermine Asian women and bar them from being given the benefit of the doubt or being treated as equals. More recent work by Goode (2019) and Hanley (2016) tells stories of how painful and paralysing achieving social mobility can be for some people from working-class backgrounds, giving rise to genuine rupture in their lives. The challenges experienced by BAME staff in workplaces is only touched upon in this research, but the wider context of the Black Lives Matter movement reveals how pervasive racist barriers are, while at the same time offering hope of greater understanding and hence improvement. However, the likely effects of austerity due to COVID-19 and the consequences of Brexit on poor Muslim communities suggest that navigating will remain arduous and perilous for working-class British Pakistani women.[5]

In this research, I have attempted to show that while the families and local community into which my informants were born placed significant constraints on their chances of educational success and upward social mobility, in the way that Bourdieu suggested, nevertheless these background factors also provided them with some resources as cultural capital that they *were* able to use. To some extent, these can also be understood in terms of spiritual capital. Similarly, while the education system placed some barriers in their paths, it also opened up opportunities for acquiring and developing cultural capital. Moreover, in line with the arguments of

[5] See Shain (2020) for a discussion of the impact of austerity and discrimination on the aspirations of British Pakistani schoolgirls and young women forming Generation 9/11.

Giddens and Beck and Beck-Gernsheim I have emphasised the importance of my informants' exercise of agency, in the form of navigational capacity.

The concept of navigation enables us to conceptualise how the past influences the future, how present fields evolve and how strategies to pursue success in achieving an imagined future can work. Navigation involves a consciousness and a capacity to steer towards a goal by circumnavigating obstacles, whether they be gender, class, racial or religion-based, or a combination of them. My informants' trajectories showed that they had the 'capacity to aspire' in a process of 'bringing the future back in' (Appadurai, 2004, p. 62). Their aspirations and their navigational abilities were facilitated by their *simultaneous* immersion in two socio-cultural worlds: that of their families and local community and that of the mainstream society. They understood the different ways that the self is orientated in each field. They could use this understanding to widen the choices for their futures. They became accustomed to the:

> game that is played out between agents in cultural fields, which involves a knowledge of the various rules (written and unwritten), genres, discourse, forms of capital, values and imperatives which inform and determine agents' practices. This knowledge allows agents to make sense of what is happening around them, to make strategic decisions as to how a field or fields should be negotiated. (Webb et al., 2002, p. 50)

Informants' immersion in these two cultural fields also facilitated an awareness of the different stakes that exist within them (Devine & Savage, 2005, p. 15). This is an advantageous capability which Bourdieu attributes mainly to those from the dominant class (Webb et al., 2002):

> Bourdieu's work offers a distinctive paradox of reflexivity. As people move between fields they become aware of the different kinds of stakes that exist in diverse fields, and hence can become more reflexive about the kinds of practices they can pursue, their respective ethics, strategies and tactics. As McNay (1999) and Adkins (2002) explore with respect to gender, reflexivity arises through mobility between fields. However, the ability to move between fields is itself variable and dependent on particular kinds of habitus that support mobile personality characteristics, personal flexibility and

> so on. It is those with stakes in many fields, namely male members of dominant social classes, who thereby find it easier to develop various kinds of reflexivity. (Devine & Savage, 2005, p. 15)

However, my informants seem to have been able to develop such reflexivity, which helped them through this liminal stage of career building. Navigating on career journeys took them into new fields, such as the university and the workplace, not experienced by earlier generations of their families. Their presence as women from a British Pakistani background was in turn new to such fields. Informants also had to navigate within the familiar fields of the family and Pakistani community, having acquired bodily comportments and attitudes that were also new to those fields. These young women's experiences within the two fields, provided stimulus and knowledge to support new futures for British Pakistani women. Their good practical sense of different fields explains the expectations and experiences that underpinned their aspirations. It helped them to become conscious of alternative futures, based on the differences in gender expectations presented by the two fields. Rather than choosing one over the other, they navigated their way between these alternatives.

Immersion in a neighbouring culture gave them access to the strategies they could employ to negotiate the conditions and contexts 'of the moment' and to make changes in their lives (Webb et al., 2002, p. 57). They could use their knowledge and opportunities to shape their futures in active ways. Since their orientations in the different habituses were learned over the course of years, choices could be carefully made without giving rise to feeling uprooted. Successful navigation depended on being able to make relational claims on other players in the field. They also reassured others by maintaining aspects of their identities unchanged, avoiding any serious rupture within the family.

In Hoggart's (1957) work, the working-class youth who succeeded in the education system experienced alienation as a result of the fact that the culture transmitted by the school was antithetical to that of the home. My research showed that my informants did sometimes experience alienation but did not experience rupture to any great degree because they found ways of bridging home and school cultures. On the one hand, they were not able to ignore the rules, derived from the home and school fields, that governed what was possible and not possible for them within education. The habitus of the home continued into other areas of life. At the same time, they found ways to achieve their new and unexpected aims. This shows how hybrid identities create complexity but also offer different possibilities in people's lives. Whilst such hybrid identities intersect with the real world of dynamic relationships to create new possibilities, these however depend as much on having structural opportunities as creating one's own. In the same way, a multiculturalism that holds a static view of culture and does not appreciate changing identities limits such opportunities. Bourdieu's view that the reproduction of educational inequality allows only fixed trajectories for members of the working class also views culture in a fixed, rather than a fluid and changing, way.

For my informants navigation required agency and creativity. In the family, educational institutions and the workplace, they strove to develop their identities in ways that realised their ambitions. They found the means to circumvent obstacles in all these fields, by broadening their range of cultural experiences, choosing alternative routes, asserting their own values firmly grounded in Islam, while conforming where necessary so as not to disrupt the changing expectations of home or the workplace.

Their stories relate to particular family situations and dynamics, and the wider experiences of a community which migrated at a time of economic expansion, with expectations of skilled employment and a better life. Their experiences are intertwined with a particular set of religious beliefs, a version of Islam mediated by life in Pakistan and Britain. The experience of these aspiring young women is also affected by the economic geography of English regions; growing up in the former textile belt of Lancashire and West Yorkshire is very different in terms of opportunities and horizons than London and the South East. At the same time, their aspirations and navigations sit within a larger history of the barriers and divisions of modern Britain and its class-bound education system: a story which connects Thomas Hardy's tragic novel Jude the Obscure, written in the 1890s, with Richard Hoggart's 1950s 'grammar school boy' in Uses of Literacy and Diane Reay's personal experiences in Miseducation: Inequality, Education and the Working Classes (2017). The burden of overcoming barriers should not rest on the shoulders of individuals; instead, the obstacles should be removed and the environment changed. Nor should this study give false hope or generate 'cruel optimism' (Berlant, 2011): given the scale of inequalities in our society, we must recognise that social and economic improvement depends primarily on structural change rather than individual pathways of mobility. However it is hoped that this particular study will add to the growing literature on how schools and colleges, employers and universities can best engage with young people from a variety of communities and help them find their way towards a more satisfying and happy life.

## References

Adkins, L. (2002). *Revisions: Gender and Sexuality in Late Modernity*. Open University Press.

Ahmad, F. (2001). Modern Traditions? British Muslim Women and Academic Achievement. *Gender and Education, 13*, 137–152.

Ahmad, F. (2012). Graduating Towards Marriage? Attitudes Towards Marriage and Relationships Among University-Educated British Muslim Women. *Culture and Religion, 13*(2), 193–210.

Appadurai, A. (2004). The Capacity to Aspire: Culture and the Terms of Recognition. In V. Rao & M. Walton (Eds.), *Culture and Public Action*. Stanford University Press.

Appiah, K. A. (1992). *In My Father's House Africa in the Philosophy of Culture*. Methuen London.

Archer, L., Hutchings, M., & Ross, A. (2003). *Higher Education and Social Class Issues of Exclusion and Inclusion*. Routledge Falmer Taylor and Francis Group.

Ball, S. (2003). *Class Strategies and the Education Market the Middle Classes and Social Advantage*. Routledge.

Becher, H. (2008). *Family Practices in South Asian Muslim Families Parenting in a Multi-Faith Britain*. Palgrave Macmillan.

Beck, J. (1998). *Morality and Citizenship Education*. Bloomsbury Publishing.

Beck, J. (2003). Citizenship and Citizenship Education in England. In J. Beck & M. Earl (Eds.), *Key Issues in Secondary Education* (2nd ed.). Continuum.

Beck, U., & Beck-Gernsheim, E. (1995). *The Normal Chaos of Love*. Polity Press, in association with Blackwell Publishers.

Beck, U., & Beck-Gernsheim, E. (2008). *Individualisation*. Sage.
Berlant, L. (2011). *Cruel Optimism*. Duke University Press.
Bertaux, D., & Thompson, P. (2007). *Pathways to Social Class: A Qualitative Approach to Social Mobility*. Transaction Publishers.
Bok, J. (2010). The Capacity to Aspire to Higher Education: 'It's Like Making Them Do a Play Without a Script'. *Critical Studies in Education, 51*(2), 163–178.
Bourdieu, P. (1977). *Outline of a Theory of Practice* (R. Nice, Trans.). Cambridge University Press.
Bourdieu, P. (1986). The Forms of Capital. In J. G. Richardson (Ed.), *Handbook of Theory and Research for the Sociology of Education*. Greenwood Press.
Bourdieu, P., & Passeron, J. (1977). *Reproduction in Education, Society and Culture* (R. Nice, Trans.). Sage.
Brah, A., & Minhas, R. (1985). Structural Racism or Cultural Difference: Schooling for Asian Girls. In G. Weiner (Ed.), *Just a Bunch of Girls*. The Open University Press.
Certeau, M. (1984). *The Practice of Everyday Life*. University of California Press.
Devine, F., & Savage, M. (2005). The Cultural Turn, Sociology and Class Analysis. In F. Devine, M. Savage, J. Scott, & R. Crompton (Eds.), *Rethinking Class: Culture, Identities and Lifestyles*. Palgrave Macmillan.
Exley, D. (2019). *The End of Aspiration? Social Mobility and Our Children's Fading Prospects*. Policy Press.
Franceschelli, M., & O'Brien, M. (2014). Islamic Capital and Family Life: The Role of Islam in Parenting. *Sociology, 48*(6), 1190–1206.
Friedman, S., & Laurison, D. (2020). *The Class Ceiling: Why It Pays to Be Privileged*. Policy Press.
Giddens, A. (1990). *The Consequences of Modernity*. Polity.
Giddens, A. (1992). *The Transformation of Intimacy Sexuality, Love and Eroticism in Modern Societies*. Polity Press.
Giddens, A. (2007). Living in a Post-Traditional Society. In U. Beck, A. Giddens, & S. Lash (Eds.), *Reflexive Modernisation Politics, Tradition and Aesthetics in the Modern Social Order*. Polity Press.
Gonzalez, N., Moll, L., & Amanti, C. (2005). *Funds of Knowledge: Theorising Practices in Household Communities and Classrooms*. Lawrence-Erlbaum and Associates.
Goode, J. (2019). *Clever Girls. Autoethnographies of Class, Gender and Ethnicity*. Palgrave Macmillan/Springer Nature.
Hanley, L. (2016). *Respectable: The Experience of Class*. Allen Lane.

Hoggart, R. (1957). A Scholarship Boy. In R. Hoggart (Ed.), *The Uses of Literacy Aspects of Working-Class Life with Special Reference to Publications and Entertainments* (pp. 238–249). Chatto and Windus.

Hussain, Y., & Bagguley, P. (2007). *Moving on Up. South Asian Women and Higher Education.* Trentham Books Limited.

Lareau, A. (1989). *Home Advantage: Social Class and Parental Intervention in Elementary Education.* Falmer Press.

Littler, J. (2018). *Against Meritocracy: Culture, Power & Myths of Mobility.* Routledge.

Maton, K. (2010). Habitus. In M. Grenfell (Ed.), *Pierre Bourdieu Key Concepts.* Acumen Publishing.

McNamee, S. (2018). *The Meritocracy Myth.* Rowman & Littlefield Publishers.

McNay, L. (1999). Gender, Habitus and the Field: Pierre Bourdieu and the Limits of Reflexivity. *Theory, Culture and Society, 16*(1), 95–117.

Mohamed, H. (2020). *People Like Us. What It Takes to Make It I Modern Britain.* Profile Books.

Mohammad, R. (2005). Negotiating Spaces of the Home, the Education System, and the Labour Market: The Case of Young Working-Class, British Pakistani Muslim Women. In G.-W. Falah & C. Nagel (Eds.), *Geographies of Muslim Women: Gender, Religion and Space* (pp. 178–200). Guildford Press.

Moll, L., & Greenberg, J. (1990). Creating Zones of Possibilities: Combining Social Contexts for Instruction. In *Vygotsky and Education.* Harvard University Press.

Oakley, A. (1974). *Housewife.* Penguin.

Reay, D. (2017). *Miseducation: Inequality, Education and the Working Classes.* Policy Press.

Reay, D., David, M., & Ball, S. (2005). *Degrees of Choice: Class, Race, Gender and Higher Education.* Trentham Books Limited.

Sayer, A. (2005). *Moral Significance of Class.* Cambridge University Press.

Shahrokni, S. (2018). The Collective Roots and Rewards of Upward Educational Mobility. *The British Journal of Sociology, 69*(4), 1175–1193.

Shain, F. (2020). Navigating the Unequal Education Space in Post-9/11 England: British Muslim Girls Talk About Their Educational Aspirations and Future Expectations. *Educational Philosophy and Theory.* https://doi.org/10.1080/00131857.2020.1769604

Spohrer, K., Stahl, G., & Bowers-Brown, T. (2018). Constituting Neo-Liberal Subjects? "Aspirations" as Technology of Government in UK Policy Discourse. *Journal of Education Policy, 33*(3), 327–342.

Thomson, P. (2006). Miners, Diggers, Ferals and Show-Men: School-Community Projects that Affirm and Unsettle Identities and Place? *British Journal of Sociology of Education, 27*(1), 81–96.

Webb, J., Schirato, T., & Danaher, G. (2002). *Understanding Bourdieu.* Sage Publications.

Williams, R. (1979). The Long Revolution. In R. Williams (Ed.), *Politics and Letters Interviews with New Left Review.* Verso.

Williams, R. (1980). Base and Superstructure in Marxist Cultural Theory. In *Problems in Materialism and Culture, Selected Essays.* Verso.

Wrigley, T. (2000). *The Power to Learn. Stories of Success in the Education of Asian and Other Bilingual Pupils.* Trentham.

Yosso, T. (2005). Whose Culture Has Capital? A Critical Race Theory Discussion of Community Cultural Wealth. *Race Ethnicity and Education, 8*(1), 69–91.

# Appendix: The Schools Informants Attended

Most of the women interviewed lived in Milltown. They all attended local state secondary schools and colleges serving different catchment areas. Their age differences and preferences resulted in their going to different schools and colleges at parallel stages in their educational trajectories.

After 1991, the middle school system came to an end in Milltown. While it operated, secondary schools were either middle schools or upper schools. Queensmead was a middle school and Alderfield and Nofields were the two upper schools. Alderfield for some of the time had a sixth form attached to it too.

Queensmead middle school was located two miles out of the town centre. It served predominantly White catchment areas that varied in terms of their economic profiles. When Raheela and Noreen attended it there was a strong Christian ethos in the school. At the end of their third year, the closest upper school was Alderfield. Some of the catchment areas of both these schools now feature in the one hundred most deprived wards in the country. Interestingly, Queensmead middle school changed its name to Summerfield, and became an 11–16 school, which Shaheena, Ghazala, Nasreen, Robina, Ayesha and Shamila attended.



A. Saeed, *Education, Aspiration and Upward Social Mobility*,
https://doi.org/10.1007/978-3-030-82261-3

Nofields Upper School was in the very centre of the town. Raheela and Noreen attended this school. A large proportion of the students who attended were of Pakistani and Bangladeshi heritage. The school eventually closed because of continually poor exam results.

Grange Park replaced Nofields as a school in the centre of town, and aimed to attract students from Milltown and surrounding areas. Even now two-thirds of the pupils are from Pakistani and Bangladeshi backgrounds and one-third are White.

Oldfields was three miles away from the centre of Milltown and was a secondary school with superior facilities and its own sixth form. The student catchment areas were affluent. Ghazala, Shaheena, Nasreen and Shamila attended this sixth form.

Ashwood college was located in the centre of town and offered courses for those in post-compulsory education. This included vocational courses, re-sit GCSE and A Level courses.

Ditchley College was a tertiary college six miles from Milltown. For Tahira it had a reputation of success for those wanting to do A Level subjects.

Robina obtained her A Levels at Kirkley High School sixth form where almost all the students were White.

# References

Abbas, T. (2002). Teacher Perceptions of South Asians in Birmingham Schools and Colleges. *Oxford Review of Education, 28*(4), 447–471.

Abbas, T. (2003). The Impact of Religio-Cultural Norms and Values on the Education of Young South Asian Women. *British Journal of Sociology of Education, 24*(4), 411–428.

Abbas, T. (2004). *The Education of British South Asians Ethnicity, Capital and Class Structure*. Palgrave Macmillan.

Adegoke, Y., & Uviebinene, E. (2018). *Slay in Your Lane the Black Girl Bible*. 4th Estate.

Adkins, L. (2002). *Revisions: Gender and Sexuality in Late Modernity*. Open University Press.

Afshar, H. (1994). Muslim Women in West Yorkshire Growing Up with Real and Imaginary Values Amidst Conflicting Views of Self and Society. In H. Afshar & M. Maynard (Eds.), *The Dynamics of 'Race' and Gender: Some Feminist Interventions* (pp. 127–147). Taylor and Francis.

Ahmad, F. (2001). Modern Traditions? British Muslim Women and Academic Achievement. *Gender and Education, 13*, 137–152.

Ahmad, F. (2012). Graduating Towards Marriage? Attitudes Towards Marriage and Relationships Among University-Educated British Muslim Women. *Culture and Religion, 13*(2), 193–210.



A. Saeed, *Education, Aspiration and Upward Social Mobility*,
https://doi.org/10.1007/978-3-030-82261-3

Alexander, C. E., & Knowles, C. (2005). *Making Race Matter: Bodies, Space and Identity*. Palgrave Macmillan.
Allen, A. (1998). What Are Ethnic Minorities Looking For? In T. Modood & T. Acland (Eds.), *Race and Higher Education* (pp. 51–73). PSI.
Allen, S., & Wolkowitz, C. (1987). *Homeworking: Myths and Realities*. Macmillan Press.
Ansari, H. (2004). *'The Infidel Within': Muslims in Britain*. Hurst & Company.
Anwar, M. (1979). *Myth of Return: Pakistanis in Britain*. Heinemann Educational Publishers.
Anwar, M. (1985). *Pakistanis in Britain*. New Century.
Anwar, M. (1998). *Continuity and Change in the Lives of Young Asians*. Routledge.
Appadurai, A. (2004). The Capacity to Aspire: Culture and the Terms of Recognition. In V. Rao & M. Walton (Eds.), *Culture and Public Action*. Stanford University Press.
Appiah, K. A. (1992). *In My Father's House Africa in the Philosophy of Culture*. Methuen London.
Archer, L. (2003). *Race, Masculinity and Schooling. Muslim Boys and Education*. The Open University Press.
Archer, L., Hutchings, M., & Ross, A. (2003). *Higher Education and Social Class Issues of Exclusion and Inclusion*. Routledge Falmer Taylor and Francis Group.
Archer, L., Halsall, A., & Hollingworth, S. (2007). Class, Gender, (Hetero) sexuality and Schooling: Paradoxes Within Working-Class Girls' Engagement with Education and Post-16 Aspirations. *British Journal of Sociology of Education, 28*(2), 165–180.
Arnot, M. (1993). A Crisis in Patriarchy? British Feminist Educational Politics and State Regulation of Gender. In M. Arnot & K. Weiler (Eds.), *Feminism and Social Justice in Education: International Perspectives*. The Falmer Press.
Arnot, M., Gray, J., James, M., & Rudduck, J. (1998). *A Review of Recent Research on Gender and Educational Performance*. OFSTED Research Series.
Arnot, M., David, M., & Weiner, G. (1999). *Closing the Gender Gap Postwar Education and Social Change*. Polity.
Arshad, R., Wrigley, T., & Pratt, L. (2020). *Social Justice Re-Examined: Dilemmas and Solutions for the Classroom Teacher*. UCL IOE Press.
Aston, J., Hooker, H., & Page, R. (2007). *Pakistani and Bangladeshi Women's Attitudes to Work and Family*.
Atkinson, R. (1998). *The Life Story Interview*. Sage.
Ball, S. (2003). *Class Strategies and the Education Market the Middle Classes and Social Advantage*. Routledge.

Ballard, R. (1994). Introduction: The Emergence of Desh Pradesh. In R. Ballard (Ed.), *Desh Pradesh: The South Asian Presence in Britain*. Hurst & Company.

Banks, O. (1971). *The Sociology of Education* (2nd ed.). Batsford.

Barnett, T., & Noriega, C. (2013). *Oral History and Communities of Color*. UCLA Chicano Studies Research Centre Press.

Basit, T. (1997). *Eastern Values, Western Milieu*. Ashgate.

Basit, T. (2012). 'I've Never Known Someone Like Me Go To University': Class, Ethnicity and Access to Higher Education. In T. Basit & S. Tomlinson (Eds.), *Social Inclusion and Higher Education*. The Policy Press.

Becher, H. (2008). *Family Practices in South Asian Muslim Families Parenting in a Multi-Faith Britain*. Palgrave Macmillan.

Beck, J. (1998). *Morality and Citizenship Education*. Bloomsbury Publishing.

Beck, J. (2003). Citizenship and Citizenship Education in England. In J. Beck & M. Earl (Eds.), *Key Issues in Secondary Education* (2nd ed.). Continuum.

Beck, U., & Beck-Gernsheim, E. (1995). *The Normal Chaos of Love*. Polity Press, in association with Blackwell Publishers.

Beck, U., & Beck-Gernsheim, E. (2008). *Individualisation*. Sage.

Berlant, L. (2011). *Cruel Optimism*. Duke University Press.

Bernstein, B., Elvin, L., & Peters, R. (1966). Ritual in Education. *Philosophical Transactions of the Royal Society of London B, 251*(*B*), 429–436.

Bertaux, D. (1981). *Biography and Society the Life History Approach in the Social Sciences*. Sage Publications.

Bertaux, D., & Bertaux-Wiame, I. (1997). Heritage and Its Lineage: A Case History of Transmission and Social Mobility Over Five Generations. In D. Bertaux & P. Thompson (Eds.), *Pathways to Social Class*. Oxford University Press.

Bertaux, D., & Thompson, P. (Eds.). (1993). *International Yearbook of Oral History* (Vol. 2). Oxford University Press.

Bertaux, D., & Thompson, P. (1997). *Pathways to Social Class: A Qualitative Approach to Social Mobility*. Clarendon Press.

Bertaux, D., & Thompson, P. (2007). *Pathways to Social Class: A Qualitative Approach to Social Mobility*. Transaction Publishers.

Bertaux-Wiame, I. (1993). The Pull of Family Ties: Intergenerational Relationships and Life Paths. In D. Bertaux & P. Thompson (Eds.), *International Yearbook of Oral History and Life Stories Volume II Between Generations Family Models, Myths, and Memories*. Oxford University Press.

Bhachu, P. (1996). Identities Constructed and Reconstructed: Representations of Asian Women in Britain. In G. Buijs (Ed.), *Migrant Women Crossing Boundaries and Changing Identities*. Berg.

Bhopal, K. (1997). *Gender, Race and Patriarchy*. Ashgate.

Bhopal, K., & Myers, M. (2008). *Insiders, Outsiders and Others Gypsies and Identity*. University of Hertfordshire Press.

Bok, J. (2010). The Capacity to Aspire to Higher Education: 'It's Like Making Them Do a Play Without a Script'. *Critical Studies in Education, 51*(2), 163–178.

Bourdieu, P. (1973). Cultural Reproduction and Social Reproduction. In R. Brown (Ed.), *Knowledge, Education and Social Change*. Tavistock.

Bourdieu, P. (1977). *Outline of a Theory of Practice* (R. Nice, Trans.). Cambridge University Press.

Bourdieu, P. (1984). *Distinction*. Routledge and Kegan Paul.

Bourdieu, P. (1986). The Forms of Capital. In J. G. Richardson (Ed.), *Handbook of Theory and Research for the Sociology of Education*. Greenwood Press.

Bourdieu, P. (1990). *The Logic of Practice* (R. Nice, Trans.). Polity.

Bourdieu, P. (1996). *The State Nobility: Elite Schools in the Field of Power*. Polity.

Bourdieu, P., & Passeron, J. (1977). *Reproduction in Education, Society and Culture* (R. Nice, Trans.). Sage.

Bourdieu, P., & Passeron, J. (1979). *The Inheritors: French Students and Their Relation to Culture* (R. Nice, Trans.). University of Chicago Press.

Bourdieu, P., & Passeron, J. C. (1990). *Reproduction in Education, Society and Culture*. Sage.

Bourdieu, P., & Wacquant, L. (1992). *An Invitation to Reflexive Sociology*. University of Chicago Press.

Bowes, A. M., Dar, N. S., & Sim, D. F. (2002). Differentiation in Housing Careers: The Case of Pakistanis in the UK. *Housing Studies, 17*(3), 381–399.

Brah, A., & Minhas, R. (1985). Structural Racism or Cultural Difference: Schooling for Asian Girls. In G. Weiner (Ed.), *Just a Bunch of Girls*. The Open University Press.

Brah, A., & Shaw, S. (1992). *Working Choices: South Asian Women and the Labour Market*. Department of Employment Research Paper, No 91.

Broecke, S., & Nicholls, T. (2007). *Ethnicity and Degree Attainment*. Research Report RW92. Department for Education and Skills.

Brown, J. (2006). *Global South Asians Introducing the Modern Diaspora*. Cambridge University Press.

Brown, P., Reay, D., & Vincent, C. (2013). Education and Social Mobility. *British Journal of Sociology of Education, 34*(5–6), 637–643.

Bukodi, E., & Goldthorpe, J. H. (2018). *Social Mobility and Education in Britain. Research, Politics and Policy*. Cambridge University Press.

Butler, J. (1997). *Excitable Speech: A Politics of the Performative*. Routledge.

Cantle, T. (2001). *Community Cohesion: A Report of the Independent Review Team*. Home Office.

Carey, S., & Shukur, A. (1985). A Profile of the Bangladeshi Community in East London. *Journal of Ethnic and Migration Studies, 12*(3), 405–417.

Casey, L. (2016). *The Casey Review: A Review into Opportunity and Integration*. www.gov.uk/dclg. ISBN: 978-1-4098-4953-7.

Certeau, M. (1984). *The Practice of Everyday Life*. University of California Press.

Chamberlain, M. (2006). *Family Love in the Diaspora*. Transaction Publishers.

Chamberlayne, P. (2002). Second-Generation Transcultural Lives. In P. Chamberlayne, M. Rustin, & T. Wengraf (Eds.), *Biography and Social Exclusion in Europe Experiences and Life Journeys*. Policy Press.

Chamberlayne, P., Bornat, J., & Wengraf, T. (2000). Introduction: The Biographical Turn. In P. B. Chamberlayne, J. Bornat, & T. Wengraf (Eds.), *The Turn to Biographical Methods in Social Science Comparative Issues and Examples*. Routledge.

Clarke, C. (2003). *The Future of Higher Education*. The Stationery Office Limited.

Clarricoates, K. (1987). Dinosaurs in the Classroom – The 'Hidden' Curriculum in Primary Schools. In M. Arnot & G. Weiner (Eds.), *Gender and the Politics of Schooling*. Unwin Hyman.

Cohler, B. (1988). The Human Studies and Life History: The Social Service Review Lecture. *Social Service Review, 62*(4), 552–575.

Colley, H. (2006). Learning to Labour with Feeling: Class, Gender and Emotion in Childcare Education and Training. *Contemporary Issues in Early Childhood, 7*(1), 15–29.

Colley, H., James, D., Tedder, M., & Diment, K. (2003). Learning as Becoming in Vocational Education and Training: Class, Gender and the Role of Vocational Habitus. *Journal of Vocational Education and Training, 55*(4), 471–496.

Craft, M. (1970). *Family, Class and Education: A Reader*. Longman.

Crossley, M. (2000). *Introducing Narrative Psychology Self, Trauma and the Construction of Meaning*. The Open University Press.

Dale, A., Shaheen, N., Kalra, V., & Fieldhouse, E. (2002). Routes into Education and Employment for Young Pakistani and Bangladeshi Women in the UK. *Ethnic and Racial Studies, 25*(6).

Dearing, R. (1996). *National Inquiry into Higher Education Department for Education and Employment*.

Denzin, N. K. (1989). *Interpretive Biography*. Sage.

Devine, F., & Savage, M. (2005). The Cultural Turn, Sociology and Class Analysis. In F. Devine, M. Savage, J. Scott, & R. Crompton (Eds.), *Rethinking Class: Culture, Identities and Lifestyles*. Palgrave Macmillan.

DFES. (2007). *Gender and Education: The Evidence on Pupils in England*. DfES Publications.

Dingwall, R. (1997). Accounts, Interviews and Observations. In G. Miller & R. Dingwall (Eds.), *Context and Method in Qualitative Research*. Sage.

Dore, R. (1976). *The Diploma Disease Education, Qualification and Development*. University of California Press.

Dunkley Jones, R. (2007). *Understanding Race Relations in Oldham*. Unpublished Paper.

Dwyer, C. (1998). Contested Identities: Challenging Dominant Representations of Young British Muslim Women. In T. Skelton & G. Valentine (Eds.), *Cool Places: Geographies of Youth Cultures* (pp. 50–64). Routledge.

Dwyer, C., Modood, T., Sanghera, G., Shah, B., & Thapar-Bjorkert, S. (2011). Educational Achievement and Career Aspirations for Young British Pakistanis. In T. Modood & J. Salt (Eds.), *Global Migration, Ethnicity and Britishness*. Palgrave Macmillan.

Elver, H. (2012). *The Headscarf Controversy Secularism and Freedom of Religion*. Oxford University Press.

Emirbayer, M., & Mische, A. (1998). What Is Agency? *American Journal of Sociology, 103*(4), 962–1023.

EOC. (2006). *Moving on Up? Bangladeshi, Pakistani and Black Caribbean Women and Work*. Equal Opportunities Commission.

Erben, M. (1998). *Biography and Education: A Reader*. Falmer Press.

Erel, U. (2009). *Migrant Women Transforming Citizenship: Life Stories from Britain and Germany*. Ashgate Publishing Limited.

Erikson, R., & Goldthorpe, J. H. (1993). *The Constant Flux: A Study of Class Mobility in Industrial Societies*. Clarendon Press.

Exley, D. (2019). *The End of Aspiration? Social Mobility and Our Children's Fading Prospects*. Policy Press.

Figueroa, P. (1995). Multicultural Education in the United Kingdom: Historical Development and Current Status. In J. Banks & C. Banks (Eds.), *Handbook of Research on Multicultural Education* (pp. 778–800). Macmillan.

Fisher, K., Egerton, M., Gershuny, J. I., & Robinson, A. (2007). Gender Convergence in the American Heritage Time Use Study (AHTUS). *Social Indicators Research, 82*(1), 1–33.

Foster, P., Gomm, R., & Hammersley, M. (1996). *Constructing Educational Inequality*. Falmer Press.
Franceschelli, M., & O'Brien, M. (2014). Islamic Capital and Family Life: The Role of Islam in Parenting. *Sociology, 48*(6), 1190–1206.
Friedman, S. (2013). The Price of the Ticket: Rethinking the Experience of Social Mobility. *Sociology, 48*(2), 352–368.
Friedman, S., & Laurison, D. (2020). *The Class Ceiling: Why It Pays to Be Privileged*. Policy Press.
Furlong, V. (1976). Interaction Sets in the Classroom: Towards a Study of Pupil Knowledge. In M. Stubbs & S. Delamont (Eds.), *Explorations in Classroom Observation*. John Wiley and Sons.
Gannaway, H. (1976). Making Sense of School. In M. Stubbs & S. Delamont (Eds.), *Explorations in Classroom Observation*. Wiley.
Garner, S., & Bhattacharyya, G. (2011). *Poverty, Ethnicity and Place*. Joseph Rowntree Foundation.
Garratt, E. (2016). Do British Muslims Face Employment Penalties? In *CSI 26: Muslim Employment*. Centre for Social Investigation, Nuffield College. http://csi.nuff.ok.ac.uk/?page_id=718
Gershuny, J. (2000). *Changing Times: Work and Leisure in Post-Industrial Society*. Oxford University Press.
Ghuman, P. (2002). South Asian Adolescents in British Schools: A Review. *Educational Studies, 28*(1), 47–59.
Giddens, A. (1984). *The Constitution of Society Outline of the Theory of Structuration*. Polity Press.
Giddens, A. (1990). *The Consequences of Modernity*. Polity.
Giddens, A. (1991). Structuration Theory: Past, Present and Future. In C. Bryant & D. Jary (Eds.), *Giddens' Theory of Structuration: A Critical Appreciation*. Routledge.
Giddens, A. (1992). *The Transformation of Intimacy Sexuality, Love and Eroticism in Modern Societies*. Polity Press.
Giddens, A. (2007). Living in a Post-Traditional Society. In U. Beck, A. Giddens, & S. Lash (Eds.), *Reflexive Modernisation Politics, Tradition and Aesthetics in the Modern Social Order*. Polity Press.
Gillborn, D., & Gipps, C. (1996). *Recent Achievements of Ethnic Minority Pupils* (HMSO, Ed.). London.
Gilliat-Ray, S. (2010). *Muslims in Britain: An Introduction*. Cambridge University Press.

Glennerster, H. (1972). Education and Inequality. In P. Townsend & N. Bosanquet (Eds.), *Labour and Inequality*. Fabian Society.

Goffman, I. (1956). *The Presentation of Self in Everyday Life*. University of Edinburgh Social Sciences Research Centre.

Goldthorpe, J. H. (2003). The Myth of Education-Based Meritocracy. Why the Theory Isn't Working. *New Economy, 10*(4), 234–239.

Goldthorpe, J. H., & Mills, C. (2008). Trends in Intergenerational Class Mobility in Modern Britain: Evidence from National Surveys 1972–2005. *Journal of the National Institute of Economic and Social Research, 205*(83), 83–100.

Gonzalez, N., Moll, L., & Amanti, C. (2005). *Funds of Knowledge: Theorising Practices in Household Communities and Classrooms*. Lawrence-Erlbaum and Associates.

Goode, J. (2019). *Clever Girls. Autoethnographies of Class, Gender and Ethnicity*. Palgrave Macmillan/Springer Nature.

Goodson, I., & Sikes, P. (2001). *Life History Research in Educational Settings Learning from Lives*. The Open University Press.

Gomm, R. (1993). Figuring Out Ethnic Equity. *British Educational Research Journal, 19*(2), 149–165.

Grenfell, M., James, D., Hodkinson, P., Reay, D., & Robbinds, D. (1998). *Bourdieu and Education Acts of Practical Theory*. Falmer Press Taylor and Francis Group.

Grey, C. (1994). Career as a Project of the Self and Labour Process Discipline. *Sociology, 28*(2), 479–497.

Halsey, A. H. (1977). Towards Meritocracy? In J. Karabel & A. H. Halsey (Eds.), *Power and Ideology in Education*. Oxford University Press.

Halsey, A. H., Heath, A. F., & Ridge, J. M. (1980). *Origins and Destinations Family, Class, and Education in Modern Britain*. Clarendon Press.

Hammersley, M. (2003). Recent Radical Criticism of Interview Studies: Any Implications for the Sociology of Education? *British Journal of Sociology of Education, 24*(1), 119–126.

Hammersley, M. (2008). *Questioning Qualitative Inquiry: Critical Essays*. Sage.

Hammersley, M. (2011). *Methodology: Who Needs It?* Sage.

Hanley, L. (2016). *Respectable: The Experience of Class*. Allen Lane.

Hannerz, U. (1996). Cosmopolitans and Locals in World Culture. In *From Transnational Connections Culture, People, Places* (pp. 102–111). Routledge.

Hardill, I. (2002). *Gender, Migration and the Dual Career Household*. Routledge.

Hardy, T. (1979). *Jude the Obscure*. Penguin Books Ltd.

Hart, C. S. (2013). *Aspirations, Education and Social Justice Applying Sen and Bourdieu*. Bloomsbury.

Haw, K. (1998). *Educating Muslim Girls*. The Open University Press.

Hawkes, N. (1966). *Immigrant Children in British Schools*. Pall Mall Press.

Heath, A. (1981). *Social Mobility*. Fontana Paperbacks.

Heath, A., & Cheung, S. Y. (2006). *Ethnic Penalties in the Labour Market: Employers and Discrimination*. Department for Work and Pensions.

Heath, A., & McMahon, D. (1997). *Education and Occupational Attainments: The Impact of Ethnic Origins*. The Stationery Office.

Heath, A., Mills, C., & Roberts, J. (1992). Towards Meritocracy? Recent Evidence of an Old Problem. In A. Heath & C. Crouch (Eds.), *Social Research and Social Reform*. Clarendon Press.

Hirst, P. (1974). The Nature and Structure of Curriculum Objectives. In P. Hirst (Ed.), *Knowledge and the Curriculum a Collection of Philosophical Papers*. Routledge.

Hoggart, R. (1957). A Scholarship Boy. In R. Hoggart (Ed.), *The Uses of Literacy Aspects of Working-Class Life with Special Reference to Publications and Entertainments* (pp. 238–249). Chatto and Windus.

Hussain, Y., & Bagguley, P. (2007). *Moving on Up. South Asian Women and Higher Education*. Trentham Books Limited.

Ingram, N. (2011). Within School and Beyond the Gate: The Complexities of Being Educationally Successful and Working-Class. *Sociology, 45*(2), 287–302.

Iqbal, M. (1930). *Six Lectures on the Reconstruction of Religious Thought in Islam*. The Kapur Art Printing Works.

Islam, A. (2020). 'It Gets Really Boring If You Stay at Home': Women, Work and Temporalities in Urban India. *Sociology, 54*(5), 867–882.

Jackson, B. (1972). *Working-Class Community; Some General Notions Raised by a Series of Studies in Northern England*. Pelican Books.

Jackson, B., & Marsden, D. (1986). *Education and the Working-Class*. Ark Paperbacks.

Jewkes, Y., & Letherby, G. (2001). Insiders and Outsiders: Complex Issues of Identification and Difference in Social Research. *Auto/Biography, 9*(1/2), 41–50.

Josselson, R., & Lieblich, A. E. (1993). *The Narrative Study of Lives* (Vol. 1). Sage.

Kalra, V. (2000). *From Textile Mills to Taxi Ranks: Experiences of Migration, Labour and Social Change*. Ashgate.

Kalra, V., Hepburn, P., & Penhale, B. (1999). *Tackling Barriers into Employment for Pakistani and Bangladeshi Young People*. Oldham Metropolitan Borough Council.

Kay, T. (2007). Daughters of Islam, Sisters in Sport. In C. Aitchison, P. Hopkins, & M. Kwan (Eds.), *Geographies of Muslim Identities*. Ashgate.

Keddie, N. (1971). Classroom Knowledge. In M. Young (Ed.), *Language and Control*. Collier-Macmillan.

Keddie, N. (1973). Introduction: Tinker, Tailor…The Myth of Cultural Deprivation. In N. Keddie (Ed.), *Tinker, Tailor… The Myth of Cultural Deprivation*. Penguin.

Khan, D., & Shaheen, F. (2017). Introduction: Analysing and Responding to Racial and Class Inequalities. In D. Khan & F. Shaheen (Eds.), *Minority Report: Race and Class in Post-Brexit Britain*. Runnymede.

Klockars, C. (1974). *The Professional Fence*. Tavistock Publications.

Krais, B. (2006). Gender, Sociological Theory and Bourdieu's Sociology of Practice. *Theory, Culture and Society, 23*(6), 119–134.

Labov, W. (1969). The Logic of Non-Standard English. In P. Giglioli (Ed.), *Language and Social Context* (pp. 179–215). Penguin.

Lamaison, P., & Bourdieu, P. (1986). From Rules to Strategies: An Interview with Pierre Bourdieu. *Cultural Anthropology, 1*(1), 110–120.

Lareau, A. (1989). *Home Advantage: Social Class and Parental Intervention in Elementary Education*. Falmer Press.

Lareau, A. (2003). *Unequal Childhoods: Class, Race and Family Life*. University of California Press.

Lawler, S. (1999). 'Getting Out and Getting Away': Women's Narratives of Class Mobility. *Feminist Review, 63*(Autumn), 3–24.

Leese, M. (2010). Bridging the Gap: Supporting Student Transitions into Higher Education. *Journal of Further and Higher Education, 34*(2), 239–251.

Lewis, O. (1961). *The Children of Sanchez. Autobiography of a Mexican Family*. Random House.

Lewis, O. (1964). *Pedro Martinez*. Random House.

Li, Y. (2017). Persisting Disadvantages: Barriers to Ethnic Social Mobility in the UK. In D. Khan & F. Shaheen (Eds.), *Race and Class in Post-Brexit Britain*. Runnymede.

Lindley, J. K., Dale, A., & Dex, S. (2006). Ethnic Differences in Women's Employment. *Oxford Economic Papers, 58*(2), 351–378.

Liodakis, N. (2006). Review of 'Mobility and Inequality: Frontiers of Research in Sociology and Economics' by Morgan, S., Grusky, D., and Fields, G. *Canadian Journal of Sociology Online November–December*. http://www.cjonline.ca/reviews/mobility.html

Littler, J. (2018). *Against Meritocracy: Culture, Power & Myths of Mobility*. Routledge.

LMP. (1983). *Linguistic Minorities in England: A Report by the Linguistic Minorities Project for the Department of Education and Science*. University of London, Institute of Education.

Loury, G., Modood, T., & Teles, S. (2005). *Ethnicity, Social Mobility and Public Policy: Comparing the USA and UK*. Cambridge University Press.

Lovell, S. (Ed.). (2007). *Generations in Twentieth-Century Europe*.

Maton, K. (2010). Habitus. In M. Grenfell (Ed.), *Pierre Bourdieu Key Concepts*. Acumen Publishing.

McDermid, J. (2000). Women and Education. In J. Purvis (Ed.), *Women's History: Britain, 1850–1945*. Routledge.

McDermott, M., & Ahsan, M. (1986). *The Muslim Guide*. The Islamic Foundation.

McIntyre, D., Bhatti, G., & Fuller, M. (1993). *Educational Experiences of Ethnic Minority Students in the City of Oxford*. Oxford University Department of Educational Studies.

McLeod, J., & Thomson, R. (2009). *Researching Social Change*. Sage.

McNamee, S. (2018). *The Meritocracy Myth*. Rowman & Littlefield Publishers.

McNay, L. (1999). Gender, Habitus and the Field: Pierre Bourdieu and the Limits of Reflexivity. *Theory, Culture and Society, 16*(1), 95–117.

Mead, G. (1934). *Mind, Self and Society*. University of Chicago.

Merton, R. K. (1968). Patterns of Influence: Local and Cosmopolitan Influentials. In *Social Theory and Social Structure* (Enlarged Ed.). The Free Press.

Merton, R. K. (1972). Insiders and Outsiders: A Chapter in the Sociology of Knowledge. *American Journal of Sociology, 78*(1), 9–47.

Mishler, E. (1999). *Storylines: Craftartists' Narratives of Identity*. Harvard University Press.

Modood, T. (2004). Capitals, Ethnic Identity and Educational Qualifications. *Cultural Trends, 13*(2), 87–105.

Modood, T. (2005). The Educational Attainments of Ethnic Minorities in Britain. In G. Loury, T. Modood, & S. Teles (Eds.), *Ethnicity, Social Mobility and Public Policy: Comparing the US and the UK*. Cambridge University Press.

Modood, T., & Shiner, M. (1994). *Ethnic Minorities and Higher Education – Why Are There Different Rates of Entry?* PSI.

Modood, T., Berthoud, R., Lakely, R., Nazroo, J., Smith, J., & Beishon, S. (Eds.). (1997). *Ethnic Minorities in Britain: Diversity and Disadvantage.* Policy Studies Institute.

Mohamed, H. (2020). *People Like Us. What It Takes to Make It I Modern Britain.* Profile Books.

Mohammad, R. (2005). Negotiating Spaces of the Home, the Education System, and the Labour Market: The Case of Young Working-Class, British Pakistani Muslim Women. In G.-W. Falah & C. Nagel (Eds.), *Geographies of Muslim Women: Gender, Religion and Space* (pp. 178–200). Guildford Press.

Mohammad, R. (2010). Gender, Space and Labour Market Participation: The Experiences of British Pakistani Women. In S. Mc-Grath-Champ, A. Herod, & A. Rainnie (Eds.), *Handbook of Employment and Society. Working Space.* Edward Elgar Publishing.

Moll, L., & Greenberg, J. (1990). Creating Zones of Possibilities: Combining Social Contexts for Instruction. In *Vygotsky and Education.* Harvard University Press.

Moore, R. (2004). Cultural Capital: Objective Probability and the Cultural Arbitrary. *British Journal of Sociology of Education, 25*(4), 445–456.

Motzafi-Haller, P. (1997). Native Anthropologists and the Politics of Representation. In D. Reed-Danahay (Ed.), *Auto/Ethnography: Rewriting the Self and the Social* (pp. 169–195). Berg Publishers.

Oakley, A. (1974). *Housewife.* Penguin.

Oakley, A. (1982). Interviewing Women: A Contradiction in Terms. In H. Roberts (Ed.), *Doing Feminist Research.* Routledge.

ODPM. (2006). *The State of the English Cities Report.* ODPM Publications.

Pahl, K. (2014). The Aesthetics of Everyday Literacies: Home Writing Practices in a British Asian Household. *Anthropology & Education Quarterly, 45*(3), 293–311.

Parekh, B. (1989). The Hermeneutics of the Swann Report. In G. Vera (Ed.), *Education for All: A Landmark in Pluralism.* Falmer Press.

Payne, G. (2007). Social Divisions, Social Mobilities and Social Research. *Sociology, 41*(901), 901–915.

Peach, C. (2005). Social Integration and Social Mobility: Spatial Segregation and Intermarriage of the Caribbean Population in Britain. In G. Loury, T. Modood, & S. Teles (Eds.), *Ethnicity, Social Mobility and Public Policy: Comparing the USA and UK* (pp. 178–203). Cambridge University Press.

Phizacklea, A. (1988). Entrepreneurship, Ethnicity and Gender. In S. Westwood & P. Bhachu (Eds.), *Enterprising Women: Ethnicity, Economy and Gender Relations*. Routledge.

Phizacklea, A., & Wolkowitz, C. (1993). *Homeworking Women: Gender, Racism and Class at Work*. Sage.

Pilcher, J. (1994). Mannheim's Sociology of Generations: An Undervalued Legacy. *British Journal of Sociology, 45*(3), 481–495.

Platt, L. (2011). *Understanding Inequalities Stratification and Difference*. Polity Press.

Plummer, K. (1983). *Documents of Life, an Introduction to the Problems and Literature of a Humanistic Method*. George Allen and Unwin.

Plummer, K. (2001). *Documents of Life 2 an Invitation to a Critical Humanism*. Sage.

PMG. (1982). Popular Memory: Theory, Politics, Method. In R. Johnson, G. McLennan, B. Schwarz, & D. Sutton (Eds.), *Making Histories Studies in History-Writing and Politics*. Hutchinson and the Centre for Contemporary Cultural Studies, University of Birmingham.

Potter, J., & Hepburn, A. (2005). Qualitative Interviews in Psychology: Problems and Possibilities. *Qualitative Research in Psychology, 2*(4), 281–307.

Power, S., Whitty, G., Edwards, T., & Wigfall, V. (2004). Schools, Families and Academically able Students Contrasting Modes of Involvement in Secondary Education. In S. J. Ball (Ed.), *The RoutledgeFalmer Reader in Sociology of Education*. Routledge.

Probyn, E. (1993). *Sexing the Self: Gendered Positions in Cultural Studies*. Routledge.

Probyn, E. (2004). *Blush: Faces of Shame*. University of Minnesota Press.

Purvis, J. (1989). *Hard Lessons. The Lives and Education of Working-Class Women in Nineteenth-Century England*. Polity Press.

Qureshi, K., & Moores, S. (1991). Identity and Remix: Tradition and Translation in the Lives of Young Pakistani Scots. *European Journal of Cultural Studies, 1999*(2), 311.

Reay, D. (2017). *Miseducation: Inequality, Education and the Working Classes*. Policy Press.

Reay, D., David, M., & Ball, S. (2005). *Degrees of Choice: Class, Race, Gender and Higher Education*. Trentham Books Limited.

Reed-Danahay, D. (1997). *Auto/Ethnography: Rewriting the Self and the Social*. Berg.

Reeves, F., & Chevannes, M. (1988). The Ideological Construction of Black Underachievement. In M. Woodhead & A. McGrath (Eds.), *Family, School and Society*. Hodder and Stoughton.

Richardson, C. (1977). *Contemporary Social Mobility*. Frances Pinter.

Richardson, J. (2008). The Attainment of Ethnic Minority Students in UK Higher Education. *Studies in Higher Education, 33*(1), 33–48.

Riessman, K. (2008). *Narrative Methods for the Human Sciences*. Sage Publications Inc.

Robbins, D. (2004). The Transcultural Transferability of Bourdieu's Sociology of Education. *British Journal of Sociology of Education, 25*(4), 415–430.

Roberts, B. (2002). *Biographical Research*. The Open University Press.

Robinson, J. (2010). *Bluestockings the Remarkable Story of the First Women to Fight for an Education*. Penguin.

Rollock, N., Gillborn, D., Vincent, C., & Ball, S. (2011). The Public Identities of the Black Middle Classes: Managing Race in Public Spaces. *Sociology, 45*(6), 1078–1093.

Rose, N. (1998). Governing Enterprising Individuals. In N. Rose (Ed.), *Inventing Our Selves Psychology, Power and Personhood*. Cambridge University Press.

Rosen, H. (1972). Language and Class: A Critical Look at the Theories of Basil Bernstein. Reprinted in J. Richmond (Ed.), *Harold Rosen: Writings on Life, Language and Learning 1958–2008*. UCL IOE Press.

Rozbicki, M., & Ndege, G. (2012). *Cross-Cultural History and the Domestication of Otherness*. Palgrave Macmillan.

Rupp, L. (2001). Feminist Movements. In N. Smelser & P. Baltes (Eds.), *International Encyclopedia of the Social and Behavioral Sciences* (Vol. 8). Elsevier Science.

Saeed, T. (2016). *Islamophobia and Securitization. Religion, Ethnicity and the Female Voice*. Palgrave Macmillan.

Saifullah-Khan, V. (1976). Purdah in the British Situation. In A. L. Barker & S. Allen (Eds.), *Dependence and Exploitation in Work and Marriage* (pp. 224–245). Longman.

Salerno, R. (2007). *Sociology Noir Studies at the University of Chicago in Loneliness, Marginality and Deviance, 1915–1935*. McFarland and Company, Inc.

Savas, O. (2010). The Collective Turkish Home in Vienna: Aesthetic Narratives of Migration and Belonging. *Home Cultures, 7*(3), 313–340.

Sayer, A. (2005). *Moral Significance of Class*. Cambridge University Press.

Scheurich, J. (1995). A Postmodernist Critique of Research Interviewing. *International Journal of Qualitative Studies in Education, 8*(3), 239–252.

Schuetz, A. (1944). The Stranger: An Essay in Social Psychology. *American Journal of Sociology, 49*(6), 1944.

Seabrook, J. (1971). *City Close Up*. Allen Lane.

Shah, B., Dwyer, C., & Modood, T. (2010). Explaining Educational Achievement and Career Aspirations Among Young British Pakistanis: Mobilising 'Ethnic Capital'? *Sociology, 44*(6), 1109–1127.

Shahrokni, S. (2018). The Collective Roots and Rewards of Upward Educational Mobility. *The British Journal of Sociology, 69*(4), 1175–1193.

Shain, F. (2020). Navigating the Unequal Education Space in Post-9/11 England: British Muslim Girls Talk About Their Educational Aspirations and Future Expectations. *Educational Philosophy and Theory*. https://doi.org/10.1080/00131857.2020.1769604

Shaw, C. (1930). *The Jack Roller A Delinquent Boy's Own Story*. The University of Chicago.

Shostak, M. (1982). *Nisa, The Life and Words of a !Kung Woman*. Allen Lane.

Shostak, M. (1998). 'What the Wind Won't Take Away' The Genesis of Nisa – The Life and Words of a !Kung Woman. In R. Perks & A. Thomson (Eds.), *The Oral History Reader*. Routledge.

Shostak, M. (2000). *Return to Nisa*. Harvard University Press.

Silva, E. B. (2005). Gender, Home and Family in Cultural Capital Theory. *The British Journal of Sociology, 56*(1), 83–103.

Singh, R. (1990). Ethnic Minority Experience in Higher Education. *Higher Education Quarterly, 44*(4), 344–359.

Skeggs, B. (1997). *Formations of Class and Gender: Becoming Respectable*. Sage.

Skeggs, B. (2002). Techniques for Telling the Reflexive Self. In T. May (Ed.), *Qualitative Research in Action*. Sage.

Slootman, M. (2019). Ethnic Minority Climbers: Evaluating 'Minority Cultures of Mobility' as a Lens to Study Dutch Minority Student Organisations. *Ethnic and Racial Studies, 42*(5), 838–856.

Smith, D. J., & Tomlinson, S. (1989). *The School Effect: A Study of Multi-Racial Comprehensives*. Policy Studies Institute.

Smyth, J., & Wrigley, T. (2013). *Living on the Edge: Rethinking Poverty, Class and Schooling*. Peter Lang.

Spender, D. (1980). *Man Made Language*. Routledge.

Spohrer, K., Stahl, G., & Bowers-Brown, T. (2018). Constituting Neo-Liberal Subjects? "Aspirations" as Technology of Government in UK Policy Discourse. *Journal of Education Policy, 33*(3), 327–342.

Stanley, L. (2008). Madness to the Method? Using a Narrative Methodology to Analyse Large-Scale Complex Social Phenomena. *Qualitative Research, 8*(3), 435–447.

Stanley, L. (2013). *Documents of Life Revisited: Narrative and Biographical Methodology for a 21st Century Critical Humanism*. Ashgate.

Strand, S. (2007). *Minority Ethnic Pupils in the Longitudinal Study of Young People in England (LSYPE)*. University of Warwick.

Strauss, A. L., & Corbin, J. (1998). *Basics of Qualitative Research. Second Edition. Techniques and Procedures for Developing Grounded Theory*. Sage.

Sullivan, A. (2001). Cultural Capital and Educational Attainment. *Sociology, 35*(4), 893–912.

Swann, M. (1985). *Education for All the Report of the Committee of Inquiry into the Education of Children from Ethnic Minority Groups*. Her Majesty's Stationery Office.

Syed, J. (2009). Reconstruction of Gender in Islamic Thought: Iqbal's Vision of Equal Opportunity. *Women's Studies International Forum, 32*(6), 435–444.

Taylor, C. (1994). *Multiculturalism: Examining the Politics of Recognition*. Ed. and Introduced by A. Gutman. Princeton University Press.

Tenvir, F. (2015). *The Educational Experiences and Life Choices of British Pakistani Muslim Women: An Ethnographic Study*. Unpublished PhD Thesis, University of Worcester.

Thapar-Bjorkert, S., & Sanghera, G. S. (2010). Social Capital, Educational Aspirations and Young Pakistani Muslim Men and Women in Bradford, West Yorkshire. *The Sociological Review, 58*(2), 244–264.

The Change Institute. (2009). *The Pakistani Muslim Community in England Understanding Muslim Ethnic Communities*. Queen's Printer and Controller of Her Majesty's Stationery Office.

Thomas, W. (1958). *The Polish Peasant in Europe and America* (Vol. II). Dover Publications.

Thompson, P. (1981). Life Histories and the Analysis of Social Change. In D. Bertaux (Ed.), *Biography and Society. The Life History Approach in the Social Sciences*. Sage.

Thompson, P. (2000). *The Voice of the Past*. Oxford University Press.

Thomson, P. (2006). Miners, Diggers, Ferals and Show-Men: School-Community Projects that Affirm and Unsettle Identities and Place? *British Journal of Sociology of Education, 27*(1), 81–96.

Thomson, A. (2007). Four Paradigm Transformations in Oral History. *Oral History Review, 34*(10), 49–71.

Thomson, P. (2010). Field. In M. Grenfell (Ed.), *Pierre Bourdieu Key Concepts*. Acumen Publishing.

Tomlinson, S. (1984). *Home and School in Multicultural Britain*. Batsford.

Tomlinson, S. (1987). *Ethnic Minorities in British Schools a Review of the Literature, 1960–82*. Gower Publishing Company.

Tomlinson, S. (2008). *Race and Education Policy and Politics in Britain*. The Open University Press.

Treanor, M. (2020). *Child Poverty: Aspiring to Survive*. Policy Press.

Troyna, B. (1984). Fact or Artefact: The 'Educational Underachievement' of Black Pupils. *British Journal of Sociology of Education, 5*(2), 153–166.

Troyna, B. (1991). Underachievers or Underrated? The Experience of Pupils of South Asian Origin in a Secondary School. *British Educational Research Journal, 17*(4), 361–376.

Vincent, C., Ball, S., Rollock, N., & Gillborn, D. (2013a). Three Generations of Racism: Black Middle-Class Children and Schooling. *British Journal of Sociology of Education, 34*(5–6), 929–946.

Vincent, C., Rollock, N., Ball, S., & Gillborn, D. (2013b). *The Educational Strategies of the Black Middle-Classes*. Institute of Education University of London.

Wacquant, L. J. D. (1989). Towards a Reflexive Sociology: A Workshop with Pierre Bourdieu. *Sociological Theory, 7*, 26–63.

Warsi, S. (2017). *The Enemy Within: A Tale of Muslim Britain*. Penguin UK.

Watkins, M., & Noble, G. (2013). *Disposed to Learn Schooling, Ethnicity and the Scholarly Habitus*. Bloomsbury Academic.

Webb, J., Schirato, T., & Danaher, G. (2002). *Understanding Bourdieu*. Sage Publications.

Weiner, G., & Arnot, M. (1987). *Gender Under Scrutiny: New Inquiries in Education*. Hutchinson in association with The Open University.

Werbner, P. (1988). Taking and Giving: Working Women and Female Bonds in a Pakistani Immigrant Neighbourhood. In S. Westwood & P. Bhachu (Eds.), *Enterprising Women: Ethnicity, Economy and Gender Relations* (pp. 177–202). Routledge.

Werbner, P. (1990). *The Migration Process, Capital, Gifts and Offerings Among British Pakistanis*. Berg.

Whittier, N. (2007). Social Movements and Gender. In G. Ritzer (Ed.), *The Blackwell Encyclopedia of Sociology Volume IV F-HE*. Blackwell Publishing.

Williams, R. (1979). The Long Revolution. In R. Williams (Ed.), *Politics and Letters Interviews with New Left Review*. Verso.

Williams, R. (1980). Base and Superstructure in Marxist Cultural Theory. In *Problems in Materialism and Culture, Selected Essays*. Verso.

Wilson, A. (2006). *Dreams, Questions, Struggles South Asian Women in Britain*. Pluto Press.

Wollstonecraft, M. (1792). *Vindication of the Rights of Woman*. Penguin.

Wrigley, T. (2000). *The Power to Learn. Stories of Success in the Education of Asian and Other Bilingual Pupils*. Trentham.

Yosso, T. (2005). Whose Culture Has Capital? A Critical Race Theory Discussion of Community Cultural Wealth. *Race Ethnicity and Education, 8*(1), 69–91.

Youdell, D. (2006). Subjectivational and Performative Politics – Butler Thinking Althusser and Foucault: Intelligibility, Agency and the Race-Nationed-Religioned Subjects of Education. *British Journal of Sociology of Education, 27*(4), 511–528.

# Index[1]



[1] Note: Page numbers followed by 'n' refer to notes.



A. Saeed, *Education, Aspiration and Upward Social Mobility*,
https://doi.org/10.1007/978-3-030-82261-3

The manufacturer's authorised representative in the EU is Springer
Nature Customer Service Centre GmbH, Europaplatz 3, 69115 Heidelberg,
Germany. If you have any concerns regarding our products, please
contact ProductSafety@springernature.com

Printed and bound by CPI Group (UK) Ltd, Croydon, CR0 4YY
30/09/2026
02225701-0005